The Magical Art of Virgil

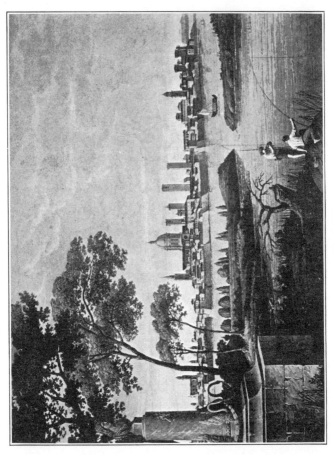

MANTUA

THE MAGICAL ART
OF VIRGIL

BY

EDWARD KENNARD RAND

ARCHON BOOKS
Hamden, Connecticut
1966

ITINERIS · VERGILIANI
OMNIVMQVE · ITINERVM
COMITI
D ·

PREFACE

IN honor of the two-thousandth anniversary of Virgil's birthday one might more profitably imitate the poet's art of reticence than add one more to the innumerable books that have been written about him. I yield to the general temptation, or, in the poet's words that Warde Fowler was fond of quoting,

iuvat insano indulgere furori,

for three reasons.

First, under the spell of that epoch-making work of my friend John Livingston Lowes, *The Road to Xanadu*, I should like to suggest, though I have by no means adequately illustrated, how the true method of examining an author's relation to his "sources" may be applied not only to a modern writer, like Coleridge, the background of whose poetic fancy can, with the help of Mr. Lowes, be so minutely traced, but also to an ancient like Virgil, even though his note-books, if he had such, have long ago crumbled into dust. Impressed with our poet's ability to convert most heterogeneous, sometimes absurdly heterogeneous, substances into a harmonious unity, I have given this art the name of magic.

Illustrations of this magic were presented in a series of six lectures on "Virgil the Magician," delivered on the Norman Wait Harris Foundation at Northwestern University, from April 29 to May 6, 1930. The titles of the lectures were:

I. Virgil's Magic. II. Epic from Pastoral. III. Arcadia from Actualities. IV. Philosophy from Farming. V. Tragedy from Romance. VI. Primitive Simplicity from Imperial Rome.

The substance of Lectures I, II, III, and IV will be found within Chapters I, III, IV, V, VI, and VII of the present book; Lectures V and VI reappear, with some modifications, in Chapters X and XII. I wish to express my thanks for the courtesy of the Trustees of the Harris Foundation, who allowed me to fulfil in this way the requirement that lectures on the Foundation should be published.

By invitation of the directors of the American Classical League and the Bureau of University Travel I repeated the Harris Lectures during the second Virgilian Cruise made in August, 1930, under the auspices of those organizations. I am grateful to them and to my fellow sea-farers, who were willing to listen to lectures during the excitements of that voyage.

I am also indebted to the editors of the *American Journal of Philology* for the privilege of using again in Chapters VI and VII part of an article on "Horatian Urbanity in Hesiod's Works and Days" (Vol. XXXII, 1911, pp. 131–165) and to the editors of the *Classical Journal* for permission to reprint, with modifications, an article, now Chapter X, on "Virgil and the Drama"

(Vol. IV, 1908, pp. 22–33, 51–61). The first of the Harris Lectures was originally composed for the October number of the *Classical Journal* for 1930, with the title of "Virgil the Magician." The matter included there differs in part from that of the lecture and from that of an article called "Salute to Virgil" and published, with the consent of the editors of the *Classical Journal*, in the *Saturday Review of Literature* for October 25, 1930. Finally, in Chapter II, I have drawn extensively on an article on "Young Virgil's Poetry" published in Vol. XXX (1919) of *Harvard Studies in Classical Philology*.

The second motive that prompted the writing of this book was to illustrate those epic tendencies which were an essential part of the poet's temperament and which at last found a free, though not — so the poet believed — a perfect, expression in the *Aeneid*. It was precisely this temperamental trait that impelled Virgil to new and daring creations in which the epic impulse was allowed a certain course in alien forms — pastoral and didactic poetry. He had the magical touch that, like the climate of Italy (as he reconstructed it), could create

alienis mensibus aestas.

With the growth of this power to harmonize incongruities it is natural that he should still exercise it when the moment for epic pure and simple came: it is not epic pure and simple, but an epic into which tragedy has been absorbed.

Finally, I have believed for some time that lovers of Virgil would profit not only by essays on his qualities and by translations of his works, but by a treatment of his poetry that sought to combine these two aims in an exposition of the contents of his poems accompanied by an interpretation of his purpose and his art. That plan has been carried out for the *Bucolics* and the *Georgics* and for most of the minor poems attributed to Virgil. It would seem peculiarly necessary for the *Bucolics*, about which

> quot homines tot sententiae;

if the reader would appraise the explanations here offered, the substance of the poems should be outspread for his contemplation. I had originally intended to treat the *Aeneid* in the same way, but so much has been written on that poem of late that I preferred to present merely certain aspects of the poet's magic, as appears in the last three chapters of the book.

No attempt has been made either to amass a bibliography on Virgil (which would have crowded out the rest of the book) or to mention in the notes every recent work that might have been cited. Two works have been so constantly cited that I have referred to them merely by the names of their authors. They are J. Brummer, *Vitae Vergilianae*, Leipsic, 1912; and Thilo and Hagen, *Servii Grammatici qui feruntur in Vergilii Carmina Commentarii*, recens. Georgius Thilo et Hermannus Hagen, Leipsic, 1881–1902. Needless to say, I owe much to such writers as Mackail and Warren, Norden and Heinze, Conington and Conway, Glover and Fowler, Frank and Prescott, even when the views to which I have been led may not agree with what started my thinking in the books of these eminent Virgilians. Still towering above works of a comprehensive nature written since its appearance is Sellar's volume on Virgil in his *Roman Poets of the Augustan Age*, first published in 1876.

To my kindly colleague, Bruno Nardi, I owe the view of Mantua reproduced in the frontispiece from an eighteenth-century engraving entitled "Veduta Esterna dalla R. città di Mantova (F. L. Montini disegnò; Lanfranco Puzzi incise; Mantova, Calcografia Negretti)." My thanks are due to the Harvard Service Bureau, in particular to Miss Marjorie Green, for the careful preparation of my manuscript for the printer and to the Harvard University Press, in particular to Mr. Joseph T. Day, for its customary expedition in issuing the book. The index was made by Charlotte P. Gilliland. My friend Bernard M. Peebles weeded the proofs of error and improved them with various other changes; it is he who noted that the *Copa* included melons in her store of attractions. Finally I am grateful, as ever, to my wife for helpful scrutiny and suggestion.

E. K. RAND

CAMBRIDGE, MASSACHUSETTS
February 1, 1931

CONTENTS

The Magical Art of Virgil

Artis poeticae est non omnia dicere.

Servius, in *Aen.* I, 683.

CHAPTER I

VIRGIL'S MAGIC AND HIS LITERARY GOAL

VIRGIL was born to write epic. His countrymen were an epic race, impressed with the dignity of their traditions and accustomed in early times, the elder Cato tells us, to hear the glorious deeds of their ancestors proclaimed at banquets by minstrels. Perhaps Niebuhr and Macaulay go too far in reconstructing a Golden Age of the primitive ballad, but some such poetry there must have been, and its spirit is not ignobly rendered into modern terms in the *Lays of Ancient Rome*. The more the critical investigator detracts from the veracity of early Roman history, the more he adds to the imaginative resources of the ancient Romans. Splendid poetic material abounded in the old legends, and later was wrought into actual poetry by various writers, among whom the historian Livy should be numbered. The crowning achievement in this effort of a race to set forth epically its past and its ideals belongs to Virgil. He stands on the crest of the hill. Epic poets had been before him and epic poets in plenty followed him. The work of his predecessors was overladen with history. Ennius, despite his flashes of genius and his sturdy Roman sentiment, works toilsomely and often prosaically with crude material. Even from his fragments we may infer the scope of his whole poem and find it well named *Annales*. The work of Virgil's successors is overladen with rhetoric. With Virgil and Ovid to teach them, they have mastered all the tricks of the trade; they can turn the proper simile and learnedly adjust their divine machines. We would gladly surrender Silius Italicus, Valerius Flaccus, and Statius for a complete copy of the *Annales*, leaving Lucan to represent the rhetorical epic at its best and its worst. Virgil came at the favored moment, or rather created it. Absorbing his country's history into the mythical and ideal, he gave it a typical and permanent expression; studying the old masterpieces reverently and submitting to the conventions of the schools, he yet achieved new creations in a delicate and impressionistic art. His success made emulation tempting and impossible. Only Dante and Milton understood and, in varying ways, expressed his spirit.

I

The poet was born in 70 B.C. in the humble village of Andes, probably the modern Pietole, a few miles south of Mantua. His father, for whose name there is no sure tradition, was either a potter or the hired man of a petty official named Magius, whose daughter Magia Pollia he married. Shortly before her child came into the world, the ancient biographer Donatus[1] says, the good woman

---

[1] The ancient Life is best cited by Brummer. The reader can easily find in his text the various statements and anecdotes included in the present chapter.

dreamed that she bore a laurel bough which, when it touched the earth, waxed at once into a mighty tree, laden with blossoms and fruit. The next day, when with her husband she was trudging along the country road, she stopped of a sudden and was delivered of the child in a ditch. The branch of poplar planted, according to the custom of the country folk, in token of the birth grew rapidly to a mature height, and was widely known as "Virgil's Tree." The infant uttered never a cry, but looked about him with a mild effulgence that indubitably portended high destiny. Virgil, ushered into the light in this lowly fashion, lived to write perhaps the most aristocratic verse that the world has ever seen. But he never looked down upon his origin or failed to extol, in his latest as in his earliest works, the wholesome virtue of simplicity well typified in country life.

The lad received a varied education. He attended a country school at Cremona till his fifteenth or his seventeenth year, when he assumed the *toga virilis*. Thence he went to Milan, and shortly thereafter to Rome, where his most noted teachers were the Epicurean philosopher Siro and the rhetorician Epidius. He included medicine in his programme, and devoted himself with special zeal to mathematics. For Virgil, like any true humanist, could harmonize poetry and science; indeed, for a brief period, he committed himself heart and soul to science. His profession was the law; for the soldier's life, the other normal career of the young Roman of family or ambition, he had no inclination. He soon abandoned law as well. He appeared in court once, and only once; for he was slow of speech, a contemporary informs us, and almost boorish in appearance. Poetry, in which he had dabbled in his schooldays, opened a surer avenue to fame.

After various preludes and experiments, Virgil turned to pastoral poetry. The *Bucolics*, written between the years 42 and 38, or thereabouts, was partly occasioned by the disturbances in the Mantuan district, where the victors of Mutina and Philippi had assigned land to their veterans. When the property of Virgil's father was thus confiscated, or in danger of confiscation, the poet found a particular champion in Asinius Pollio, to whom, with others, he made ample amends in the homage of the *Bucolics*. Octavian and Maecenas were the last in this series of patrons. The *Georgics*, written between 37 and 30, is dedicated, in different ways, to them both. From his friends and patrons the poet received the tidy sum of ten million sesterces, — about five hundred thousand dollars, — and had a house on the Esquiline near the gardens of Maecenas. But he did not care for Rome; he preferred his quiet retreats by the bay of Naples or in Sicily. Whenever he chanced to come to town and bystanders pointed out the famous bard, he would make for the nearest doorway; this anecdote, so true to Virgil's temperament as his poetry reveals it, would almost induce us to accept everything else that the ancient biographer tells of him. The *Aeneid*, the achievement toward which the poet's genius had ever tended, was begun about the year 30.

In the year 19, the fifty-second of his life, Virgil took his poem to Greece, meaning to give it the final touches there, and to devote his remaining days to philosophy. But meeting Augustus in Athens, homeward bound after journeying in the East, Virgil decided to return with him. A fatal visit to Megara on a hot day induced an attack of malaria. The illness increased during the voyage, and a few days after landing at Brundisium the poet died, on the twentieth of September, 19 B.C. He had left instructions with his fellow-poet Varius to burn the *Aeneid*, to us a work of exquisite art of which even the unfinished edges are delightful, but to the sensitive artist himself a statue not yet chiselled out in every part, and therefore meet for the flames. Virgil had also, after the precedent of the great Ennius, written his epitaph, which somehow seems too prosaic, not to say telegraphic, for the full Virgilian style:

> Mantua me genuit: Calabri rapuere: tenet nunc
> Parthenope: cecini pascua, rura, duces.[1]

His bones were buried in Naples hard by the road to Pozzuoli. The traditional site of his tomb is visited by the devout today, and still awaits the archaeologist's spade. Probably the digging should be undertaken under the waves nearby.

---

[1] "Mantua brought me to birth and Calabria snatched from the living; Naples entombs me: I sang pastures and corn-land and arms."

II

Such, briefly, is Virgil's career. I would put into special prominence the epic quality of his temperament, first making clear what I mean by this term. The Century Dictionary, adapting Aristotle to modern needs, defines epic as "an heroic poem, narrating at length and in metrical form as a poetic whole, with subordination of parts, a series of heroic achievements or of events under supernatural guidance." But the epic spirit may manifest itself in flashes, in the course of any poem of a different sort. Dante's *Divine Comedy* is not an epic, but the stories of Paolo and Francesca, of Ulysses and of Ugolino, in the *Inferno* have the surge of epic narrative and are modelled in places on the *Aeneid*. To frame a definition that will include such passages as these, we may perhaps call epic "poetic narrative ennobled," leaving the poet to select his heroes and to magnify what he will.

> If woodland be our song, then let the woods
> Be worthy of a consul.[1]

Virgil understood his own processes completely, and Calpurnius detected the flavor that he could not reproduce. For he calls Virgil

> That seer divine whose oaten reed
> Sounded the music of the lyre.[2]

[1] *Ecl.*, IV, 3. So *Georg.*, III, 290:
angustis hunc addere rebus honorem.
[2] IV, 65:   Ille fuit vates sacer, et qui posset avena
praesonuisse chelyn.

Various other pastoral singers tried to blow the same music from that reed, but it only gave forth scrannel puffings, until Milton in his *Lycidas* made it sound. This is Virgil's most significant innovation, and his boldest.

Another of Virgil's traits finds expression in what I should call the magic of his poetry. In the Dark and Middle Ages, the poet Virgil was seen through a haze of romance. His reading of life was, with the help of allegory, magnified into omniscience, and he himself assumed the rôle of prophet, theologian, and wizard. Strange tales were told of his magical powers, and strange adventures were associated with his name. It is not my purpose to repeat these well-known fables, or to show — what sadly needs showing — that an eminent Italian authority has grossly exaggerated mediaeval credulity and misinterpreted the spirit in which the romance of Virgil was fashioned. I am concerned rather with the actual temperament of Virgil as set forth in his poetry, which for astounding feats of magic may challenge comparison with the wildest inventions of mediaeval myth.

The art of magic, according to the Oxford Concise Dictionary, derives in part from an "inexplicable or remarkable influence producing surprising results," as when, we may add, an alchemist turns lead to gold, or a conjurer extracts alien objects from a hat, or Medea rejuvenates Aeson by plunging him in a medicated bath

— in a word, magic is the skilful and unanalyzable transformation of one substance into another. How truly Virgil had this power we appreciate only when we examine in some detail the diverse elements of which his poetical creations are composed. And this means a study of his literary sources.

One might imagine that Virgil's sources had been studied enough. In one way they have been studied too much. A scholar today, equipped with a good memory or a copious collection of *indices verborum*, may readily collect so many coincidences between Virgil and his masters in incident and plot, in imagery and phrase, that after one has scanned the long array of deadly parallels the place for originality in Virgil's art seems small. We are tempted to form a picture of the poet in his workshop. He sits at a long table with many volumes of his sources before him; from one he abstracts a line, from another a half-line, from another a quarter-line, and turning them into Latin metre — if they are not already in Latin metre — he adds, by a special providence, a quarter-line of his own, and thus has two verses done. Such a procedure, as one patient source-tracker remarked, is *Mosaikarbeit*. Doubtless if the poet had had the mind of the source-tracker he would have built his lofty rhyme in precisely this way.

No study of the workings of a poet's mind should be attempted today without much pondering of that remarkable book by John Livingston Lowes, *The Road to*

Xanadu. With the help of Coleridge's notes on his own reading, and after much travelling in the realms through which the poet's inquisitive mind had wandered, Mr. Lowes has set forth with an uncanny and indisputable exactness the mental processes that preceded the creative act; the adventures of Mr. Lowes, his intellectual voyages from China to Peru and from the Golden Age to the present time, are hardly less exciting than those of the Ancient Mariner himself. Virgil's note-books have disappeared, but he, too, had a "falcon eye" that pounced on rare matter for poetry in the multitudinous things that he read. He, too, had a "deep well" of retentive memory in which diverse impressions were stored; for those ancient wells, sunk before the invention of printing had brought bane as well as blessing to the world, were roomier and deeper than those of the modern mind. The same mysterious, unconscious union of impressions must likewise have gone on in that deep well, whence the shaping spirit of the poet's imagination drew what he demanded from the chaos, and moulded it into perfect art.

We do not possess Virgil's note-books, but certain priceless little anecdotes have been transmitted in the ancient Life of him that was compiled by Donatus from Suetonius, who doubtless took from sources contemporary, or almost contemporary, with the poet himself. The source-tracker was active in Virgil's day. Quintus Octavius Avitus collected eight volumes of "Coincidences" ('Ομοιότητες), with each pilfered verse and its author exactly labelled. Alas for the modern *obtrectatores* of the poet, these eight volumes have not come down to our times. Source-trackers would number them among the major losses of Latin literature. How many extra bushels could one have collected of chips *aus Vergils Werkstätte*! But the lost work would have been no less valuable for one in search of the poet's originality. Virgil himself answered his detractors neatly with the remark that if they thought he had stolen his best things from Homer, why did they not attempt the same theft themselves? "They will find it easier," he declared, "to steal his club from Hercules than a verse from Homer." To steal bits here and there and fit them into a mosaic — no, that is not Virgil's way. The verse of Homer would still be Homer's, and the thief would be caught in the act. Many things from Homer have gone into Virgil's poetry, but not until they have been absorbed into the mass of his memories and his fancies, not until there have occurred, in the words of Keats, "the innumerable compositions and decompositions which take place between the intellect and its thousand materials before it arrives at that trembling delicate and snail-born perception of beauty."[1] Whatever emerges then from Virgil's mind belongs not to Homer or to anybody else, but is all his own.

[1] Letter 46, to Benjamin Robert Haydon (*The Complete Poetical Works and Letters of John Keats*, Cambridge Edition, Boston, 1899, p. 296).

The ancient Life also tells us that Virgil, in the fashion followed by some other poets, notably Goethe, made a prose draft of the *Aeneid* — how detailed we do not know — and wrought it into verse as inclination prompted, in no particular order. The mood for the downfall of Troy, or for the prophecy in the Elysian fields, or for morning birds on the primitive Palatine, would come, and everything else stood aside. When the inspiration began to fade, he would write temporary verses, which he likened to scaffolding that at least gave the outlines of the structure till the solid columns should be brought. And sometimes he knew he must pause in the middle of a verse, since the Muse dictated no further; but the message of the Muse had been crystal-clear up to that point. Such lapses of inspiration account for those "pathetic half-lines" which were deplored by Virgil's literary executors and by the stupid folk who tried to fill them out, but which, with their wild, informal grace, come to modern readers as a happy surprise.

We are told, further, that the poet would read his verses aloud in a voice of sweetness and of wondrous charm. Taking turns with Maecenas, he read the *Georgics* to Octavian when the victor returned from Actium. He read him later, at his urging, the Second and the Fourth and the Sixth Books of the *Aeneid*, and so matched his voice with the spirit of the poem that when he had finished the lines on the hapless Marcellus,

Octavia, the boy's mother, whom her consort had invited to the reading, fainted and fell and hardly could be restored —

> e cade come corpo morto cadde.

At such moments the poet and his Muse were one. Sometimes as he read his verse aloud to himself his inspiration would carry him on and supply the fitting words at the points where he had halted before. Virgil's amanuensis, who bore the name Eros, perhaps by the compliment of his master, once heard him read on through one of the unfinished half-lines,

> Misenum Aeoliden,

and the other half came to him at once,

> quo non praestantior alter.

The next line too was unfinished,

> aere ciere viros,

but in the same heat of inspiration he uttered the rest of it,

> Martemque accendere cantu,

and ordered Eros to write down the new inventions in the text. These are not the most notable of Virgil's inventions, but they indicate that his inventiveness, like that of Coleridge's, involved no *creatio ex nihilo*, but that the product of his fancy germinated and grew, and at times was checked in its growth before of a sudden, in the twinkling of an eye, it burst into full flower.

Not all of Virgil is perfect art. A poet may conceive a great plan; he may jot down in a note-book, or immediately consign to the deep well of memory, images or designs of poetic significance, which there await the flash of creation that never comes. Instead, the poet draws them out before the time and arranges them in a seemly order that lacks the magic touch. This, in the phrase of Mr. Lowes, is "joiner's work," which may be found in abundance in the minor poems ascribed to Virgil. Assuming, on good ancient evidence, their genuineness, we may trace in them the growth of a poetic genius, not forgetting the prayer of a witty postprandial orator that it would be a graceful tribute on Virgil's birthday to relieve him of the authorship of at least some of them, and not forgetting either that the poet himself had left them unmentioned in his backward glances at his earlier works. For the moment, I am assuming, as I have assumed in an article written on this question a decade ago, that most if not all of the works on the ancient list are genuine. I am aware of the difficulties in the way and wish to make quite plain the nature of the assumption and its consequences. The outcome is, briefly, that from the matter of these little poems one may construct a consistent picture of the development of the young poet's mind and thought before he achieved his first great work of art, the *Eclogues*. This development may not be plotted too nicely or associated too closely with what little we know about his experience and his career.

But the picture that may be formed is too striking and too plausible lightly to be thrown aside. As I try to paint it in the following chapter let us not forget the cloud of hypothesis in which painter and portrait are enveloped.

III

The art of the minor poems, with some significant exceptions, as we shall see, is crude. There is little magic there. That of the *Eclogues* is, in comparison, astonishing. To illustrate this difference I select two passages, one from the *Eclogues* and one from Virgil's schoolboy poem, the *Culex*. With the characteristics of the latter piece I will deal more elaborately in the following chapter.

The theme of the *Culex* — "The Gnat," or "The Mosquito" — is humble. It seems natural enough to any traveller who has spent a summer's night at Mantua; a humble theme it is, but treated in the grand style. It is the story of a shepherd, who drives his flocks afield at dawn. While the goats are cropping the grass, or hanging from cliffs, he soliloquizes on the pleasures of rural simplicity. At noon he retires with his herd to the shelter of a grove, where every tree suggests the story of its metamorphosis. While the shepherd is taking his siesta, a huge spotted snake glides up and, angry that his wonted bed has been preoccupied, is about to make trouble for the intruder, when a little gnat wakes the shepherd by stinging him on the forehead. The shep-

herd, starting in pain, slays his benefactor. Then, seeing the greater peril, still drowsy and not so frightened
as he would normally have been, he tears a bough from
the tree and crushes the serpent. That night the gnat
comes to the shepherd in a vision, even as Patroclus
appears to Achilles in the *Iliad*, and tells of his wanderings in the world below. Next morning the shepherd,
touched with pity, builds a burial-mound for his little
friend, plants flowers about it, and carves an epitaph:

> PARVE CULEX PECVDUM CUSTOS TIBI TALE MERENTI
> FUNERIS OFFICIUM VITAE PRO MUNERE REDDIT.

This runs in the poet Spenser's translation —

> To thee, small Gnat, in lieu of his life saved,
> The Shepherd hath thy death's record engraved

This is a work of no little promise.

In a word, the youthful poet took his initial inspiration from the prevailing modes of his day. He had read
widely in diverse sorts of poetry and he had something
to say on the larger issues of life. All these things were
stirring within him, composing and decomposing and
awaiting the summons to emerge — and some of them
emerged too soon.

The story as I have just outlined it flows rapidly
enough; not so, I am sorry to say, the story that the
reader will find in the text. He will enjoy but a brief
repose with the shepherd in a grove where each and
every tree must tell the story of its human descent —
where one cannot see the woods for these trees and can-

not hear anything but them. Then the gnat's adventure among the shades is told at merciless length and with no suggestion of the delicate art that Virgil had learned when he reverted to the same subject in the Sixth Book of the *Aeneid*. Finally — and this is the passage to which I would call your particular attention — there is the abundant, and redundant, botanical garden that the shepherd plants about the tomb of the little gnat. To make it as fragrant as possible, let us have it in Spenser's verse:

> And round about he taught sweete flowres to growe;
> The Rose engrained in pure scarlet die;
> The Lilly fresh; and Violet belowe;
> The Marigolde; and cherefull Rosemarie;
> The *Spartan* Mirtle, whence sweet gumb does flowe;
> The purple Hyacinthe; and fresh Costmarie;
> And Saffron, sought for in *Cilician* soyle;
> And Lawrell, th' ornament of *Phœbus* toyle.
>
> Fresh *Rhododaphne*; and the *Sabine* flowre;
> Matching the wealth of th' auncient Frankincence;
> And pallid Yuie, building his owne bowre;
> And Box yet mindfull of his olde offence;
> Red *Amaranthus*, lucklesse Paramour;
> Oxeye still greene; and bitter Patience;
> Ne wants there pale *Narcisse*, that, in a well
> Seeing his beautie, in loue with it fell.

Bitter Patience must be plucked by the modern reader even before he reaches the mention of this flower, and when, at the end, Narcissus falls into the well, he drops in alongside him. There is no artful variety in the planting of these eighteen specimens of flora. They follow the one after the other, in the Latin lines, heralded no less than five times by *hic*, which thrice stands in the same position in the verse.

But the poet is not done. As though fearing that some omitted plant may take offence, he adds an omnibus clause, as in a Roman prayer, to include all the fair flowers of spring:

> And whatsoever other flowre of worth,
> And whatso other hearb of louely hew,
> The ioyous Spring out of the ground brings forth,
> To cloath her selfe in colours fresh and new;
> He planted there, and reard a mount of earth,
> In whose high front was writ as doth ensue.

I will refrain from citing the Latin verse; it has no music; the singer grates on a scrannel pipe of wretched straw, and knows not the tender stops of various quills. The description of the garden about the tomb, like that of the metamorphosed trees and like the gnat's story of the lower regions, is replete with unassimilated matter. The poet gets interested in a detail and loses his design. For one so very young he displays a commendable acquaintance with mythology, with Greek and Roman history, and with the flowers of the field or those of his favorite authors. He forgets where he is — and his reader, awaiting the magic act, waits in vain.

Virgil's failure here becomes the more conspicuous when we contrast it with a brilliant success in the earliest of his pastorals, that which today stands second in the collection of these works. Again it is a shepherd who

offers a profusion of flowers to one beloved of him. Here
are the words of Corydon's appeal, as presented in the
admirable translation of the late Theodore Chickering
Williams:

> Come hither, loveliest boy!
> The wood-nymphs bear thee lilies heaping high
> In osier baskets; and a naiad white
> Plucking pale violets and poppies tall,
> Wreathes scented fennel with narcissus bloom,
> And lavender with all sweet herbs she binds,
> And bids sad-vestured hyacinth look gay
> Mated with sprays of saffron marigold.
> I'll pluck thee apricots of velvet skin,
> And chestnuts such as Amaryllis loved,
> And waxen plums to top my basket well —
> An honored fruit.   And O ye laurels green,
> Ye myrtles set near by, I cull ye both,
> That thus your mingled breaths may sweeter be!

This is a good translation; it is better than was Spenser's from "The Gnat." Then we did not want to read
the original, and now we do:

> Huc ades, o formose puer: tibi lilia plenis
> ecce ferunt Nymphae calathis; tibi candida Nais,
> pallentes violas et summa papavera carpens,
> narcissum et florem iungit bene olentis anethi;
> tum casia atque aliis intexens suavibus herbis
> mollia luteola pingit vaccinia calta.
> Ipse ego cana legam tenera lanugine mala
> castaneasque nuces, mea quas Amaryllis amabat.
> addam cerea pruna: honos erit huic quoque pomo;
> et vos, o lauri, carpam et te, proxima myrte,
> sic positae quoniam suaves miscetis odores.[1]

[1] *Ecl.*, II, 45–55.

Here is a sweet and resonant music from the pastoral pipe, and here is the perfect art that absorbs incongruities into a harmonious mass. When Polyphemus, in Theocritus's idyll, would present Galatea with flowers, he observes the proprieties:

> Oh why was I not born a finny thing,
> To float unto thy side and kiss thy hand,
> Denied thy lips — and bring thee lilies white
> And crimson-petalled poppies' dainty bloom!
> Nay — summer hath his flowers and winter his;
> I could not bring all these the selfsame day.[1]

This is Calverley's translation; I have changed his "autumn" to "winter," for that is what Theocritus says, whatever his "lilies" may be. Polyphemus is a realist. In his fervor of adoration, he promises his beloved a botanical impossibility, and quickly corrects himself. Corydon is a magician and, like a later master of the art, plucks flowers from different seasons as from different beds. What is time to a magician?

> Bring the rathe primrose that forsaken dies,
> The tufted crow-toe, and pale jessamine,
> The white pink, and the pansy freak'd with jet,
> The glowing violet,
> The musk-rose, and the well-attired woodbine,
> With cowslips wan that hang the pensive head,
> And every flower that sad embroidery wears:
> Bid amarantus all his beauty shed,
> And daffadillies fill their cups with tears
> To strew the laureat hearse where Lycid lies.

---

[1] *Idylls*, XI, 54-59.

We need not imagine that Virgil's magic came all in a flash. Immediacy there was, and also the quiet fashioning by chisel and by file. Yet here, too, a happy combination, a delicate adjustment, a neat transposition, though small in extent, is no mechanical affair; and a series of such retouchings often transmutes some baser metal into gold. We shall see how the poet worked when we turn, before this chapter closes, to the *Georgics*. For the moment, we have only to glance again at the amorphous catalogue in the *Culex* and contrast it with the finished art in the passage from the *Eclogues*. The later passage contains virtually the same number of lines as the earlier, and almost as many objects are specified; but its wealth of description is without confusion. Obvious anaphora is avoided, and has emotional value when it appears (*tibi — tibi*). Verbs and participles are sprinkled in with the nouns, to prevent the effect of a list. The flowers are not merely named; they form part of the action. The action is distributed by the introduction of other persons besides the shepherd himself. The offering is diversified by the presence of fruit among the flowers, by its distribution among different actors, and finally by its personification and the use of the case of address. Not all of this delicacy was impromptu; a touch here and a touch there had preceded the finished form.

Where had Virgil learned his art? Twelve years had elapsed since he wrote his schoolboy poem, and the twelve years from incipient youth to the flush of young

manhood is a long time. The art of constantly retouch-
ing affects the poet's mind as well as his work; he re-
touches his temperament; he moulds it into a more
delicate and responsive instrument, until it can produce
spontaneously what once was the culmination of refin-
ing toil. Magic, like genius, — if the definition in either
case is not too frugally Scotch, — is an infinite capacity
for taking pains. At any rate we may say that a magician is made as well as born. Start such a process and a
man's later art will bear slight resemblance to that
which he first displayed. Who would have prophesied
Schubert's final expression of his genius from the Mo-
zartian Symphony in B flat major of his early youth?
Who would have thought that the author of *Love's
Labour's Lost* would have lived to write *Hamlet*? Who
would have prophesied that from the art of a *Culex* an
Aeneid would grow? Look backwards, however, from the
Aeneid or from the *Georgics* or from the *Eclogues* to Virgil's schoolboy poem, and upon his early work in general:
you will find there what the author of the verses appended to some of the minor poems thought he found —
the seeds of poetry divine, and the epic Muse breathing
in diverse forms of verse:

> illius haec quoque sunt divini elementa poetae
> et rudis in vario carmine Calliope.

Varium carmen, diverse experiments, amid which are
glimpses of a temperament essentially epic struggling for
expression — somebody who knew Virgil wrote these

words. The promises found in the minor poems are later fulfilled. We will examine them more minutely in the succeeding chapter, noting particularly the impulses that led Virgil to the pastoral.

IV

Virgil's master in the pastoral was Theocritus, a genius of a different order, to whom he dutifully and gladly paid the homage due to the greatest name among singers of the field and fold. The idylls of Theocritus were woven into the tissue of his mind. They lay in the deep well, along with the best of other poetry, Greek and Roman, and with visions of his native Mantua and the Brescian Alps, of the splendor of the bay of Naples, the river Galaesus, and the mountains of Sicily. Hero-worship was also there, with a lineage of heroes — Pollio, the first, then Varus and Gallus, and last and not least the godlike Octavian. The wrongs of his countrymen, ejected to make room for the veterans of Antony and Octavian, were borne on his heart, and they mingled with the discordant pastoral scenes that his fancy was reshaping. There is, further, the surging prophecy of a new Rome under a new leader, the heir of all the ages and the ruler of a new and golden age. Here is tumultuous chaos, and from it there took form under the poet's creative touch an Arcadian fairyland, harmonious and real. The magic of the *Eclogues* would take a volume to unfold. We will pry into its mysteries later.

As Virgil wrote the closing lines of his *Georgics*, some seven years later, he looked back, with an amused affection, to what he calls the youthful hazard of his *Bucolics* —

> carmina qui lusi pastorum audaxque iuuenta
> Tityre te patulae cecini sub tegmine fagi.

The *Bucolics* are indeed of a novel type, and one most hazardous for any save a magician. But the poem that he had just finished is no less daring. It is a poem on farming, eminently practical, full of sound precepts, and of delight in the dirty actualities of the soil. At the same time, in a way that I shall attempt to set forth in a later chapter, it is a moral satire in which the larger ideas of the poem of Hesiod, who also was no simple farmer, are woven into a new design. It is a rhapsody with no touch of the sentimental. It is at once a tribute and a challenge to Lucretius, the master of his youthful mind. It is a philosophy of life, gained after turbulent reflections, and perhaps not permanently gained. It is a tract for the times, though in no sense a document of propaganda written to order. Rather it is a warning to the state and an exhortation to its ruler to establish the strength of Rome, as of yore, in industry, contentment, religion, and peace. It is, finally, another bold flight into epic, in which the poet aspires to give the business of the farm a heroic setting —

> angustis hunc addere rebus honorem —

in sounding verse, the epic tone rising or falling as the theme requires, now thundering against the menace of war, now moving calmly on high levels as it proclaims the glory of the countryside divine, now gliding on with exquisite grace in the sprightly mock-heroic of the bees, and at last speaking out loud and bold in the story of Orpheus, as Virgil, knowing that the moment has come, meets Homer on his own ground. Here is diversity, incongruity, enough, in the elements from which the poem is wrought, but only a golden harmony in the finished work. There are no patches here, purple or drab; there is no line, no word, that does not play its part in a manual, and an epic, of farming. The *Georgics*, as Dryden observed, displayed Virgil's most finished art. What magic had created, patient care wrought into perfection.

We have no ancient manuscripts preserved which, like the successive editions of *The Ancient Mariner*, show where, and why, the poet made over the verses that first had flashed from him. But again we have a precious bit of information preserved by the ancient biographer,[1] who states that when Virgil was at work on the *Georgics* he would write a great many verses — *plurimos versus* — and spend the whole day in reducing them to as few as possible — *ad paucissimos* — "not inaptly remarking that in the manner of a mother bear he gave his poem birth and licked it into shape." Tennyson did not quite accurately describe

[1] Brummer, p. 6.

Old Virgil who would write ten lines, they say,
At dawn, and lavish all the golden day
To make them wealthier in his reader's eyes.

Virgil wrote more than ten lines at dawn — he wrote
plurimos versus in the rush of inspiration. At the end of
the day, some ten remained, all of burnished gold. As
we have already learned from the *Eclogues*, miracles are
wrought not only by lightning stroke, but by patient
mixing and re-mixing of the elements in a crucible.

Who shall set forth the magic of the *Aeneid* in a page?
It would take a magician to do it. The design of the
epic, of which from his boyhood the poet had dreamed,
was of amazing proportions, and, like all his works, replete with incongruities. A lucky chance shows us how
the plan developed in his mind. He, first, as is set forth
at the beginning of the Third Georgic, would build by
the banks of his native Mincio a temple to the victor,
his hero Octavian. He will write in his honor, he means,
an epic poem to celebrate his triumphs. The poem is
concerned, accordingly, with contemporary events. There
is, to be sure, an inferno, designed for the enemies of
state, and the lineage of the Julians is deduced from
Troy; here is a tiny seed of mythology, from which the
real poem was destined to grow. For, as it matured in
his mind, the contemporary and historical elements
withdrew to the background, the mythical and universal
advanced to the fore. And yet the meaning of the poem
is for Virgil's generation. Just as the subject of the

Georgics is farming, although farming is glorified in its setting of ideals, so is the subject of the *Aeneid* still the rule of Augustus, the hopes of Rome, the mission of the present age — seen, however, from the remote past *sub specie aeternitatis.*

To form this design, much mellowing of the incongruous was needed in the deep well of the poet's mind. His sovereign master was Homer, whose verses none could steal, but there were minor masters of the epic and the epyllion to whom he turned — notably, Apollonius Rhodius, and Catullus, and Father Ennius. Furthermore, the dramatic poets — and not Aeschylus alone — had taken slices from the Homeric feast. The characters of ancient epic had played their part in tragedy. It was through a tragic atmosphere that Virgil looked back at Homer. Tragedy is an essential part of Virgil's poem — he was forever joining together what critics would keep asunder. He was confronted, also, with a tangled mass of tradition, partly preserved for us by the historians and the ancient commentators on his poems, and all this he had to unfashion and remould. Yes, much was stirring in the deep well.

No less complex was the development of the characters in the poem. The greatest triumph is the creation of Dido. Much reading, observing, pondering, combining, fashioning, unfashioning, went on in the poet's mind before that radiant being stepped out on the scene —

matri longa decem tulerunt fastidia menses.

Dido had probably appeared in the story of Aeneas as told by the Roman predecessors of Virgil, but she must be made worthy of Homer, since in the *Odyssey*, too, a hero had been diverted from his objective by an enchantress — by more than one enchantress. Then, too, the legends of maidens abandoned by false lovers must contribute to the picture. Medea stirred the poet's fancy, and she was also an enchantress. Something could be garnered from Apollonius's *Argonautica* and from the tragedy of Euripides. Tragedy, again, was demanded, and a transmutation of Catullus's Ariadne from pathos into the sterner sentiment of the drama. But all these suggestions from masterpieces of the past would amount to nothing by the mere assembling of them. They are absorbed into a creature of flesh and blood, true queen and true woman, whose charm and whose betrayal bring every masculine reader to his knees and fill him with a sovereign contempt for the pious cad who preferred a hazy Italy to her. There is no need to debase this perfect art by imagining that Dido points a moral lesson, typifying some naughty Cleopatra for the shame of Mark Antony, who ought to have shown himself a good Stoic like Aeneas.

But there is magic in Aeneas too. The masculine reader admits it when his indignation has cooled. The task for the poet, seemingly easier, proved harder. The material to be moulded is less ductile. The triumph, if triumph there is, will be all the greater. Aeneas, the

emissary of the *fatum Romanum*, must be modelled to a
certain extent on the heroes of Homer and Apollonius
of Rhodes and Greek tragedy. He must be human. If
he would win our sympathies the tragedy must be his, no
less than Dido's. How can that be done? Only by the
art of magic.

We have seen what sort of task the poet had set himself when he shifted the scene of his epic from his own day
to the dawn of history, or rather to an age when myth
and history were inextricably confused. His object was
not to disentangle, but to select whatever fitted his new
design. The schoolboy, gliding along, or stumbling
along, the lines of the *Aeneid*, imagines that all the poet
had to do was to tell an old story in hexameter verse.
But nobody had told that story before. The reader of
the ancient historians and of the ancient commentators
on Virgil becomes aware of a tangle of traditions cluttered with inconsistencies and absurdities through which
the poet had to cut his way. From such matter he makes
his story and his characters, with an eye to Homer and
Greek tragedy and the whole lineage of noble poetry.
But more than that, — more than Homer had had to
attempt, — the story, the characters thus formed,
though located in the past, must shine through the
varied mists of the ages to the poet's day. And cor-
respondingly, present conditions and persons and places
must be disguised and metamorphosed until their outlines melt into the ancient setting. The mansions on the

Palatine must be laid low that Aeneas may be wakened
in a cottage there by the song of birds, and near the
spot where Agrippa had put through one of the great
engineering feats of the day the hero must go downward
on his mystic journey to the shades. A hundred such
acts of creation confronted the poet's mind. I could not
begin to suggest them in these slender discussions,

> non mihi si linguae centum sint oraque centum
> aurea vox.

Enough magic is in all that to madden an ordinary brain.

We forget, sometimes, that the *Aeneid* did not, like
the *Georgics*, receive the poet's finishing touch. He had
taken the poem with him to Greece; in violet-crowned
Athens or on the coast of Asia he would bring it to perfection, devoting three years to the task. His plans
changed when he met Augustus there, and his change of
plans meant the fatal visit to Megara and his death.
Why did he wish to burn his masterpiece? It had meant
a mighty wrestling with the magic art. He had written
Augustus, when halfway along in his task, that it was
well-nigh in a fit of insanity — *paene vitio mentis* — that
he had attempted it. Doubtless his confidence was
stronger when he had finished what we have today; yet
he knew that some joiner's work was still there, some
scaffolding that awaited the solid columns. There were
the truncated verses; there were the inconsistencies in
the plot. A happy idea had occurred to him before he
took up in the Third Book the story of the hero's voyage;

he would now represent the true goal of that voyage as only gradually revealed to Aeneas — but this notion of deferment, of uncertainty, does not tally with various passages elsewhere in the poem. Similarly, when he adds the council of the gods at the beginning of the Tenth Book, he makes Jupiter decree that Olympus will abstain from further interference with the conflict of Trojans and Italians. That is a brilliant and a novel idea, to make epic battles purely human — but the idea is not carried out (possibly it could not entirely be carried out) in the narrative from that point to the conclusion of the poem. A delicate adjustment was demanded. And then the battle-scenes! Homer had enjoyed them, and had bequeathed them to his successors in epic. But who else could reproduce the hero whom Holmes calls

πόδας ὠχὺς Achilles,
Homer's ferocious old boy?

Only the conscience of an Aeneas could induce Virgil to cultivate bloodthirstiness for bloodthirstiness' sake. And there was Aeneas himself. The poet knew what he had meant to make of him, but would the reader see? Three years of Athens and the cities of Asia. Golden mornings undisturbed. More acts of magic, transforming a word, a line, a book. But that was not to be. Virgil lies on his deathbed. Well, burn the poem, then. What, the Emperor forbids? Then let true poets, Varius and Tucca, take the work in hand, if they will have their way. They may cut it, for he would have cut — but let them not emend. Leave the rude work to be called, with its imperfections, his own.

It were ungracious on Virgil's birthday to point these imperfections out — ungracious to him, and probably unkind to ourselves. For many critics who have been most alive to his defects have written their own sentence. Like the emenders of texts of whom Quintilian speaks, *dum poetae insectari volunt inscientiam, suam confitentur.* It is a more profitable pastime to train ourselves to the detection of magic in the *Aeneid* as in Virgil's other works. And a plenty of magic, of more than mediaeval magic, remains.

CHAPTER II

THE PRELUDE TO THE *BUCOLICS*

VIRGIL was born a poet, but he was also made. He was not born a magician, but he gradually acquired the magical art. As with most writers whose works have lasted, his genius found expression in a thoroughly harmonious form only after varied experiments in alien fields. Epic was his goal. His temperament as revealed in his mature productions is imperial and Augustan. But Virgil started, naturally, with the literary fashions which prevailed when he began to write. Catullus and Calvus were the popular poets of the day. Their themes were largely those of their Greek masters of the Alexandrian age, who had practised mainly the smaller literary varieties — mime, pastoral, elegy, and epigram. They had maintained drama in a new and important species of comedy, but tragedy had disappeared. Epic either had dwindled into short narrative poems, or *epyllia*, or else, if it retained its length, had submitted in spirit to the pervasive influence of erotic elegy. The genius of Catullus lifted his work high above his models; however we technically class him, for sheer lyric intensity he is the peer of Sappho, or of Burns. But his craftsmanship is Alexandrian. In the earlier Republican period, national desires had found expression, however imperfectly, in epic and tragedy, the forms which were best suited to the Roman temperament, and which the writers of the day, Ennius, Naevius, Pacuvius, found lacking in contemporary Greek literature. They turned to the older authors for their vital needs. Nothing could better show, however much they depended on Greek forms, the individuality and sincerity of their effort to create a national and Roman literature. Virgil's ambition, developing slowly at first in an alien atmosphere, was eventually the same.

The record of our poet's progress from Alexandrian to Augustan — a more pleasant history to follow than Milton's transformation from Elizabethan to Puritan — is partly displayed in the ascent from *Bucolics* to *Georgics* to *Aeneid*. It may be more minutely traced if we may regard as genuine certain of the minor poems attributed to him. The question of their genuineness has been hotly argued. Once universally accepted, they fell easy prey to the higher critics of the nineteenth century; the little poems were unworthy of the author of the *Bucolics*, the *Georgics*, and the *Aeneid*, and were therefore spurious. What modern poet would not like his *juvenilia* treated in the same way? In recent years, however, more than one scholar of eminence has declared that the Virgilian authorship of some if not all the pieces can no longer be denied.

Our chief source of information regarding the minor poems is the Life of Virgil adapted by Donatus in the fourth century of our era from that by Suetonius in the second. Donatus tells us that Virgil began his poetical career when a schoolboy with an epigram on Ballista, schoolmaster and robber; in justice to both Ballista and the studious Virgil it should be said that the school probably consisted of gladiators. Ballista at any rate was stoned to death.

> Under this mountain of stone lies buried the robber Ballista;
> Safely by night and by day, traveller, go on your way.[1]

Besides this bit, Donatus adds, he wrote *Catalepton*, including *Priapea* and *Epigrammata*, also *Dirae*, likewise *Ciris*, and, at the age of sixteen, *Culex*. He also ascribes *Aetna* to Virgil, though admitting that the work is in doubt. Since the commentator Servius, who writes in the early fifth century and uses the same sources as Donatus, cites the *Copa* too, this poem may also be included in the list. Certain mediaeval manuscripts likewise attribute to Virgil both the *Moretum* and several short pieces that are obviously not his. The information given in the ancient list was taken by the latter commentators from Suetonius's treatise on the poets; that writer had used reliable and contemporary sources for his chapter on Virgil. Some of the poems, finally, are quoted or mentioned by authors like Lucan, Statius, Martial, and Quintilian. Though we must make some

---

[1] See Brummer, p. 4:
> Monte sub hoc lapidum tegitur Ballista sepultus;
> Nocte die tutum carpe viator iter.

discount for the accretion of later error, such evidence deserves serious consideration. We may at least start with it, as I have indicated above,[1] in our quest of the early development of the poet's art.

I

CULEX

The earliest of the poems is the *Culex*, the plan of which has already been sketched. Virgil dedicates his work to a certain Octavius, whom we shall meet again, and apologizes for a *jeu d'esprit*; there will come a time when he will write of his friend in a loftier strain. Octavius is still very youthful, though his youth inspires respect; "worshipful Octavius," "holy lad," the poet calls him. Phoebus and Pales, pastoral deities, are invoked, for though the spirit of the little poem is mock-epic, its contents, as we have seen, are largely pastoral. The verse shall sing not the sad wars of gods and giants or battles of Persians and Greeks, but the story of the shepherd, the serpent, and the gnat.

For a lad of sixteen, our poet has scored a success, not to say a triumph. Nor does the triumph seem too great for one of sixteen when one considers the performances of John Milton in Latin verse at virtually the same age. There are youthful infelicities, prolixities, and lame verses, but the little parody is cleverly managed, and has pleasant touches of humor, good observation, and a

[1] P. 15.

genuine feeling for nature. The poem is just what a
country boy with the spark of genius might have written
after a certain amount of schooling. He has read his
Homer and his Hesiod. In the latter he discerns, with
no little penetration, not a weary pessimist, as Hesiod
is sometimes portrayed, but a tranquil sage who has
caught the secret of simple delights.[1] The young poet
had also read something of Greek tragedy and medi-
tated on the tragic interplay of fate and human wills.
Fate brought about Eurydice's doom, and yet Orpheus
deserved a share, perhaps the larger share, of the blame.

Sed tu crudelis, crudelis tu magis Orpheu.[2]

Virgil may have known, besides, Alexandrian poems
on love and metamorphosis and journeys to the lower
world. The Inferno portrayed shows none of the special inventions conspicuous in that of the Sixth *Aeneid*;
the gnat goes about indiscriminately as at a circus —
surely an imitator of Virgil writing after the *Aeneid*
would not have been guilty of such chaos. The pastoral
elements in the *Culex* also suggest an Alexandrian
source, though not Theocritus. Of course the whole
poem may be a rendering of some lost Greek work.
I prefer to give Virgil the benefit of the doubt; John
Stuart Mill had read at least an equal bulk of Greek
literature at half the age. Virgil's greatest master, how-

---

[1] L. 96:   aemulus Ascraeo pastor sibi quisque poetae
securam placido traducit pectore vitam.

[2] L. 292.

ever, at this time was his own countryman Lucretius, whose poem had appeared not long before. The pastoral passages in the *De Rerum Natura* and the splendid bursts of moral satire, in which senseless human conventions are matched with the quiet joys of nature, explain the serious part of the *Culex*, supply some of its phrases, and justify, in part, its tautologies and crudities of construction. Catullus is not so much in evidence. Perhaps the latter's poems had not yet been widely circulated; or perhaps the lad had not read them. Soon, at any rate, he attached himself devotedly to the school of Catullus. Possibly he was led to write his epyllion on the gnat by a study of Catullus's Sixty-fourth Poem; though the two pieces are very different, they agree at least in their Alexandrian character. The mock-heroic element in the *Culex* is Alexandrian; so is its abjuration of the lofty but well-worn themes of myth or history in preference for something new or something humble. The new impulse stirring in the poem is Lucretian moral earnestness and the promise of genius in the young poet himself; for the time, he is under the spell of environment, nor has he acquired the magical power of blending discordant notes into a harmony.

II

CATALEPTON—PRIAPEA AND *EPIGRAMMATA*

If the *Culex* is Lucretian, the *Catalepton* attests a vigorously Catullan period in Virgil's career. The title

Κατὰ Λεπτόν, used by Alexandrian poets, means "In Trifling Vein" or "Trifles." The collection comprises the *Priapea* and the *Epigrammata*. The pieces are not all of the same period, but most date from Virgil's youth and immediately suggest Catullus. Indeed, Catullus had borrowed the same title, translating it *Nugae*, for one of his volumes of verse.

PRIAPEA

The *Priapea* are graceful and sprightly soliloquies by the scarecrow-god, who figures also in the *Georgics* and the *Bucolics*. The three little poems are in different metres, one in elegiacs, one in iambics, and one in the beautiful and impetuous Priapean verse which Catullus had employed with effect. In the first poem the god tells of the presents — roses, fruit, and sheaves of grain — given him in the three pleasant seasons of the year, and fears that he may become fire-wood in the fourth. In the second poem a bit of the conventional coarseness is treated with a light humor, and indeed involves a moral lesson for would-be suitors of Priapus. In the third, the god boasts of the pretty offerings which he receives from the farmer's household, and, faithful to his charge, suggests that the youthful marauders will find a wealthier and less vigilant Priapus at the next-door neighbor's, to which he kindly points the nearest path. Virgil would not have been ashamed of this perfect little poem in any period of his career.

EPIGRAMMATA

The *Epigrammata* include fourteen pieces in various Catullan metres, elegiac, iambic, and choliambic; the familiar hendecasyllabic Virgil did not try. Virgil's elegiacs are always of the Catullan and never of the Ovidian type; the later practice of invariably ending the pentameter with a dissyllable is not observed here. The poems are of different dates, but most of them are Catullan in character and probably early. Some [1] show us the youthful Virgil among the poets of love — nothing to wonder at, when we consider the Second Eclogue and the Tenth, with its tribute to Gallus and the school of elegiac poetry. Then there are boisterous invectives, recalling those of Catullus without their inexpressible filth.[2] There is a direct and clever parody of Catullus, at the expense of some upstart.[3] In another,[4] the downfall of some mighty lord of men, perhaps Alexander, is used to point, in a rather boyish and obvious fashion, recalling a passage in the *Culex*,[5] the moral of the uncertainties of fortune; again it would appear that the young poet had read something of Greek tragedy.

Some of the poems are biographically important. The Fourth is addressed to a learned devotee of Clio, a certain Musa, to whom Virgil shows an affectionate respect natural in accosting a patron. The Eleventh laments the death of Octavius, a writer of Roman history, who,

---

[1] Nos. 1, 7. [2] Nos. 2, 6, 12. [3] No. 10.
[4] No. 3. [5] Ll. 339 ff.

rumor had it, died from excessive fondness of the bowl; this, then, is not the sainted Augustus, who spared the bowl and lived till A.D. 14. Piecing together the two poems we find them concerned with the same man, Octavius Musa, who was a member of the literary circle to which Horace, Virgil, and Maecenas belonged,[1] and one of the agents of Octavian during the disturbances at Cremona. He paid off an old grudge on the Mantuans by taking a slice from their territory too; it looks as if he were, or had been, a resident of Cremona.[2] We now may guess, with some probability, who the Octavius is in whose honor the boy Virgil wrote his *Culex* — a somewhat younger boy of higher station, whom Virgil met in his schooldays at Cremona, of whose career we get glimpses down to 35 B.C., when Horace published his first book of *Satires*, and whose unfortunate death is recorded in the Eleventh Poem of the *Catalepton*.

Another biographical poem is the Ninth, a panegyric of Messalla written in 27 B.C. on his triumph over the Aquitanians. Messalla, as the dedication of the *Ciris* shows, had been interested in Virgil's youthful work. Virgil, like Horace, though specially of the circle of Maecenas, was not thereby debarred from friendship with other patrons of literature. Horace made Messalla the fine present of his best convivial ode, *O nate mecum consule Manlio.*[3] Virgil contributed the present piece, a

---

[1] Horace, *Sat.*, I, 10, 82.   [2] See Servius on *Ecl.*, IX, 7.
[3] *Carm.*, III, 21.

distinctly mediocre affair, such as great poets sometimes produce when writing from a sense of duty. And yet there are touches of the real Virgil in the poem, particularly in the neat compliment to Messalla's Greek pastorals, which Virgil describes with a reminiscence of his own.[1]

A poem often believed Virgilian by various scholars who do not accept the *Catalepton* as a whole, is the boyish farewell to poetry as the sterner training in philosophy under Siro comes in prospect.

> Hence, rhetoricians! Pompous herd,
> Whom breath of Greece has never stirred,
> Ye portly pedants known to fame,
> Well-padded folk, your verse the same,
> Tinkling your cymbals to deaf youth,
> Avaunt! Sweet mates, I'm sad, in truth,
> To leave you. Sextus, heart of hearts,
> Goodbye! I sail for fairer parts;
> To Siro's wisdom I repair,
> Who'll rid my soul of every care.
> Muses! I bid ye too, farewell.
> Sweet were ye Muses, truth to tell.
> Aye sweet! So guide ye still my pen,
> Coming discreetly, now and then.[2]

The vigor of this little poem suggests the bits of Catullan invective in the *Catalepton*. It also ushers in an important period in Virgil's youthful career. It must have been written after the *Culex*, but not very long after.

[1] L. 17. Cf. *Ecl.*, I, 1:
> molliter hic viridi patulae sub tegmine quercus.

[2] No. 5.

We hear of Siro some years later, in a poem,[1] or little prayer, addressed to the humble villa, once Siro's, which now was to shelter Virgil, his father, and others of his family, "If sadder news comes from my native town." The circumstances suggest a time either after the battle of Mutina in 43, or after Philippi in 42. The poet writes presumably from Rome. Wherever the little villa was, its philosophical owner had found it, as Horace found his Sabine farm, stocked with that abiding wealth which the young author of the *Culex* had praised.[2] Whether Virgil and his family actually had recourse to this villa, we do not know.

The latest poem in the *Catalepton* [3] is also a prayer. Virgil is at work on the *Aeneid*; in a moment of pious confidence he makes a vow to Venus.

> Grant me but strength and skill,
>   My purpose to fulfil,
> Lady of Paphos and the Idalian shrine;
>   To sing him fairly home,
>   At last thro' his own Rome,
> Sharing thy state, that Trojan son of thine!
>   Not paltry frankincense
>   Or painted board's pretence
> I'll vow, nor homely wreaths with pious finger twine;
>   But a horned victim high,
>   A bull, no ram, shall die,
> Proudly thy hallowed hearth to incarnadine:
>   And sculptured Love shall stand,
>   Hard at his mother's hand,

[1] No. 8.
[2] Cf. l. 2, *verum illi domino tu quoque divitiae*, with *Culex*, ll. 58–97.
[3] No. 14.

With quiver gay and wings of rainbow shine;
　　Set, then, from thine isle thy sails,
　　O Queen; thy Caesar hails
From Heaven, and thine own shore invites, thy Sur-
　　rentine![1]

It is tempting for those who love the bay of Naples, as the poet did, to accept the truth of this picture. It seems too good not to be true — Virgil building an altar on the beach at Sorrento.

Only one number in the collection gives rise to serious suspicion, the Thirteenth Poem, which in metre and matter is an epode. A certain Lucius has declared our poet so enfeebled by dissipation that he can no longer endure the toils of the sea or the camp. Virgil describes the vices of his critic in billingsgate so abusive that it suggests a literary exercise. Virgil had not served in the army or the navy and his life had been singularly pure; even Suetonius could rake together only a few dubious items for the chapter of scandals with which he regularly equipped his biographies of illustrious men. May we not father the contents of this poem on the patient Greeks? There is distinctly a liturgy of abuse, which Archilochus and Catullus, Cicero and Filelfo and Milton, well knew, and which relieves us of taking their invectives as narrative truth. Horace in his *Epodes* can also use autobiographical fiction with effect, satirizing the third person in terms of the first. The present piece might have been prompted by the *Epodes*, which Virgil doubt-

---

[1] Translated by T. H. Warren, *The Death of Virgil*, ll. 756 ff.

less knew considerably before the volume appeared in
30 B.C., or perhaps it occurred to him even earlier, in the
storm and stress of youth, to turn into an Archilochian
epode the material of a Catullan invective. In that
case, Virgil pointed the way for what Horace rightly
claimed as his literary creation, just as he called lyric
poetry his own despite the few essays of Catullus with
Sapphics, and just as Ovid is the original author of
heroines' love-letters, though Propertius hit the idea
first.

The *Catalepton* closes with a quatrain from the editor
of the collection or, more probably, of a larger collection
embracing other minor poems as well.

> Who sang more sweetly the Sicilian song,
>   Greater than Hesiod and Homer's peer,
> To him the epic seeds belong
>   That stir unseen in varied verses here.[1]

If Varius or Tucca, Virgil's literary executors, did not
write this envoy, some other expert did, who knew that
"sweet" was a favorite word with Theocritus and that
Virgil's temperament was epic. The Fourteenth Poem
has the right ring, but otherwise there are no conspicuously epic seeds in the *Catalepton*; to justify the eulogy,
we must examine the other poems that led to Virgil's
Bucolics.

[1] Vate Syracosio qui dulcior, Hesiodoque
      maior, Homereo non minor ore fuit,
    illius haec quoque sunt divini elementa poetae
      et rudis in vario carmine Calliope.

III

CIRIS

The *Ciris* seems at first reading curiously unlike Virgil. The author, who confesses his youth in no uncertain terms, is devoutly attached to the garden of Epicurus. He scorns the prizes of the fickle mob [1] and craves above all things the glory of some philosophic achievement. He would look down on the passing show from a Lucretian ivory tower, which rests, in a more eclectic fashion than Lucretius would have approved, on the pillars of the four ancient schools. Feeling that his scientific powers need development, he will for the moment give his patron, the young Messalla, the best that he can.

It shall be the story of Scylla's unhallowed passion for her country's enemy Minos, which led her to cut from her father's head the sacred purple lock on which the safety of the city depended. The young poet soberly rejects the legend of that other Scylla, who,

> Girding with yelping monsters her fair loins,
> Tossed in deep pools the ships of Ithaca
> Whose men were mangled by her sea-born hounds. [2]

He declares with a certain wit that neither Homer, who preserves the yarn, nor Ulysses, who tells it, has the best reputation for veracity. At most, it is an allegory of vicious passion, which he would destroy. In the *Culex*,[3] he had given the Homeric version in language

---

[1] L. 2. Cf. *Catal.*, IX, 64.   [2] Ll. 56–61.   [3] L. 331.

similar to that here. In the *Eclogues*,[1] he fuses the two legends and, using again the lines of our passage, declares it is the very daughter of Nisus who became the sea-monster; artistic unconcern is as natural in the *Eclogues* as tremendous scientific seriousness is in the present poem. In the *Georgics*,[2] Scylla is the bird once more, but in the *Aeneid*,[3] the monster. Virgil could alter his treatment of the legend to suit his varying purpose. We may not infer, therefore, that the *Ciris* is not his work just because he there condemns the version of the myth that elsewhere he accepts.

After a brief invocation of the Pierides, the poet is ready for the story, which he tells with a firm dignity and a certain mystic wonder, of which the exclamations over the metamorphosis of Scylla are typical.[4] Despite occasional roughness in verse and phrasing, the poem is a noteworthy success. Scylla deserves a place with the characters of tragedy. The moment when her old nurse overtakes her in the act of stealing by night to her father's chamber in quest of the fatal lock is full of tragic feeling. Despite the horror of the deed, we have the sense of some uncanny destiny that overrules poor mortals and occasions part at least of their guilt — *crudeles vos quoque superi*. A touch of this idea, we saw, was present in the very earliest of young Virgil's works. As a whole, the epyllion of *Ciris* is in the manner of Catullus and his contemporaries. It also shows some of

[1] VI, 74–77.   [2] I, 404 ff.   [3] III, 420 ff.   [4] Ll. 195 ff.

their minor traits of versification and language, such as the diminutive adjectives *frigidulus* and *tabidulus*. Indeed, the combination of *Catalepton* and *Ciris* suggests a thorough-going emulation of the two varieties of Catullus's work, the *Nugae* and the longer poems. No touch of his wistful romanticism, the yearning for a Golden Age, appears; its nearest approach is the sense of wonder and mystery. The laments of Scylla and Carme are inferior in pathos to that of Ariadne in Catullus, but the tragic element gives the *Ciris* a peculiar intensity which the latter wholly lacks. Virgil entered the lists against his master another time when in his story of Dido he again transformed pathos into tragedy. A dim prophecy of this achievement is given in the present poem.

Another prophecy of the later Virgil consists in the identity of phrases, lines, and passages with portions of the *Bucolics*, the *Georgics*, and the *Aeneid*. These are so extensive that many believe that the *Ciris* is a later imitation, in places almost a cento, from Virgil's genuine works. And yet the piece seems clearly of the school of Catullus. It is hardly conceivable that some belated admirer of the late Republican poets wrote it toward the end of the Augustan period, incidentally making large appropriations from poetry of a different sort. The perplexities raised by this hypothesis are cleared by the testimony of tradition. The poem does belong to the earlier period, but it is by Virgil himself. To see how a later Augustan used the same material, we can turn to Ovid's story of Scylla, or of Byblis, or of Myrrha,[1] where dapper rhetoric and expert mastery of pathological impossibilities replace the sober and somewhat archaic art of Catullus and the author of the *Ciris*; technique has developed and grandeur disappeared, as in Bernini's sculpture after that of Giovanni Pisano. Two ingenious theories, neither supported by external evidence, have been proposed, one[2] that the *Ciris* is a collaboration by Virgil and his beloved friend Cornelius Gallus, brother-poets like Coleridge and Wordsworth, the other[3] that the author is Gallus, to whom Virgil paid the compliment of constant borrowing. But Virgil also paid the same compliment to his own works — to the *Bucolics* in the *Georgics*, and to both of these in the *Aeneid*. He reverted to what was good to make it better.

Since the *Culex* was written in 54 B.C., and Virgil's youthful revolt from rhetoric took place not long thereafter, we may plausibly assign the year 50 as the approximate date of the *Ciris*. Since it is more mature than any of the works that we have examined, Virgil may have devoted three or four years to its composition, emulating the careful method of Helvius Cinna and his nine-years-pondered lay on a similar story of filial impiety.

[1] *Metam.*, VIII, 1; IX, 450; X, 298.
[2] J. W Mackail, *Lectures on Poetry* (London), 1911, pp. 48 ff.
[3] F. Skutsch, *Aus Vergils Frühzeit*, pp. 61-102.

IV

AETNA

The philosophical achievement to which the poet of the *Ciris* looked forward perhaps lies before us in the *Aetna*. This work is included only doubtfully in Donatus's list, but its theme might have led critics in antiquity, as it does today, to question the attribution to Virgil. Furthermore, the language of Donatus, which may be that of Suetonius, need not involve the writer himself in the doubt which he reports.[1] Modern scholars have assigned it to various dates ranging from 45 B.C. to 79 A.D., present opinion inclining to an author of the time of Nero. But though Virgil would hardly have devoted a poem to natural science in his later days, it is precisely the subject which would appeal to him in the brief period when he had turned from the glamour of letters to sterner training under Siro the Epicurean. For Epicureans of the type of Lucretius and the young Virgil were more interested in the physical laboratory than in roses and wine.

Our poet starts off with an invocation to Phoebus, not too poetical a beginning for an imitator of Lucretius, who called Venus to aid him in the building of his philosophic verse. There follows a bit of satire on the Golden Age, which poets, the writer says, seem to know better than their own times, and on the stale fables which

---

[1] Scripsit autem de qua ambigitur Aetnam (Brummer, p. 5). Servius in his comment on *Aen.*, III, 571, quotes the *Aetna* as Virgil's.

everyone has sung; among them is included the tale of
Ariadne abandoned on the barren shore — this looks
like a hit at Catullus and the kind of poetry which
the young philosopher himself had shortly before been
writing. This despite of mythology might seem unlike
Virgil, if there were not the same sort of thing in the
Culex and the Third Book of the *Georgics*. The tone is
milder, naturally, in both cases. He would not later, as
here, call the poet's function the dissemination of false
report. Ovid blithely uses a similar phrase,[1] and Lucretius likes to harp on the splendid lies that are fed to
mankind by poets and allegorists. As early as the wise
Solon,[2] in fact, a poet could declare

πολλὰ ψεύδονται ἀοιδοί.

Of course this is one way for a poet to establish his own
reputation for veracity.

The subject of the poem, doubtless inspired by the
Sixth Book of Lucretius, is the real cause of volcanoes.
Here is a matter in which the gods are not involved, for,
free from sordid cares, they dwell in the palaces of the
sky and mind not our concerns; the poet, like Lucretius
and the author of the *Ciris*, is of the school of Epicurus.
The tale of Vulcan and the Cyclops and Enceladus's
fate in the battle of gods and giants is an idle affair, our
poet declares, a concession to mendacious rumor; how-

[1] *Fasti*, VI, 253.   [2] *Fragm.* 26.

ever, he takes a certain pleasure in telling it. Most of
the staging of life, he continues, is falsity.[1] The poets
have invented Hades and its famous sinners and Jove's
amours and the rest. That is well enough for poetry,
but our present concern is truth — it would not be impossible, perhaps, for our philosopher to turn to mere
poetry again if occasion arose. The real explanation of
Aetna is that air works into the crevices of the earth,
induces fire by its action, and thus ignites and sets in
motion masses of earth and stones. The theme is high
and difficult, but fertile in reward [2] and worthy of the
dignity of man, who was born not like the beasts to
grovel in the earth, but to raise his head to the skies and
to inquire proudly into the laws that govern the heavens
and the earth. Scientific discovery is a rare and sacred
pleasure, the veritable thrill of religious awe that the
vision of raining atoms inspired in Lucretius. The ordinary pursuits of mankind are idle — the quest of gold in
the veins of the earth, or the farmer's struggle for fertile
soil and bursting crops and lusty herds, with the ignoble
lure of wealth ever in the foreground. This disillusioned
picture of the agricultural career suggests the toils of
Lucretius's unhappy farmer rather than the cheerful
gospel of labor set forth in the *Georgics*, though the latter
work contains an inconspicuous passage on that round

[1] L. 76: plurima pars scaenae rerum est fallacia.
[2] Cf. *Georg.*, IV, 6:
        in tenui labor; at tenuis non gloria.

of chores and calamities which justify exasperation and the prompt and wise maxim,

>Praise big estates and till a tiny one.[1]

Read this passage with no knowledge of its context, and you would think it came from a satire on the farm in the vein of the present lines from the *Aetna*. The real cure for the ills of life, our author continues, is not sordid farming, but the cultivation of the richer soil of the intellect.

>Lay in a store of liberalizing arts.
>These are the mind's true crops, the richest wares.[2]

Learn of science the real secret of Aetna, and idle fears and superstitions flee apace. The fine arts are treated by our poet in a rather Stoic spirit, of which there is a touch in the *Aeneid*.[3] At least, why go sight-seeing to Thebes and Sparta, Athens and Troy, when the greater wonders of nature, such as Aetna, lie unheeded all about us? This is a familiar Horatian strain, to which the modern traveller would gladly listen and spend the remainder of his days at Taormina or the Sabine farm. There is a bit of epic in the poet's descriptions, especially in the lines on Troy. And he is by no means insensible to art after all, or he would hardly speak of the "living glory

[1] *Georg.*, II, 412:
> Laudato ingentia rura, exiguum colito.

[2] L. 274: Implendus sibi bonis est artibus.   Illae
> sunt animi fruges, haec rerum est optima merces.

[3] I, 464: animum pictura pascit inani.

of Myron";[1] his real censure is not of the enjoyment of art but of the indifference to nature.

The poem ends, as the last book of Lucretius ends, with an episode. During an eruption of Aetna, everybody was hastily carrying off his dearest possessions, one groaning under gold, one loading his stupid neck with swords, and one staggering under the weight of his poems — a terrible satire on the Muses, whom our author evidently has renounced. All these greedy folk were overtaken by the hot lava, but Amphion and his brother, catching up their best treasures, their aged parents, brought them safely through the flames, which yielded at their approach; science apparently has still room for a few miracles. The poet exclaims, in words recalling one of the mystic raptures of the *Ciris*:

> Happy that day, and happy that blameless year!
> And happy those who saw that day and year![2]

Filial devotion like that shall live forever and bards shall sing its praise; there seems to be some use for the poet after all.[3]

This little work is primarily a Lucretian affair with the attitudes and catch-phrases of Lucretius, but its author is not a profound scientist; Humboldt thought him

[1] L. 598: gloria viva Myronis.

[2] L. 637. Cf. *Ciris*, 27–28:
> felix illa dies, felix et dicitur annus,
> felices qui talem annum videre diemque,

[3] One is reminded of the proud prophecy of the poet of the *Aeneid* that, if aught his song avails, the heroism of Nisus and Euryalus shall be immortal (*Aen.*, IX, 446–449).

a bit obvious. Like the author of the *Ciris*, further, he is more tolerant and eclectic than Lucretius; he speaks of "the truest words of the book obscure" of Heraclitus,[1] whereas Lucretius charged Heraclitus with using obscure words to conceal poverty of thought.[2] The verse is much smoother than that of Lucretius, and one hears the true music of the *Georgics* now and then. The style suffers still from Lucretian prolixity. The writer, for all his scientific fanfare, is hovering on the border between science and poetry. In short, this work harmonizes completely with Virgil's sympathies at the time when he wrote the *Ciris*. We may well regard it as the final memorial of his philosophic or scientific period. Every youth of imagination goes through some telling experience which he afterwards looks back upon with kindly amusement — an Hegelian period, a Walter Pater period, a period of *vers libre*. Virgil was a kind of undergraduate, absolute and determined, in the days of his devotion to philosophy.

V

THE EPIC ON RES ROMANAE

Thus far the spell of Catullus and Lucretius has prevailed. After the *Culex*, the product of the poet's school-days, comes a Catullan period with *Nugae* and an epyllion. This is followed by a philosophic or Lucretian period, of which the crowning effort is the *Aetna*.

[1] L. 538.   [2] I, 638.

Neither of these paths led to genuine success; both gave experience of value. Virgil's thoughts now took a new turn. His biographer tells us that not long before the *Bucolics* he planned an epic on Rome, but, finding the subject difficult, abandoned it in disgust.[1] The subject may have been difficult because contemporary, for though Servius states, among other possibilities, that it was the story of the kings of Alba, the mighty events of the years of civil war in 48 and thereafter would naturally impel to epic a spirit that had been feeling the way towards it; possibly Julius Caesar, the first of Virgil's heroes, as we shall see from the *Eclogues*, was the hero of his essay in epic. There is epic material in the mock-heroic of the *Culex*, particularly its Inferno; there is epic spirit in passages of the *Ciris* and the *Aetna* — *rudis Calliope*, as Virgil's editor said. But the moment has not yet come, and Virgil took up pastoral instead.

VI

COPA

Apart from Virgil's reaction from epic, two motives prompted the *Bucolics*, resulting in two different kinds of eclogue. One is the simple expression of Virgil's fondness of the country and of poems about the country. This pastoral interest, already conspicuous in the earliest of Virgil's works, appears again in the *Copa*, if we

---

[1] Brummer, p. 5: mox cum res Romanas inchoasset, offensus materia ad Bucolica transiit.

may attribute this poem to him. It is attested by manuscripts of the ninth century and later, and though not
in Donatus's list is in that of Servius, and may have
been carelessly omitted by Donatus from Suetonius's
account. We are glad, at any rate, that the poem itself
is not lost, for its charm is unique. It represents the
proprietress of a humble tavern performing a seductive
Neapolitan tarantella outside the door and plying the
wayfarer with various inducements to turn in. In the
manner of the pastoral swain, she enumerates the attractions of the place — the rose, the bowl, and the lute, a
cool and shady pergola, the sweet sound of the shepherd's pipe in a Maenalian grotto, country wine just
broached, sparkling water, and heaps and heaps of various posies brought in a basket by the nymph Achelois
from the stream. Cheeses and plums and chestnuts and
sweet-blushing apples are there. Priapus watches the
garden, which is stocked with grapes and mulberries and
melons.[1] Come in, then, try a summer-bumper and,
twining your brow with roses, gather sweets from the
lips of a pretty girl. Why save up garlands for the sole
end of crowning your tombstone? Yielding to this irresistible appeal, the traveller calls for wine and dice and
bids the morrow look out for itself; for Death, plucking
us by the ear, cries, "Live ye; I come."

There is nothing here that Virgil might not have done.
He could interpret dramatically what is vulgarly called

---

[1] See *In Quest of Virgil's Birthplace*, Harvard University Press, 1930, p. 21.

Epicureanism, as the character of Anna in the *Aeneid* shows.[1] We need not point also to his training in Epicurean philosophy, which, indeed, as its founder preached it, stands nearer to monasticism than to the riotous joy of life. Perhaps the *Copa* marks Virgil's reaction from Epicurean philosophy, when *offensus materia* he turned to poetry again. For the art of the *Copa* is mature. By this time, Virgil has read Greek pastoral with care, and applies its devices to a novel situation; they are applied to a strictly pastoral theme in the Second Eclogue. He uses the elegiac metre, for the elegy had been associated with the pastoral in Hellenistic literature and it has a fascination for Virgil. With its bit of dialogue and its realism, the poem recalls the little one-scene plays, or mimes, which had been popular in both Alexandria and Rome. It is not entirely realistic; the ordinary barmaid would not be familiar with Maenalian grottoes or the nymph Achelois. In this very commingling of art and nature, the piece is characteristic of Virgil.

VII

MORE*T*VM

Another unique poem, of equal perfection and equal if different interest, in the history of the pastoral, is the *Moretum* or *Salad*. It is simply the description of a peasant's morning meal. If this be a sufficiently epic

---

[1] Cf. *Aen.*, IV, 32 ff., and *Copa*, 34–38. The Virgilian authorship of the *Copa* has, in my opinion, been definitely established by I. E. Drabkin in his excellent doctor's dissertation, *The Copa*, Geneva, N. Y., 1930.

subject, the poem is an epyllion. Simylus, probably a slave or a recent slave, owns a cottage and a bit of a garden

> scanty in space but rich in various herbs.[1]

He gets up while it is still dark, finds the hearth by stumbling on it, starts up the fire, grinds his meal to the accompaniment of a song, and calls to his help-mate Scybale or "Trash," a very knowingly portrayed negress.

> Africa's child, her country in her looks —
> Hair kinky, pouting lips, complexion swart,
> Broad chest, low-hanging teats and trim-set waist.
> Slim legs she had, but generous space of foot
> And stiff heels furrowed into numerous chinks.[2]

After mixing his bread — for this essential act of man is not entrusted to a woman — he allows Scybale to bake it, and proceeds himself to the great act of the story, the creation of the salad. Getting the proper herbs from the garden, not forgetting four whole cloves of garlic, he seasons them with salt and cheese, stirring them with a little oil and vinegar into a homogeneous mixture, in which the individual ingredients lose their original virtues to form the new harmonious whole, the perfect salad. Scybale, meanwhile, has taken out the bread and breakfast is ready. Fortified therewith for that day, Simylus draws on his boots, drives his team to the corn-land, and plunges the plough in the soil.

[1] L. 62: exiguus spatio variis sed fertilis herbis.   [2] Ll. 31 ff.

The art of this delightful and original production is not such as one associates with Virgil. It does not, like *Culex* and *Copa* and *Bucolics* and *Georgics*, present a harmony of realistic observation and literary allusion. It is all realism; the names of gods are used for the substances with which they are associated,[1] but this common device does not affect the prevailing tone of matter-of-fact veracity. The author is not, like Virgil in the *Georgics*, concerned with country life as a symbol of simplicity; he is interested in a situation, which he sets before us with vividness and charm. Virgil might indeed have passed through a brief period of realism in the prelude of his career; supposing that unquestionable external evidence vouched for the *Moretum*, we should add it to the list of his experiments. The fact is that, though the poem is ascribed to Virgil in manuscripts from the ninth century on, it is not in the ancient lists. We are relieved of the necessity of adjusting it to the other poems. The quest of its talented author, presumably a writer of the Augustan age, need not engage us here.

VIII

DIRAE

The second and more elaborate type of pastoral is represented by the *Dirae*, "Curses," the remaining name on the ancient list. These curses are pronounced by the poet on his own estate, of which he has been robbed

---

[1] L. 111: Palladii guttas olivi. Cf. vv. 51, 54.

for the benefit of an old soldier. Battarus, a fellow-shepherd, who like Mopsus in the Fifth Eclogue [1] is skilled in accompaniment, plays his pipe while the poet delivers the imprecation, or, more exactly, a kind of summary and reminiscence of an imprecation already delivered; [2] he changes his tones from lively to severe at the other's bidding. The poet prays that the pleasant breezes and the sweet breath of the soil may change to pestilential heat and fell poison; he invites fires and floods to do their worst with his favorite grove and all of his little estate that the impious surveying-rod has now measured off. The pipe plays a more cheerful note as he imagines the new occupant gathering rushes in the swamps where grain flourished before, and hearing the croak of the garrulous frog in the ancient domain of the grasshopper. With the thought that the curse of civil war has brought the evil to pass, the shepherd prepares to leave his estate and his beloved Lydia. His sheep climb slowly down the hills, as he takes a farewell look and vows that nothing can drive from his heart the love of his little farm.

This poem seems sufficiently in Virgil's manner, and is not far removed in time from the *Bucolics*. There are various coincidences in phrase with several of the

---

[1] L. 2: tu calamos inflare leves, ego dicere versus.
[2] Ll. 1–3:

> Battare, cycneas *repetamus* carmine voces:
> divisas *iterum* sedes et rura canamus,
> rura quibus diras *indiximus*, impia vota.

eclogues, and the closing scene notably recalls that of
the first. The verse is firm and strong; the description
contains touches altogether worthy of Virgil, like the
line on the sweet breezes scented with the fields —

> hinc aurae dulces, hinc suavis spiritus agri,

or the smoking showers sweeping down from the high
hills —

> praecipitent altis fumantes montibus imbres.

But these bucolic and realistic elements are combined,
in a more elaborate kind of pastoral, with actual history.
The poem reflects the woes of the Mantuan district,
rather after Mutina in 43 than after Philippi in 42, as the
art of the *Dirae* is less perfect than that of the *Bucolics*,
which Virgil began writing in the latter year. The earlier
poem has not quite received the magic touch. It is interesting for this very reason. It is also interesting because
it helps us understand, in large measure, the motive for
historical allegory in Virgil's pastorals. A real disaster
has come to the poet, if not to himself at least to his
townsfolk. For the purpose of his poem, he plays the rôle
of a shepherd who has lost his farm. He looks for an appropriate form in which to express his indignation, and
selects the poet's curse, 'Aρά, a form of poetry that Ovid
also found useful in his exile. But the curse is fitted to
the situation. Shepherds have lost their farms; it is
a pastoral curse. The next step is to write an actual
bucolic on the same theme. Thus contemporary history

creeps into the pastoral, not because the poet, starting
with the pastoral convention, seeks to enliven it with a
rather questionable novelty, but because, impelled to
write of contemporary events, he adapts them to an appropriate poetical form. The one undertaking is artificial; the other is sincere. But Virgil is never crassly
historical; that is the secret of the *Bucolics* and the
Aeneid alike. So in the *Dirae* it is hard to localize the
poet's farm at either Mantua or Cremona; in fact, it lies
on the shore of the sea,[1] and, if the curse avails, will be
deluged with salt waves and be called another Syrtis —
a disconsolate shepherd in the *Bucolics* makes the same
prayer, which is taken by condescending editors for a
mistranslation of Theocritus.[2] It is ever Virgil's way to
merge the actual in the typical and ideal, and thus to
make its reality the brighter.

LYDIA

The *Dirae*, which is found in manuscripts of the ninth
century and later, is immediately followed, as though it
were part of the same text, by a surely different piece,
the *Lydia*. The poet, driven from his estate, turns back
his thoughts to his love Lydia, whom he has had to leave
behind. He envies his former fields their fair possession.

Invideo vobis agri —

he repeats the words in a lovesick refrain. The maiden
coquettishly, perhaps symbolically, plucks green grapes

[1] Ll. 48–53.
[2] See Conington's note on *Ecl.*, VIII, 58, and below, p. 125.

with rosy fingers, or, crushing the soft grass on which she lies, tells the secret of her love to the listening woods and fields and fountains and the silent birds. Meanwhile the poet is slowly pining away. Never maiden prettier or wittier than she, or, whether Jove come in form of bull or gold, — may this information never reach Jove's ears! — none more worthy of his love. The happy animals are all mated. The moon has her Endymion and Phoebus his Daphne. The sky is populated with the sweethearts of the gods. Why then has so dreary a lot befallen humankind? Or is the poet's passion a sin? Was he the first in history to know the joys of stolen love? Would indeed that he had gained this proud distinction! His name would go ringing down the corridors of time. There follows another series of divine exempla, the amours of gods and heroes in the Golden Age. Ah, why was not the poet born then, rather than in the day when passion is out of date? Such is the rack and ruin wrought on him by pitiless fate, that scarce enough of him remains to make out with the eye:

> tantam fata meae carnis fecere ruinam,
> ut maneam quod vix oculis cognoscere possis.

With that, this belated Jupiter melts away literally into an ounce or two of decadence.

The author of this poem does not seem like Virgil. He is a descendant of the later Hellenistic poets, in whose work pastoral was submerged in the erotic. He is delicately erotic in the description of the dainty maiden and the green grapes; there is a delicacy in the picture of the pale stars in the green firmament [1] — he rather runs to green. There is a touch of humor in his appeal to Jupiter not to listen too closely to the praise of Lydia, and there is a startling paucity of humor elsewhere. Morbid refinement, romantic yearnings, and lack of humor are not Virgilian. The only bond of connection between the two poems agglutinated by chance is that the shepherd's love in both cases is Lydia. That does not prove it is the same shepherd — or the same Lydia. The poem gives an important glimpse into the literary history of the day and puts the originality of Virgil's achievement in higher relief. As the Ninth Eclogue indicates, he may have found a group of pastoral poets in existence, amongst whom he came, as Theocritus amongst the Alexandrians, like a refreshing wind, blowing aside the vapors of decadence and sentimentality. Should a minute comparison of *Dirae* and *Lydia* establish identity of authorship, then we must say that if Virgil himself tried his hand at the decadent style he did not abide by it.

A pastoral mock-heroic at the age of sixteen, Catullan *Nugae* and a Catullan epyllion, a period of stern Lucretian science and revolt from the Muses culminating in a poem on a volcano, a frustrated epic during the civil

[1] L. 39: sidera per viridem redeunt cum pallida mundum.

wars and epic stirrings in the other poems, pure pastoral delight expressed in various forms, a pastoral imprecation inspired by an actual grievance and reflecting contemporary affairs — such is the prelude to Virgil's *Bucolics*. It is an Alexandrian prelude, with signs of some larger impulse. Neither the temperament nor the art of our poet is fixed. His mind is filled with chaotic images and designs, awaiting the magic touch of creation. He reflects without harmonizing the varying literary and philosophical tendencies of the day. With an imagination kindled by the appeal of the moment, he follows now the Muses, from whom he could never wholly escape, and now the sterner daughters of science; it is that ancient battle of which Plato speaks between philosophy and poetry, a battle that Virgil fought till his dying day. Underneath the fluctuation of his youthful interests we may discern here and there that current of epic feeling that later swelled to the full stream of the *Aeneid*.

CHAPTER III

EPIC FROM PASTORAL

(ECLOGUES II, III, V, IV)

WE HAVE followed step by step the varied calls to poetry that came to young Virgil up to the moment when his creative power became confident and steady. The story of this progress lies before us in the minor poems, and even if the verdict of critical scholarship be the exclusion of them all from the number of Virgil's authentic works, we may be positive that the poet experiencèd some such development before he captured the Roman world of letters with the mature art of the *Bucolics*. At least as early as 35 B.C., and perhaps as early as 38, his pastorals are proclaimed by Horace, spokesman of the modern school, as models of the tender grace of that simple style on which the country Muses had nodded approbation:

> Molle atque facetum
> Vergilio adnuerunt gaudentes rure Camenae.

Even if we restrict the number of the genuine pieces among the minor poems to just two — the two which, to the best of my knowledge, everybody who accepts any of them accepts — even so the outlines of the development that I have traced remain. These poems are the

Culex and the Fifth Poem of the *Catalepton*, *Ite hinc inanes, ite rhetorum ampullae*.[1] In those two pieces we see a young poet who begins with the literary interests and standards of the day, with special homage to Lucretius and Catullus. We see a poetical temperament inclined to epic and fond of the quiet joys of the country. We see also, however, a young mind ready to revolt against rhetorical artifice and to turn heart and soul to stern science with a follower of Epicurus for guide. He is not entirely emancipated; he knows that the Muses will come again to him discreetly, now and then. He prophesies for himself a period of fluctuation, which we know gave place to one of matured control. Accept as many others of the mooted poems as you please, and they will only fill in this outline of young Virgil's experience as we read it in the *Culex* and the Fifth Poem of the *Catalepton*. I am accepting hypothetically, as explained above, all, or almost all, the poems on the ancient list, awaiting the presentation of convincing proof that Virgil did not write them, or that some known author, for instance (God save the mark!) Ovid, did.

I

We have noted the impulses that led Virgil to the pastoral, and we have also noted, not adequately but sufficiently for our purpose, the waves of epic feeling and the attempts at epic expression illustrated in his early work.

[1] See above, p. 43.

These two passions of the poet's mind, his ruling passions, were destined like two chemical substances to be fused in a third which is neither one nor the other but both.

The country about Pietole is flat and marshy. It is fertile in grain and vegetables and fruits. The splendid white oxen for which north-central Italy is famous troop the roads, dragging full wagons of hay or the larger wine-carts; the less epic but lovable donkey carries the inferior loads. The most conspicuous trees are the slim poplars, which border the road or divide farm from farm. The vines are wedded in the ancient way to rows of small trees — the profitable mulberry now replacing the ancient elm — with supporting poles on either side; as the traveller spins past, they appear to circle in a joyous dance. The Mincio not infrequently glides over its fringing reeds, and women wash clothes in its pools. Willows grow by and in these pools; if Galatea fled to their not too dense covert today, she would often have to wade. The sea is far away, but a flooded farm or any of the three lagoons into which the Mincio swells at Mantua might seem oceanic to the despairing shepherd of the *Bucolics*.[1] Along the road are luxuriant hedges of white thorn, astir with bees and other flying creatures; sleep in their shade amid the gentle buzzing would be an easy thing. There are no prominent hills. The ground slopes a trace in the direction of Cremona, or the

[1] *Ecl.*, VIII, 58.

Brescian Alps, but the general impression is that of a bit of a prairie, with few traces of the "groves" and no sign of the "mountains" to which the pastoral swain poured out his song. Still, it is a radiant landscape with much quiet charm. The admirable statue of Virgil erected at Pietole in 1881 seems at home there, in a little park of hemlocks, chestnuts, and poplars, full of singing birds

> Stirring with some sweet, unwonted joy.[1]

At the rear, there is a view of wedded vines and elms in the distant fields.[2]

There is no proof that Virgil wrote his *Bucolics* in Mantua. After his schooling in Cremona and Milan, as we have seen, he studied under Siro in Rome. *Ciris* and *Aetna*, the products of his brief scientific period, are more likely to have been written at Rome than elsewhere. With the *Aetna* we come down at least to the year 48. During the disturbances at Mantua, Virgil is in Rome, or at any rate not in his native place, when he addresses the Eighth Poem of the *Catalepton* to the hospitable villa of Siro. The poet does not state that he and his household were actually driven from their possessions and found shelter in Siro's villa; he merely looks forward apprehensively to disagreeable tidings that may

---

[1] *Georg.*, I, 412: nescio qua praeter solitum dulcedine laeti.

[2] For a discussion of Virgil's birthplace and the scenery in the whole Mantuan district, see *In Quest of Virgil's Birthplace*; and B. Nardi, *The Youth of Virgil* (trans. Belle Palmer Rand), Harvard University Press, 1930. See also below, pp. 132–134.

necessitate the change. From the evidence of his own works, then, we should infer that he had not returned to Mantua.

Donatus adds nothing in contradiction of this view. After telling how Virgil completed his studies in Rome, he makes no statement about a further change of residence, save to say that the poet, though owning a house in town, spent most of his time in Campania or Sicily. After enumerating the minor poems, he passes to the *Bucolics*, the chief purpose of which, he declares, was to sing the praises of Asinius Pollio, Alfenus Varus, and Cornelius Gallus for befriending the poet in the troubles at Mantua.[1] Maecenas also interfered in his behalf, and indeed saved his life when threatened by an exceedingly violent veteran. The scene of this episode is obviously Mantua, but Virgil might have gone there from Rome in the interest of his father and the rest of his family. In his discourse on bucolic poetry, Donatus gives further details. We learn that the veteran was a centurion named Arrius and that, sword in hand, he pursued Virgil to a river into which the poet was forced to dive and which he swam safely across. Virgil had previously determined to resist him, relying on the favor of his poems and the friendship of certain nobles. The language admits the interpretation that Virgil had already written something in honor of his powerful friends.

"But afterward," continues Donatus,[2] "gaining fame

---

[1] Brummer, p. 5, ll. 66–70.   [2] *Ibid.*, p. 16, ll. 277–280.

in poetry, he was recommended to Augustus both by Maecenas and by the three members of the Agrarian commission, Varus, Pollio, and Gallus. Thus he recovered his estate and enjoyed the emperor's intimate friendship." The names of the patrons are given in a different order from what he had before, but putting the two statements together we elicit the same information as that given in the Life of Virgil by Probus. The first, that is, to appear in Virgil's behalf are Pollio, Varus, and Gallus. Then came Maecenas, who finally introduced him to Octavian. There are thus two stages in Virgil's experience. First, he either lost his farm or ran in danger of losing it, and was helped by Pollio. Then came another moment of apprehensiveness,[1] and finally Octavian (not yet Augustus) apparently re-established him permanently.[2] The recognition of the simple historical fact that the poet had not yet reached the Augustan Age should correct various errors, ancient and modern, in the interpretation of the *Bucolics*.

Servius [3] puts the matter differently. Virgil, he says, lost his estate when Mantua was involved with Cremona, and *then came to Rome*. Using the influence of Pollio and Maecenas, he was the *only* one to win back his place. Then Pollio suggested to him that he should

---

[1] Brummer, p. 5, l. 70: deinde [edidit] georgica in honore Maecenatis, qui sibi mediocriter adhuc noto opem tulisset adversus veterani cuiusdam violentiam, a quo in altercatione litis agrariae paulum afuit quin occideretur.

[2] That not all the wrongs of Mantua were righted appears from a passage in the *Georgics*, II, 198–202.

[3] Thilo and Hagen, I, 2, 6 ff.

write a bucolic poem,[1] which he finished and revised in
a space of three years. Servius's genuine information
seems in this instance to have been lifted bodily out of
Donatus; his additions, which I have indicated by
italics, are the unfortunate product of his own or others'
fancies. He has the commendable idea, further, of citing
chapter and verse from Virgil to illustrate Donatus's
statements,[2] but stupidly concluding that all of these
must be identified, explains that Virgil's dive into the
river — an incident that the ordinary reader cannot find
in the *Bucolics* — is described allegorically in the line

> See, the old ram is drying off his fleece! [3]

This adventure took place, Servius declares, after Virgil
had his farm restored. It was later restored again and
finally by Augustus, who entrusted the affair to the com-
mittee of three. Hence we see the poet in the First
Eclogue happy over the recovery of his farm, but afterward, in the Ninth, woeful at the loss of it again — a
"verification" of Donatus no less ridiculous than the
discovery of an allegorical Virgil in ram's clothing, and
decidedly more dangerous, because soberly accepted by
generations of critics. We can clear the air by throwing
away Servius altogether and picking up our facts as best

---

[1] The term *carmen bucolicum*, as we see from the title employed by Calpurnius, Petrarch, and Boccaccio, seems to have been applied to a series of
pastoral poems which severally were called "eclogues."

[2] Cf. Thilo and Hagen, III, 3.

[3] *Ecl.*, III, 95: ipse aries etiam nunc vellera siccat.

we can from Donatus and Probus and the *Bucolics* themselves.[1]

There may be a clue, further, in Propertius's brief description of Virgil's poetry. He weaves together reminiscences of various eclogues and says of them in general:

> Thou singest 'neath Galaesus' shady pines
> Thyrsis and Daphnis of the well-worn reeds.[2]

Thyrsis and Daphnis do not, in the *Bucolics*, sing beneath the pines by the Galaesus; it is therefore the poet himself whom Propertius sets there. When Virgil writes his *Georgics*, his memory takes him back to a miraculous garden near Tarentum on the banks of the Galaesus, where one of Pompey's retired pirates cheated nature in as lordly a style as he had robbed man before.

> Spring roses first to pluck, in autumn first
> To garner fruit and when sad winter brake
> The freezing rocks and reined the streams with ice,
> Then would he clip the hyacinth's nodding locks,
> Taunting late summer and the zephyr's sloth. . . .
> He too could set in rows the full-grown elms,
> The seasoned pear and brambles bearing plums,
> And planes that tempted feasters with their shade.[3]

[1] Donatus — if I may designate by the name of Donatus the supplementary explanations in Servius — gives some of the Servian notes, which had evidently descended from earlier commentators. He was familiar, therefore, with the minute and treacherous sort of allegory that Servius adopted, and did not hesitate to include it in his "variorum" set of annotations. What he himself thought about the matter is apparently set forth in his Life of the poet.

[2] II, 34, 67–68.

[3] *Georg.*, IV, 143 ff.

If Virgil had a country-place by Tarentum, we see better why Horace wanted to spend his old age in that smiling corner of the earth.[1] If Virgil knew gardens like the above, we should not cavil at the sublimated scenery in the *Bucolics*. Not at Mantua, then, but in some place remote from it, where he could better idealize it, Virgil wrote his pastorals, creating from recollections of his native countryside, from observations of the new country about him, and from scenes in the Greek poets, his own magic Arcadia.

The *Bucolics* was begun when Virgil was twenty-eight years old and was finished in three years. The outside limits, then, would be the years 42 and 39. We may allow ourselves a certain leeway in establishing these limits. Probus, or the later scholar who made extracts from his commentary, may have depended on good evidence for the date of the first eclogue and the last, but neither he nor anybody else knew the insides of Virgil's mind well enough to tell us just when the design of his earliest eclogue came to him or just when he began its verses at dawn to lavish golden days on their perfection; it is also possible that certain finishing touches were given the last eclogue, or the collection as a whole, after the twelfth month of the third year had expired.

At the time, whatever it was, that Virgil began his pastorals, his patron was Pollio, of whom he says:

[1] *Odes*, II, 6, 9 ff.

From thee the source, with thee the end shall be,
Take thou the songs begun at thy behest.[1]

The compliment should be given its weight and not more than its weight. Virgil did not write bucolics just because Pollio told him to do so. A vivid interest in the pastoral had already appeared in various poems, and in the *Dirae* it is combined in a novel fashion with another literary form. Pollio could have seen the inevitable makings of a pastoral poet in these early works and told Virgil where his strength lay. Nor is there evidence that the earliest eclogues were a thank-offering for the poet's Mantuan estate. By the year 45, Virgil had won considerable fame for poetry of various kinds. Pollio, when praetor in Rome in 44, might have known him and helped him with counsel and inspiration. When, on the formation of the second triumvirate in 43, Antony gave over to Pollio Transpadane Gaul, which included Mantua and the neighboring country, a new bond of intimacy would be established between the poet and the statesman. The troubles at Mantua called forth a preliminary protest from Virgil in the *Dirae*, which I am inclined to set in the year 43 or 42; these troubles are not reflected, however, in the earliest eclogues. These are the Second, the Third, and the Fifth. The earlier we can date the Fifth the better, and the Fifth refers explicitly to the Second and the Third.[2]

---

[1] *Ecl.*, VIII, 11: a te principium, tibi desinet: accipe iussis
                     carmina coepta tuis.

[2] V, 86 f.

II

THE SECOND ECLOGUE

The subject of the Second Eclogue is the hopeless love of the shepherd Corydon for the young Alexis, the favorite slave of his master. The lover's consolation is to pour forth his sorrows to the hills and woods. It is the height of the hot noon, when not a sound is heard save the chirping cicada and his own laments. "Were it not better done," he muses, "to put up with tempestuous Amaryllis or dusky Amyntas? Good looks are not everything, after all. I am well-to-do in goats and lambs — if only Alexis cared to find out about me. And I, too, am fair to see, as the image in the calm water on the beach told me of late. Ah, if my love would live with me in the woods and share my humble joys, the chase, the pastoral song! The radiant Naid will bring him lilies in full canisters, pale violets and poppies, the nodding hyacinth and yellow marigold. Downy quinces there shall be, and waxen plums, with laurel and myrtle mingling their perfumes in a nosegay. But what cares Alexis for such gifts? In the contest of giving, Iollas, his master, would surely bear the prize. I was but letting in the gale on a bed of flowers or turning a herd of wild boars into a clear spring. Ah, mad boy, why flee me! The gods did not scorn the pastoral life, nor did Prince Paris of Troy. Let Pallas keep to the cities that she built — the freedom of the woods for me. Our fancies are our fates; lioness seeks wolf, and wolf the goat, and goat the flowering clover, and so Corydon Alexis, each drawn by the chain of his desire. Look, the oxen are dragging home their upturned ploughs and the sinking sun doubles the shadows. Rest for all these after toil, no rest for consuming love. Ah, Corydon, what madness is this! Your vines hang half-pruned on the elms. Seek some useful work. Try weaving baskets. If this Alexis disdain you will find another."

This poem, though we can trace its antecedents,[1] comes like a bolt from the blue. It gives no sense of the experiment. Virgil writes with the free joy of one who has found, after long searching, the appropriate form for irresistible emotions. For pastoral, he turns aside from the later Hellenistic decadence; his verse breathes again the sweet and vigorous air of Theocritus. There is the same revelry in the senses and the same protest against sentimentality. Corydon, like poor Polyphemus in the Greek poet's verses, finds balm for love in song and in his homely tasks; this lesson is suggested and not driven home, for Virgil is less obviously didactic than Theocritus. There is a touch, too, of revolt from the conventions of the town, a relish for the wilds of nature where man does not come — a sentiment, sometimes called modern, which ran riot in Alexandrian poetry and which is treated by Virgil with both sincerity and reserve.

[1] A source recently discovered is the love-poetry (epigrams) of Meleager. See J. Hubaux, *Le Réalisme dans les Bucoliques de Virgile* (Bibliothèque de la Faculté de Philosophie et Lettres de l'Université de Liège, XXXVII [1927], 47). See B. Nardi, "Alexis" in *Il Popolo d'Italia*, September 17, 1930.

And now for the poet's magic. He knows Theocritus by heart, and sometimes consciously, sometimes, it may well be, unconsciously, echoes the haunting music of his master. But he remembers, too, what he himself has seen — downy quinces and waxen plums, and, most cursed prank of Nature that a gardener knows, the wind making havoc in flower-beds. The source-tracker, setting his parallel passages in array, points out that Virgil has committed, as Conington has it, an "incongruity." He has mixed a shepherd with the Cyclops, who in Theocritus pour out their despair in similar strains. That is so. He has dismembered them and put them in a magical cauldron and, with Medea's art, creates anew. Virgil's brown Campanian rustic has a character of his own; his passion is more serious than that of Polyphemus or the melancholy swain of the Third Idyll. The critic may analyze with benefit this process of re-creation, but the result is that absolute art that defies analysis or criticism. Only an unsuccessful magician deserves ridicule. Let us see if those who have discovered the recipe can do the trick.

But there is another act of magic here. The main impulses of Virgil's early work, apart from his interest in Epicurean science, strive for expression in two poetical forms, the epic and the pastoral. The present poem fuses them in a literary creation, the epic pastoral. Into a form that he has produced from a dialect and an imagery essentially Theocritean, the poet breathes a spirit that never appears in Theocritus or in the poetry of his age. The subject is humble, but the verses are heroic. Is this the real pastoral? Is it not courtly and artificial and spurious? Perhaps it is pertinent to inquire whether Theocritus's Polyphemus is the real Polyphemus, who according to scientific authorities today was either a gorilla or a volcano; perhaps we may even inquire whether the fascinating shepherds of the Idylls are real country folk. Theocritus combines the typical and the real, in Virgil's way; he has the same magic of uniting different things. However, the spirit is wholly pastoral. Virgil, impelled by his temperament, tries a more dangerous experiment, the fusing of elements so diverse as country life and the grand style. But the fusion is successful, both in the sentiment and in the verse that embodies it, the "rich, Virgilian, rustic measure" with its Italian sweetness and strength.

> Aspice aratra iugo referunt suspensa iuvenci
> et sol crescentes decedens duplicat umbras — [1]

verses like these tell the finale of some great epic deed.

Virgil's success in this hazardous attempt is set in conspicuous relief by the disastrous failures of his imitators — of all but one.

> Yet once more, O ye laurels, and once more
> Ye myrtles brown with ivy never sere —

[1] Ll. 66 f.:
> "The oxen, look! drag home their hanging ploughs,
> And shadows lengthen with the sinking sun."

these two lines are enough to set the key which had not
been heard since the days of the verse which they echo:

> et vos o lauri, carpam et te proxima myrte.

Milton's *Lycidas* has been condemned, by Dr. Johnson
among others, for its mosaics of imitation and its incongruities; but for Walter Pater it set the high-water mark
of English poetry. He who understands *Lycidas* will not
be blind to the magic of Virgil's pastorals.

The episode treated in the Second Eclogue may not
be altogether imaginary. Servius, who here depends on
sources that go back at least to the second century,[1]
says that the shepherd Corydon is Virgil himself and
Alexis is Alexander, a beautiful slave of Pollio's, whom
Virgil had noticed at one of his patron's dinners and had
received as a gift. Rather curious, then, that the lad
should be glorified in the poem as a type of the unat-
tainable. But Servius also remarks that Corydon may
be Pollio's slave, or that Alexis is possibly Octavian or a
slave of Octavian's. These plentiful suggestions indicate that the ancient commentators started with little,
if any, information. Certainly it is too soon for Octavian
to appear on the scene, and Virgil would have turned
him a neater compliment than the last line:

> If he disdain,
> Some other good Alexis thou shalt find.[2]

---

[1] See Apuleius, *Apologia*, 10.
[2] Invenies alium si te hic fastidit Alexim.

Certain stolid critics, whom even Servius cannot approve, found no difficulty here. "Thou shalt find another emperor," the verse means, "if Augustus rejects your appeal in behalf of your farm." This is a good specimen of what we may call the false "Augustan" interpretation of the *Bucolics*, which has done more than any one error to obscure their simple intention. The name Corydon, at any rate, continues our commentator blithely, is derived from that of the sweet-singing lark, *corydalus*, and that of Alexis — from α privative and λέγειν, "not to talk" — suggests the haughty boy's taciturnity. From this welter of allegory, we may perhaps infer that Virgil, attracted by the beauty of his patron Pollio's slave, made him the hero of an imaginary pastoral, which inobtrusively honors his master too. But even that is uncertain.

III

THE THIRD ECLOGUE

There is no doubt that the Third Eclogue is dedicated to Pollio, for he is named in it. Despite this incidental touch of panegyric, for which Virgil has the sanction of similar eulogies in the idylls of Theocritus,[1] the eclogue as a whole is, like the Second, of a simple, pastoral character. Two shepherds, meeting, engage in an amount of ribald abuse, which prompts Dryden, in his *Discourse Concerning Satire*, to remark that Virgil, had he chosen,

[1] As in XIV and XV.

could have written sharper satire than either Horace or Juvenal, and, in a famous verse and a half, to put "commas after every word, to shew that he has given almost as many lashes as he has written syllables" —

> — non tu in triviis, indocte, solebas
> stridenti, miserum, stipula, disperdere carmen.

Milton's

> And when they list, their lean and flashy songs
> Grate on their scrannel pipes of wretched straw

finely renders the grating music of the pipe, but not the sharp blows of the lash. This part of the eclogue gives Virgil's nearest approach to the rude realism of Theocritus's Fifth Idyll, and yet it is a sort of epic ribaldry after all. The rustics decide to settle their quarrel by a contest of song, and at once fall to wrangling over the appropriate stakes. Menalcas is a learned shepherd even if he does forget the name of one of the astronomers pictured in the prize bowl, but he is not more learned than Theocritus's swains can be.[1] A neighbor, Palaemon, who chances to appear, is hailed as referee. He bids them begin:

> "Sing, as we sit here on the tender grass.
> And now each field, each tree young life begets,
> Now forests burgeon, now is the year most fair."[2]

[1] See the end of Idyll III.
[2] Ll. 55 ff.:
> Dicite, quandoquidem in molli consedimus herba.
> et nunc omnis ager, nunc omnis parturit arbos,
> nunc frondent silvae, nunc formosissimus annus.

At these joyous and exquisite lines, the rustics are purged of their foulness as though by some mystic rite, and the amoebaean contest begins. Virgil is a master of contrasts, learning something of his art from Theocritus, who follows the little tragedy of Daphnis with rustic jubilations,[1] and introduces the song of Adonis by the idle palaver of women.[2]

Successful amoebaean is no easy affair for either contestant. The first shepherd must invent a worthy theme. The second, though having the benefit of this suggestion, must devise a worthy reply, keeping within the lines drawn by his opponent and improving on his model. Damoetas starts with Jove, who fills the world with his presence and has a care, too, for the shepherd's songs. Menalcas responds that he is beloved of Phoebus, to whom he offers the most acceptable gifts, laurel and sweetly glowing hyacinth. This is a fine line —

> munera sunt, lauri et suave rubens hyacinthus,[3]

and the account is squared. Damoetas then tells of his love Galatea, who pelts him with an apple, merry wench, runs to the willows and, in Pope's rendering, "hopes she does not run unseen." "But my Amyntas," replies Menalcas, "comes to me unasked; my dogs know him as well as they know the moon." The next

---

[1] Idyll I, end.

[2] XV, 100.

[3] L. 63. Cf. *Ciris*, 96: suave rubens narcissus. *Priapea*, 3, 13: suave olentia mala. *Copa*, 19: suave rubentia mala. Catullus, 61, 7: suave olentis amaraci.

theme is the proper presents for the loved one; the next, their diversions together. Then, with a good-bye to Galatea, Damoetas clamors for Phyllis. "For 'tis my birthday, Iollas; when I sacrifice a heifer for my crops, why that's the time for you to come" — that is, at a festival of purification and abstinence from love. At that Menalcas does a bit of acting; for pastoral often verges on drama. The shepherd takes the part of Iollas and protests that Phyllis loves him truly. Damoetas now pays homage to his master, as any shepherd might — but the master is Virgil's own patron, Pollio. "Pollio loves my Muse, though it be rustic. Muses, offer a heifer to him who reads your songs." What shall the second shepherd reply? No other name could match Pollio's — the best reply is to repeat the name, to praise Pollio's own poetry, and to offer a larger victim. To compare small things with great, Dante uses no other word but itself to rhyme with *Cristo*.[1] Damoetas proceeds with the eulogy of Pollio. "May he that loves thee, Pollio, rise to thine own heights and live where honey flows and the rough brake bears precious spice." Pollio, it seems, busy statesman and warrior though he was, could close his eyes to actualities and live in a Golden Age. May we venture to guess that he had found the Golden Age by writing pastorals about it? Menalcas, with good taste, feels that there has been enough of Pollio. He passes to poets of the opposite sort. "Who hates not Bavius, may

[1] *Paradiso*, XII, 71.

love thy songs, O Maevius. And he may harness foxes and milk he-goats." Minor poets attempt the miraculous too, but the failure of their magic ends in contradictions and ridicule; there is a fable for Virgil's critics here. The remaining themes are pastoral, including a pair of riddles, such as shepherds liked to tell. At the end the judge cannot pronounce a verdict, and the contest closes with a simple pastoral act, told in an epic way —

Lads, stop the sluice, the fields have drunk their fill.[1]

Spenser, who turns this amoebaean into a roundelay, ends the action of several poems in the *Shepherd's Calendar* with the close of day. He adopts Virgil's device,[2] with no suggestion of his epic tone.

The judge has wisely refrained from assigning the prize, for Virgil has given his readers a perfect specimen of amoebaean, to study which is a lesson in good taste. Theocritus has one idyll, the Sixth, in which the singers come off even, but their songs are of considerable length and offer no test of amoebaean. He gives hints, as in the Fifth Idyll, of what unsuccessful amoebaean is, but only hints. Virgil, working as ever with the traditional material, creates a novelty. A hostile critic,[3] who of all his tribe has perhaps spent the most time over Virgil with the least result, patiently harnessing foxes and milking

[1] Claudite iam rivos, pueri; sat prata biberunt.

[2] Cf. the end of Eclogues I and VI.

[3] P. Jahn, *Die Art der Abhaengigkeit Vergils von Theokrit*, 1897, and numerous later articles.

he-goats, declares that this piece, a mosaic of Theocritean reminiscences, has no worth save that of a literary curiosity. He makes the valuable discovery that there is no telling whether Menalcas and Damoetas are neatherds, goatherds, or shepherds, whereas the distinction is always plain in Theocritus; Virgil has tied himself up in inconsistencies because, filching a line here and a quarter-line there, he has jumbled different contexts. That is the way that a poet of this critic's temperament might compose a Theocritean eclogue, but it is not Virgil's way. Waiving the point that a peasant might conceivably drive both sheep and goats and oxen, we see rather in this eclogue Virgil's peculiar impressionism, his mastery of that illusion which can harmonize the incongruities of prose. We must view a Monet from the proper angle and not, standing too near, pronounce it a daub of paint.

There is no allegory discoverable in this eclogue. The extraneous and contemporary character, Pollio, is mentioned outright, and perhaps, with the Golden Age at his beck and call, he is entitled to enter the pastoral without metamorphosis. Servius rejects the attempts of some allegorists to read into one of the shepherd's jibes a piece of scandal involving Virgil in both larceny and adultery — a curious thing for the poet to immortalize — and lays down the principle that the only allegory in the *Bucolics* relates to the loss of the poet's estate. This is an absurd rule, and Servius does not

always abide by it. For the moment it enables him to
identify Virgil with the ram shaking his fleece after the
bath, while the snake in the grass must be the veteran
soldiery that made life in Mantua unpleasantly insid-
ious. A still more advanced school of allegorists, whom
the cautious Servius cannot accept, find a meaning in
the shepherd's complaint that his beloved boy, though
fond of him at heart, leaves him to guard the net while
he makes for the boar; that expresses Virgil's reluctance
to stay at home while Augustus pursues Antony at
Actium. This is an exceedingly Augustan interpretation. The Berne Scholia, which consist partly of ancient
material, explain that Damoetas stands for Virgil,
Menalcas for Cornificius, and the judge Palaemon for
Octavian. More Augustan interpretation. We cannot
detect that the shepherds symbolize anybody. The one
allegorical clue visible leads us to an impasse. The rare
name Iollas, apparently the proprietor of Phyllis, recalls the Iollas of the Second Eclogue, who owns Alexis
and, as we saw, is perhaps Pollio in disguise. But he cannot be Pollio here, for Pollio is called by name a few lines
below. Possibly, then, Iollas in the Second Eclogue is also
not Pollio, after all. Virgil leaves his allegory, whatever
it amounts to, in a mystifying blur, perhaps to warn us
not to track further his glances of contemporary allusion.

Similarly, we cannot describe the scenery in this
eclogue as local. Professor Conway maintained that the
setting in the odd-numbered eclogues, I, III, V, VII,

IX, is local, while that of the even-numbered, II, IV, VI, VIII, X, is ideal.[1] The only bit of Mantua — and a real bit it is — appears in the last line, where we see the canals of irrigation such as cross all parts of that district even today. The rest is Theocritean, idyllic, Arcadian. The eclogue is a companion-piece to the Second, and is felt by the author to be of like nature to it. It has a touch more of Roman coloring, since Pollio is mentioned in it directly. But it is played on the same reed that the poet discards when the call to something in a deeper, more national strain prompts him to the writing of the poem that succeeds these earlier essays.

IV

THE FIFTH ECLOGUE

Mopsus and Menalcas meet in a grove of elms and hazels, to while away the time in song. As in the *Dirae*, there is a division of function. Menalcas proposes to indite the verses, while Mopsus plays the pipe. The reader wonders if this is the Menalcas who shared honors with Damoetas in the pastoral contest of the Third Eclogue. He is an elder poet here — older, at any rate, than the lad Mopsus. The latter respectfully obeys his senior and, with a certain aesthetic discrimination which has appeared in Virgil's earlier descriptions of nature,[2] looks about for the most attractive setting

---

[1] *The Vergilian Age*, Harvard University Press, 1928, pp. 15–17.
[2] See *Culex*, 48 ff.

for their song. Shall they rest where the zephyrs stir amidst the flickering shadows, or mount, rather, to the cave, over which the vine with its thin-set clusters is trailing? The answer is not given at once, but it is implied. The repetition of the word "cave" in the same line, the pointed "rather," and the shepherd's eager look towards the cave, indicate the choice which Virgil does not need to describe. This is the true Virgilian reticence, a quality conspicuous in the poet's art and allied with the lovable shyness of his disposition, as is finely illustrated in a recent essay by one of the most appreciative interpreters of the poet today.[1] After complimenting the young singer on his victories, over all but Amyntas, Menalcas bids him take the lead; he is not to furnish the music after all. Mopsus consents to render the song that he wrote of late on the bark of a beech and set to music. Menalcas is agreed and bids him sing, for, he adds, "We have mounted to the cave." This talk, then, has been going on during their walk to the cave. The whole picture is before us now, painted stroke by stroke, without a touch too many or too few.

Mopsus starts the song of the nymphs' laments for Daphnis, when his mother embraced his poor body and called the stars cruel. Who is this mother of Daphnis? The nymph that bore him to Hermes? If so, she figures in the story for the first time. The situation recalls

[1] R. S. Conway, "An Unnoticed Aspect of Virgil's Personality," in *Proceedings of the [British] Classical Association*, 1907.

rather the mourning of Aphrodite for her dead Adonis; it prophesies some Italian master's *Pietà*. Now Servius, abandoning his professed principle that allegory in the *Bucolics* relates solely to the loss of the poet's estate, observes that Daphnis represents Julius Caesar; the goddess Venus would appropriately be called his mother, for from her, by one of the genealogical compliments of the day, the Julian line descended. Virgil, then, is mingling the legends of Daphnis and Adonis in the interests of a purpose different from either. We must recognize this possible intent. It grows clearer in the following verses. Daphnis, as the hills and woods repeat, was mourned by Punic lions; he harnessed Armenian tigers to his chariot and led the processions of Bacchus's troupes. We can understand Punic lions in a simple pastoral; indeed they are more intelligible than Theocritus's famous Sicilian lion.[1] But Armenian tigers and the introduction of elaborate Bacchanalian rites have nothing to do with the pastoral lad Daphnis and his fatal love. Servius declares that there is again unmistakable reference to Julius Caesar, who first established the rites of father Bacchus in Rome. Though it is not strictly true, since the *Liberalia* had long existed, Caesar may have introduced some innovation into the cult, which the poet selects as the most pastoral of the

[1] *Idylls*, I, 72. The scholiast, a realist, comments on the absence of lions in Sicily and emends the text to make it read, "The lion *would* have wept, had he been there." This fidelity to geography, alas, does not correct the Greek poet's lamentable infidelity to biology.

hero's deeds and a symbol of his civic reforms in general. The remainder of Mopsus's song is purely pastoral. To Menalcas it is as refreshing as sleep in the grass to tired folk or a draught of sweet springing water to the thirsty wayfarer on a summer's day. The lad has surpassed his master now, in verse as well as music. Here, says Servius, again breaking his rule, is an allegory of Theocritus and Virgil. Mopsus, according to this suggestion, should be the young Virgil.

It is now Menalcas's turn. Consoling the despair of the other shepherd's song, he gives voice to the joy that all nature feels, as Daphnis, radiant with new godhead, mounts Olympus and sees the clouds and stars beneath his feet. The wolf does not beset the flock or the deer dread the treacherous toils, for good Daphnis loves peace; the Golden Age is returning. Yes, even the unshorn mountains cast shouts of joy to the stars; the very rocks, the very bushes, ring with song; "A god, a god is he, Menalcas." Again, this is not the shepherd Daphnis, who went down the stream to Hades, with the hatred of Aphrodite in his heart. A modern might so change tradition, but to Virgil this would seem the height of literary blasphemy and bad taste. This Daphnis, who will be "good and propitious to his people," is none other than the deified Caesar. Donatus curiously imagines that Daphnis stands for Virgil's brother Flaccus, but the poet would not venture to exalt him to so presumptuous a height.

The shepherd now points in imagination to four altars, two erected for Daphnis and two high altars for Phoebus, the great god of shepherds and later of the Augustan Age itself. Twice a year, at seed-time and harvest, there shall be an offering of foaming milk and olive oil; a banquet with a merry pastoral pantomime shall do honor to the new god, who no less than Bacchus and Ceres will fulfil the farmers' vows and be worshipped of them forever. Here, too, the specific allusions cannot be gainsaid. Julius Caesar's birthday fell on July 13, but since that day was included in the period given up to the *Ludi Apollinares*, and since the Sibylline oracles forbade the celebration of any other rite on Apollo's festival, the birthday was kept the day before the festival began. Caesar was not merely a pastoral god, but that is the aspect of his deity emphasized here.

This new song is more charming to Mopsus than the whispering south wind or breakers dashing on the beach or rivers racing down rocky dells. The shepherds exchange gifts. Menalcas presents the lad with the frail reed that sang

"Formosum Corydon ardebat Alexim"

and

"Cuium pecus? an Meliboei?" —

fragments of the opening lines of the Second and Third Eclogues. He receives from Mopsus a shepherd's staff with even nodes and rings of brass. This insignificant detail at the end is artfully placed, like the irrelevant little pictures with which Horace sometimes closes his odes. By avoiding an obvious emphasis of an important idea, the poet somehow sets it in clearer relief.

The closing lines dispose of one allegorical clue given by Servius. Mopsus cannot be Virgil after all. And yet Menalcas, though plainly enough declared Virgil in the lines that accredit him with Virgil's poems, does not seem quite true to type; it is curious for Virgil to put himself among the older pastoral singers on the strength of two eclogues. The character of Mopsus, young, ardent, and victorious, is in some respects better suited to him, though Mopsus is not conspicuous for Virgilian modesty. The master-poet seems to be Amyntas; he is also a rival of Menalcas. Stimichon, Damoetas, and others are also of the band. There are questionable attempts in the ancient commentaries to identify most of them. All ought to have historical counterparts, or the allegory breaks down. It is safer to see no such formal allegory in any of them, even Menalcas, who surely need not be the Menalcas of the Third Eclogue. Virgil's method is rather to give, in a nuance of allegory, glimpses of his own temperament and work. We may infer, perhaps, that he is one of a little group of pastoral writers. That is as far towards the identification of Virgil's comrades in poetry as the scanty evidence will take us.

The eclogue ranks in that constellation of pastoral "elegies" in which the names of Theocritus, Bion, the

Pseudo-Moschus, Spenser, Milton, Shelley, and Arnold are the brightest stars. Virgil innovates in his poem by adding a consolation to the lament, altering indeed thereby the entire character of the traditional form. The way had been prepared for him by the ritual of the festival of Adonis, for the song of the first day mourned the youth's death and that of the second glorified his resurrection. There is a touch of this contrast in Bion's *Epitaphion Adonis*, but Virgil, so far as the literary remains tell us, was the first to apportion formally in the same poem the elements of grief and cheer. His invention became a feature of the pastoral elegy thereafter, being well suited to the purposes of the Christian pastoral.

The Fifth Eclogue is new in another way. While the allegory of contemporary poets is veiled in a haze, that of the deified Caesar, Virgil's national hero, is plain, and forms the substance of the songs. This type of eclogue, Theocritean in form and Roman in substance — a fusion made already in the *Dirae* — has been well called,[1] in allusion to the two kinds of Roman comedy, a *togata*, a piece in Roman dress. The Second and Third Eclogues represent the opposite type, the *palliata*, in which the setting is Greek; they are played, the poet says, on the frail pipe which he now discards. Horace in like manner felt the moment come when he could bid his lyre strike up a Roman song.[2] Virgil's estimate of his earliest

[1] Cf. Leo in *Hermes* (1903), pp. 1 ff.
[2] *Odes*, I, 34.

eclogues is modest, from the artistic, if not from the patriotic, point of view. The Romanism in the present piece, at least in the lines on the *Liberalia*, is a bit frigid. The magician has not quite performed the miracle of playing an epic air on his shepherd's pipe.

This is the only weak spot in an eclogue perfect in its kind. The exquisite introduction, the stately liturgy of Menalcas's song, the shepherd's similes, all have the pure pastoral tone. Shouting cliffs and shaggy mountains shaking their manes and calling to the stars give a vision of nature too immediate and sincere to be dubbed the pathetic fallacy. The shepherd has heard these voices with his own ears; he reports what he has heard. The only fallacy in the interpretation of nature is the failure of a poet to paint a living picture, free from the taint of the morbid or the absurd; whether he personify Nature or reduce her to her elements is of little moment. In poetry as in Kantian philosophy, the understanding is the creator of the law of nature.

The scenery in this poem, odd-numbered though it is, cannot be called local. The only touch of Mantua is, possibly, the description of the grotto in the opening lines. Respectable grottoes may be found in the ridge of Carpenedolo, which by Conway's theory was in ancient times within Mantuan territory (though it is not there today), and the hills at the north near Valeggio would have furnished many more. But grottoes are also a feature of Theocritus's idylls, and the rest of the scenery, in which Punic lions and Armenian tigers are at home, is anything but local. The inner purpose of the poem is the exaltation of Julius Caesar; this part of its coloring is Roman. The poet feels a higher inspiration than that which dictated the Second and the Third. These earlier pieces he puts in a class by themselves, but not on the basis of the scenery that they portray.

We get in this poem for the first time some insight into Virgil's political sympathies. In the year 42, Julius Caesar by vote of the senate and people was declared a god. This was done before the battle of Philippi, which took place in the autumn. Virgil was not twenty-eight until October 15, but without stretching the ancient evidence too far we may suppose the Second and Third Eclogues written in 42, before the deification. This act appealed to Virgil's imagination and occasioned the present eclogue, in which he could better give voice to his inborn sense of epic and hero-worship than in the poems sung on the frailer reed of simple pastoral. We should set the piece late in 42 or early in 41.

From start to finish, Virgil shows himself a consistent monarchist; epic feeling and hero-worship help him to that view. Not every Roman shared his enthusiasm over the extraordinary honors paid to Caesar; Horace, who had fought for the lost cause at Philippi, returned to Rome with far less rosy presentiments. Let us note, however, with some care, that though Virgil pledges his faith to the divine Caesar he does not thereby declare himself a partisan of Octavian. There were two lines of political descent from Caesar, one through Octavian and one through Antony. For the moment these leaders were united in crushing the remnants of republican opposition; dissension was imminent, however, and came to a head in the revolt of Lucius Antony and the Perusine war in 41. In either 42 or 41, Antony seems the more likely hero for Virgil; he had contributed more to the victory at Philippi than Octavian, and he and his deputy Pollio were the governors of Virgil's province. It may be worth noting here that Agrippa, Octavian's famous general, appears among the hostile critics of Virgil.[1] Virgil's attachment to Pollio is obvious in his earliest eclogues; there has been no sign of enthusiasm for Octavian or of any acquaintance with him. Indeed we have the explicit statement in Probus and Donatus that Octavian is the last in the series of great friends who helped the poet during the disasters at Mantua. Virgil, I would conclude, was an imperialist before he was an Augustan. It has been asserted that Wordsworth's *Tract on the Convention of Cintra* anticipated by more than twenty years the nationalism of Mazzini. If this is true, Wordsworth, like Virgil, led his age.

The hope of a high destiny for his nation that rings out in clear epic tones in the Fifth Eclogue is uttered still more confidently in the poem to which we now turn.

[1] Brummer, p. 10, ll. 180–183.

V

THE FOURTH ECLOGUE

"Muses of Sicily, let us sing a somewhat loftier strain." With these words, Virgil announces that his pastoral is concerned with a novel and exalted theme. It is to be worthy of a consul; it is to be panegyric. Moreover, it is prophecy and the fulfilment of prophecy. The last of the ages foretold by the Sibyl has arrived and now is the time for the golden years to recommence. The maiden Astraea, personification of Justice, who hurried to the skies when Saturn's reign was finished, will come again to men, and heaven will send a new-born King, a Messiah, to symbolize the age and lead it. Indeed it is the very moment before the boy is born. May Diana guard his birth! The goddess should come with special favor, for her brother Apollo shall rule the new age, that of the sun, the last of the ten proclaimed by the Sibyl. And what glory to Pollio, in whose consulate the golden era begins! With him as guardian of the state, Rome shall atone for its crime and the world be freed from everlasting dread. Gods and demigods shall dwell with mighty heroes on a new earth, while the lad, with the virtues of his sire, shall govern a world at peace. Still, the universal renovation is gradual; it keeps pace with the growing boy. In his early years, it is nature that first submits to the workings of the new miracle. She lavishes her flowers without tillage; they spring up about the cradle of the child. Goats come to the milking unbidden, and the ox lies down with the lion. More wonders follow as the child grows into boyhood and learns the praises of old heroes and his parent's mighty deeds. Man's sins, however, are harder to eradicate. He still will practise those inventions — sailing, building, and agriculture—the secret of which ought never to have been wrung from the gods. Wars, too, shall not cease at once; there shall yet be foreign campaigns, another Argo shall be manned, and another Achilles dispatched with the flower of chivalry against Troy. But at last comes the consummation, when trading and navigation — war too of course, though Virgil does not stop to say so — will be no more, and every country be sufficient to itself, with nature satisfying all its needs.

"'So run on, ye Ages,' spake to their spindles the harmonious Fates, who utter the fixed will of destiny." These words show, in Virgil's allusive way, that we have been listening to a *Genethliacon*, a Birthday Song, chanted by the Fates as the child comes into the world. As they finish, all Nature, groaning and travailing until now, breaks forth into exultation; for the child is born. The poet renders homage to the mighty scion of Jove, and prays for inspiration fit to sing, in honor of his coming deeds, a pastoral which Pan himself, with Arcady to judge, will say is better than his own. "Come then, little boy, come greet thy mother with a smile. Him on whom his parents have not smiled no god deems worthy

of his board nor goddess of her bed."[1] Again Virgil
wastes no strokes in setting his picture before us; it is his
reticent method of description. The smile of the child
with the answering smile of his parents is the needful
omen of a high career, like that of Peleus, to whom the
poet here alludes. Such was the omen that attended the
birth of Virgil himself; for as we have learned from his
ancient biographer, the infant did not cry, but wore a
benign look, sure portent of some mighty destiny.

This remarkable poem is in honor of Pollio; there is a
quiet, Virgilian crescendo in the panegyric. The opening verses dedicate the poem to some consul, but we are
not told to whom. A few lines below (v. 11), he is addressed with an emphatically repeated pronoun: "In
thy consulship, in thine, the glorious epoch shall begin."
The next line names him; it is Pollio. The next declares
him savior of the state; *te duce* is an impressive and
almost technical designation of majesty, with which
Horace honors Octavian[2] and Tibullus invokes Apollo.[3]
With Pollio the mighty months of the new era begin, and
under his guidance Rome shall make her great atonement. The crime for which she does penance is obviously the succession of civil wars culminating in the
murder of Julius Caesar, whose apotheosis Virgil had
proclaimed in the Fifth Eclogue. Pollio, then, is not an

[1] There is no reason why Quintilian, or anybody else, should desert the
reading of the manuscripts in l. 62: *cui non risere parentes.*
[2] *Odes* I, 2, 52.
[3] II, 5, 15.

aside, a witness of someone else's greatness. He is the leader of his race and the mediator between it and the offended gods; he is invested with the high mission which Horace later sees fulfilled by Octavian. When, therefore, three lines below, the poet declares that the lad shall with the virtues of his sire rule a world at peace, Virgil would seem to have made it as plain as his artistic reserve permits that the sire of the child is Pollio. In 40 B.C. Pollio might well have seemed to many besides Virgil the most prominent figure on the political horizon. He was one of the consuls of the year, and represented Antony's interests at the conference that settled the peace of Brundisium, where Maecenas appeared in Octavian's behalf. Virgil had been devoted to him before, and in the following year, when he writes his Eighth Eclogue, Pollio is still the poet's hero. Now, in the year of his consulate, a son has been born to him; Virgil seizes the moment to express, with a beautiful symbolism, his gratitude to his patron and his mystical longings for a reign of peace. He composes his poem, naturally, after the child is born; the imaginative setting is the moment of birth.

The most competent ancient authorities, I am convinced, believed that the child of the Fourth Eclogue was Pollio's son, but there are rival candidates today. We may pass over various attempts to explain the child as an allegory of the Orphic mysteries or the Roman state; the closing lines would be ridiculous if they did not tell of a human mother and a human child.

Who, then, is the child? One curious notion favored today is that the child was the yet unborn offspring of Octavian and Scribonia. There is no ancient evidence in support of this theory. The commentators, as represented by Servius, wavered between two explanations; the child might be either Augustus, or the son of Pollio; or, by an artful *double entendre*, both might be meant.[1] This is a sufficiently Augustan interpretation, and yet there is no suggestion that the new-born babe is the child of Octavian.

The theory evidently favored by Servius is stated by him in his comment on the opening line. It is after the capture of Salonae by Pollio in his Dalmatian campaign that a child was born to him, named, to commemorate his father's victory, Saloninus. Thereafter Pollio was elected consul, and Virgil wrote the poem. Surely the poem was written at the time of Pollio's consulship, but just as surely is Servius wrong in dating that event after the triumph given Pollio for his Dalmatian campaign. But Pollio had another son, Asinius Gallus, who is stated, on the excellent authority of Asconius Pedianus, to have regarded himself as the hero of the poem.[2] He was born, however, before Pollio was elected consul. On

---

[1] On l. 15: sicut supra, artificiose laudem confundit ut possit esse communis: nam ad quemvis potest referri "ille," vel ad Augustum, vel ad Saloninum.

[2] Servius (= Donatus?) on l. 11: *quidam Saloninum Pollionis filium, accipiunt, alii Asinium Gallum, fratrem Salonini, qui prius natus est Pollione consule designato. Asconius Pedianus a Gallo audisse se refert, hanc eclogam in honorem eius factum.*

the basis of this fact some scholars would rule him out of consideration, insinuating, further, that Asinius Gallus had perverted his own history "that the prophecy might be fulfilled." [1]   But such insinuation is gratuitous. There is no reason why Asinius Gallus should have blinked the truth. The child had already been born before the poem was written. Just when in 41 B.C. Pollio was elected consul we do not know; the dates of elections at that time depended on circumstances. Assuming the earliest possible time in 41 for the birth of Asinius and the latest possible time in 40 for the writing of the poem, even so we cannot stretch the baby's age beyond two years. He was not too old, that is, to inspire a birthday poem of the sort that we find here. The idea of a birthday poem may well have occurred to Virgil the moment that Asinius was born; if that is so, the events that succeeded in rapid order — Pollio's election and the peace of Brundisium — made the character of the work immensely richer than he had at first intended.

Let us examine some of the other possibilities. Antony and Octavia were united in wedlock to commemorate the peace of Brundisium; the child of Octavia by

---

[1] E. Norden, *Die Geburt des Kindes* (Leipsic and Berlin, 1924), p. 11. Norden adds a word on how one should read scholia, and gives in his own Latin what Asconius probably said. Evidently, the true art of reading scholia is to interpolate one's own ideas into a simple text. I am sorry that the excellent work of J. Carcopino, *Virgile et le Mystère de la IV*e *Églogue* (Paris, 1930) was not available for me before this chapter was in print. I am delighted to find that the view of the Fourth Eclogue that I have held for years is confirmed, in its essential parts, by so eminent an authority. He may be right in regarding Galoninus as the child of the prophecy, but that point needs further argument.

her first husband may have been born at this time. But
though Antony might well have seemed heroic to Virgil
in the year 40, and though Pollio might be given incidental honor in a poem devoted mainly to Antony, we
should expect some sort of allusion to Antony; Virgil,
while reticent, is never dumb. There is no indication
that he is thinking of Antony at all; the place of distinction is Pollio's. It is still less likely that the child is that
of Octavian and Scribonia. In that event, the poem was
written before the birth, and the offspring proved to be
not a boy or a Messiah, but Julia, of unhappy memory.

Was Virgil destitute of the sense of humor? Many
seers have prophesied a Golden Age, but few have ven-
tured to proclaim the sex of an unborn child. When
Marot wrote, before the birth, a greeting to a child of
the Duchess of Ferrara, he prudently began, "Petit
enfant, quel que sois fille ou filz." If there flourished in
antiquity a prophetic song in which the assumption was
made, perhaps as a kind of spell to win the favor of
Lucina, that the offspring would surely be a boy, Virgil's hardihood is intelligible. But apart from a poem of
uncertain interpretation by the incorrigible Martial,[1]
who was audacious enough to try any novelty, no specimens of a prophetic birth-song have come down to us.
We certainly are not driven by anything in Virgil's
eclogue to assume the existence of such a literary form.

Finally, we must think back into the political situa-

[1] VI, 3.

tion of the year 40, and remember that Octavian was not yet Augustus, but only one among several possible successors to the powers once held by the great Julius. The treaty of Brundisium, though it marked a lull in the dissensions that had threatened the stability of the Roman world, did not obliterate party lines, as Actium before long made only too evident. Pollio and Octavian had been political foes and were soon to be so again. Virgil would hardly have greeted the Golden Age on the prospect of a new arrival in Octavian's household and congratulated Pollio on the event. We have as yet seen no indication that Virgil has been associated with Octavian or had any feeling about him. We have nothing to controvert the order of Virgil's patrons as given by Donatus in his life of the Poet — Pollio, Varus, Gallus, and last of all, through their and through Maecenas's kindly offices, Octavian. The testimony of the remaining eclogues will confirm this order.

To many readers besides the Church Fathers, Virgil's Fourth Eclogue, fraught with the Messianic hope, has seemed to echo directly the words of Isaiah. It were rash to deny that Virgil might have known the Old Testament at first or second hand. The Jews came in large numbers to Rome after 64 B.C., when Pompey took their holy city. Pollio knew Herod and may have had kinsmen who accepted the Jewish faith. Further, when the ancient Sibylline oracles burned with the Capitol in 83, emissaries were dispatched far and wide to make a new collection, which surely might have included some Jewish oracles reflecting the spirit or the substance of Isaiah's prophecy. However, when we compare the eclogue with one of the extant and still later Sibyllines which sets over part of the eleventh chapter of Isaiah into Homeric verse, we see the difference between obvious reproduction and random coincidence. Further, it may be that the oracle known to Virgil is of Egyptian origin or is colored with Egyptian ideas.[1] Even so, we have explained only the source and not the purpose of the riotous imagery in which the prediction is clothed. Dr. Johnson, in one of his essays in the *Adventurer*,[2] acutely remarked that, splendid as the poem is, there is no apparent connection between it and the occasion that produced it. "That the Golden Age should return because Pollio had a son appears so wild a fiction, that I am ready to suspect the poet of having written, for some other purpose, what he took this opportunity of producing to the publick."

Now a motive is not far to seek. It is revealed, I believe, by Horace's Sixteenth Epode. When in the year 42 Horace returned from Philippi, where his captains Brutus and Cassius had gone down to defeat, he penned this despairing poem in the conviction that the only salvation of the Roman people was for them to sail away to an Atlantis in the sea and found a new common-

[1] See E. Norden, *op. cit., passim*, Carcopino has now shown that the coloring is much more probably Neo-Pythagorean.
[2] No. 92 (Saturday, September 22, 1753).

wealth far from civil strife amid the miraculous bounties which flourished in that blessed island. Horace writes at the outbreak of the Perusine war and speaks for the lost cause. Virgil, a year later, proclaims the era of peace which the treaty of Brundisium had apparently secured. He retorts with the imagery that Horace had used. The vision of a Golden Age had allured Virgil before; it finds expression in the Third Eclogue and more distinctly in the Fifth. In the former it is Pollio, in the latter it is Julius Caesar, whose person somehow works miracles in the natural world; at their coming, as at the divine presence of Faunus or of Pan, the brambles bear balsam and wolves play amiably with lambs. Now, with Horace's epode before him, Virgil has a further motive for his Saturnian dream. But mark the difference. To find the Golden Age Virgil does not flee to the Happy Islands or man's primitive past; the Golden Age is in Italy and now. This is what Horace also came to think when in the year 17 B.C. he wrote his ritual ode for the festival that marked the end of an age and commemorated in an enduring monument the savior of the Roman state. The *Carmen Saeculare* records the fulfilment of what the Fourth Eclogue prophesied.

This manifest connection of Virgil's pastoral with Horace's epode obviates the wild fancy of certain recent writers [1] who, regarding the child of the Fourth Eclogue

[1] Norden and Jeanmaire. Their views are discussed by J. Hubaux, who agrees with them, in his article "Etudes récentes sur la quatrième Eglogue de Virgile," *Le Musée Belge*, XXIX (1925), 117–132.

either as an Egyptian deity or as the offspring of Antony and Cleopatra, find the work a poetic fantasy on religious themes, with particular reference to the new cults that Antony and his regal paramour were seeking to introduce. Was there some danger, then, in publishing this piece in a collection which, as we shall see, was virtually dedicated to Octavian? Virgil showed his independence by letting his praise of Pollio stand. According to one of these recent writers,[1] Virgil while laughing in his sleeve could devise a new explanation for the benefit of Octavian. Sure it is that the original sub-intention, the glorification of the proposed innovations of Antony and Cleopatra, escaped not only Octavian but everybody else, except masters of *Religionsge-schichte* in the twentieth century.

Waiving these latest attempts to solve the mystery by a solution yet more mysterious, we may still regard the poem, in one of its aspects, as a reply to Horace's Sixteenth Epode.

But the poem is aimed at Catullus too. The birth-song of the Fates recalls in the words of its refrain

> "Talia saecla" suis dixerunt "currite" fusis
> concordes stabili fatorum numine Parcae

that of the prophecy of the Fates in Catullus's Sixty-fourth Poem, the epithalamium of Peleus and Thetis:

> Currite ducentes subtegmina, currite, fusi.

[1] *Ibid.*, p. 132.

With other artful touches of allusion — the voyage of
the Argonauts, Achilles and the Trojan war, the wedding
of Peleus and his goddess bride — Virgil invites us to
compare the two poems and their different ideals; the
savage warrior Achilles is matched with the new-born
Prince of Peace.

There is another contrast, too. Catullus looks back
with longing to the heroic past and sighs that Astraea
and the blessed gods no longer walk with men.[1] Such
feeling is pure romanticism; it is the spirit of Keats's
Endymion. Catullus, in his yearning for the primitive,
idealizes the mythical world, even though his present
story contains a Theseus. Such sentiment is alien to the
classic Virgil, whose sympathies, though they sweep
through history, converge on the present; Astraea and
the gods, he declares, are now on earth, and the child is
of their number. Virgil had studied Catullus's Sixty-
fourth Poem with devotion, as the *Ciris* can show us,
but here he rebukes its dominant tone; the tide of imperial epic is rising.

The Fourth Eclogue, then, is first of all a thank-
offering to Virgil's patron Pollio, whom he reveres as the
savior of the age and the apostle of peace. It is, further,
a challenge to the pessimism of Horace and the romanticism of Catullus. For these reasons, we find very few
Greek echoes in the poem; it belongs with the *togatae*
and of all the eclogues is the most conspicuously heroic.

[1] Ll. 22 ff., 384 ff.

Lastly, though it is not necessarily connected with Hebrew tradition in any way, it is instinct with the spirit of prophecy. We laugh too easily at the Christian allegorists and their ability to discover in the poem all the meaning of the Madonna and the Child; one reason for this curious misinterpretation is a real and profound insight into Virgil's temperament, into the quality that gives the Fourth Eclogue its special and perennial charm. That *anima candida* whom Horace reverenced was also an *anima naturaliter Christiana*. Victor Hugo was impressed with this tender, brooding, mystical element in Virgil. On one of the poems of *Les Voix Intérieures*, he speaks of the strange gleam, the Orient flames that play on the summit of his verse —

> Dieu voulait qu'avant tout rayon du Fils de l'homme,
> L'aube de Bethléem blanchît le front de Rome.

The magic of Virgil's art is nowhere more clearly seen than in this poem. While its epic spirit seems anything but pastoral, the pastoral coloring is carefully maintained. The Golden Age is a theme appropriate enough, and when Pan and Arcadia are challenged we feel that the poet is not some courtly singer, but a humble shepherd to whom the Birth-Song of the Fates, a Gloria in Excelsis, has been revealed.

Such is our poet's most hazardous innovation in the pastoral. Dr. Johnson, who shows little of that Virgiliolatry which is sometimes ascribed to the eighteenth century, observes sagely: "He has written with greater splendor of diction, and elevation of sentiment: but as the magnificence of his performance was more, the simplicity was less; and perhaps, when he excels Theocritus, he sometimes obtains his superiority by deviating from the pastoral character and performing what Theocritus never attempted."

This is one way of putting the matter. It defines the danger, but not the success. It describes the substances and the poetical tones, heterogeneous and distinct, from which a poet with Virgil's magic art can make a living harmony.

CHAPTER IV

PASTORAL ALLEGORY AND CONTEMPORARY EVENTS

(ECLOGUES VII, VIII, IX, VI, I)

THE infusion of epic spirit into pastoral form is only one of the acts of magic which Virgil performed in moulding the material for his novel bucolics. Epic concerns heroes, and heroes are sung in the *Eclogues*. Of two of these, Julius Caesar and Pollio, we have seen clear signs in the poems thus far discussed. Other heroes, either directly named or plainly peering through the pastoral disguise, will meet us in the remaining eclogues. What shall we do with the other characters in Virgil's pastoral, Corydon and Menalcas, Lycidas and Moeris, Damoetas and Tityrus and the rest? Are the *Eclogues* biographical throughout? And are they autobiographical? What glimpses do they reveal of Virgil's experience, his visions, and his art?

Furthermore, some of these poems, notably the First and the Ninth, reflect a historical event, the turmoil that reigned in the fields of Cremona and of Mantua, "all too near," when the veterans of Antony and Octavian ousted the inhabitants from their estates. Was the poet or his father ejected from his farm, and if so, how many times? Where was that farm, and is its locality pictured for us in the scenery of the *Eclogues*? These are the questions that throng before the mind of the reader as he skims the flowing verse whose music is sufficient excuse for its existence.

We have noted that, in the eclogues at which we have glanced thus far, the scent of allegory that spurs the quest of the interpreter never reveals the quarry. He starts blithely to follow a clue that ultimately balks him. There are many other such clues, and the pursuit is ever the same. It begins in expectancy and ends in despair — despair if we hope for a definite goal, satisfaction if we learn the secret of the poet's art.

Before we come to the eclogues that are concerned with the confiscation of Mantuan property, there are two that we must consider, both early in type, the Seventh and the Eighth. The first of these throws an important light on the nature of Virgil's use of allegory.

I

THE SEVENTH ECLOGUE

There is no certain indication of the date of the Seventh Eclogue. It is not necessarily early because simple in type, and yet it is hardly one of the latest. It might have been written not long before the Fourth Eclogue — or not long after. The scene of the poem is laid in Mantua, though there is no allusion to the distresses of that community. The time is not the present, but the Golden Age. Like the Third Eclogue, the Seventh is an amoebaean pastoral, which here is set in a narrative of the first person. Meliboeus tells of the contest, to which Daphnis had summoned him, between Corydon and Thyrsis, two young Arcadians well matched in starting amoebaean and replying. The rivals and their auditors sit down near where the Mincio fringes its green banks with tender reeds, and swarms of bees are buzzing in the sacred oak.[1] This is Mantuan scenery. Great oaks are not a feature of the landscape at the present day, but may have been in Virgil's. Horace had a towering pine on his Sabine estate which Byron in his rambles could not find; the cypresses that Byron describes have now vanished. In contrast to the amoebaean of the Third Eclogue, in which both shepherds prove equal, the present contest results in the victory of Corydon. It will be a close call, for the singers are worthy opponents. We must watch sharply to see why the prize is assigned.

Corydon starts with a humble prayer to the Muses of Helicon to grant him a song like that of Codrus, whom only Phoebus can surpass. If such is not his luck, he will hang up his pipe as an offering on the sacred pine. Thyrsis, in rejoinder, bids the shepherds of Arcadia crown him with ivy, that Codrus may split his sides with envy. Yet, lest too much praise excite the gods' jealousy, the coming bard will put a bit of foxglove on his brow, to act as a charm against any evil tongue or evil

[1] Ll. 12 f.:

> hic viridis tenera praetexit harundine ripas
> Mincius, eque sacra resonant examina quercu.

eye. These opening quatrains neatly set before us the modest and the boastful shepherd. The note of ὕβρις, with ἄτη rumbling not far away, is sounded as plainly here as in a Greek tragedy. We are not prepossessed with Thyrsis. He has the arrogance without the saving naïveté of Polyphemus, who spits thrice into his bosom to ward off the evil eye that may be cast upon his beauty.[1]

The second theme is the shepherd's offerings to his god. Corydon, in a bit of pastoral drama, impersonates little Micon, who presents to Diana a bristly boar's-head and a pair of antlers; if she favor him, the huntress-goddess shall have a statue of herself. Thyrsis offers to Priapus, custodian of a humble garden, a bowl of milk and some cakes. A marble statue will do for the present, but if the herd breeds well, he shall be done in gold. Absurd excess is Thyrsis's failing here, in his endeavor, on the proper amoebaean principle, to go his rival one better. It was not a happy idea to erect a marble scare-crow, much less one of gold.

Corydon, in the next challenge, calls his love Galatea to meet him at twilight, when the herd returns to the stalls. Thyrsis misses the cue altogether. "May I seem to thee more bitter than the Sardinian herb," he rejoins, "rougher than butcher's-broom, more paltry than stranded seaweed, if this day is not longer to me than a whole year. Go home, for shame, my pastured herd." The similes have the delightful flavor of Virgil's occa-

[1] Theocritus, *Idylls*, VI, 39.

sional realism, but in the setting are somewhat extravagant. Instead of improvising on the theme, "the
shepherd's invitation to his love," Thyrsis, as though
aware of his failure in the preceding quatrain — could
it be that his gold Priapus had raised a laugh? — simply
gets mad and orders his herd home.

"Mossy fountains and grass more soft than sleep, and
the flecked shadows of the green arbutus, defend my
flock against the solstice; for summer has now come and
the sluggish vines have just begun to burgeon." This is
Corydon's prayer for protection against the summer's
heat. Servius notes that the description is true to conditions in northern Italy; the grapevine, though always
slow to bud, would have leaved out in more southern
districts long before the end of June. Thyrsis in reply
imagines a winter scene. "With fat pine-billets on the
fire, which blackens the rafters with its smoke, we care
as little for the blasts of Boreas as the wolf for the
fold or torrents for their banks." This is a pleasing description and makes an excellent pendant. The error of
Thyrsis here lies in the inappropriateness of his similes.
He turns his matter upside down. Shepherds clustering
about a roaring fire and sheltered from the winter's wind,
like sheep in a pen well guarded from the wolf, should
not be compared to destructive forces such as the wolf
or the rushing stream.[1]

[1] In the *Aeneid* (IX, 59–66) Virgil shows how the simile should be used.
Turnus is compared to the raging wolf, and the Trojans safe in their camp to
the huddling sheep in the fold. It is of interest that Apollonius of Rhodes,

"Chestnuts and junipers are shaking their manes. Apples lie scattered under their trees on a smiling, autumn day. But if beautiful Alexis leave these hills, even the streams will dry." Corydon's theme is the desolation of nature when his loved one departs. Nothing could be more appropriate than Thyrsis's answering theme — the joy of nature when his Phyllis returns. "Parched is the land; the thirsty herb dies in the tainted air. The wine-god has withheld the vine-leaves' shade from the hillsides. At Phyllis's coming all the wood will turn to green and Jupiter descend in copious, glad showers." Beautiful lines, but it is somewhat unfortunate for Phyllis to get caught in a shower. Pope, in his tame but very proper adaptation of the lines, avoids the error in taste.

> All nature mourns, the skies relent in showers;
> Hushed are the birds, and closed the drooping flowers;
> If Delia smile, the flowers begin to spring,
> The skies to brighten, and the birds to sing.

Lastly, Corydon tells of his favorite tree. "Hercules has his poplar, Bacchus his vine, fair Venus her myrtle, and Phoebus his bay. Phyllis loves hazels, so that's the tree for me." Thyrsis: "Ash trees are fine in forests, pines in gardens, poplars by rivers, firs on high moun-

whom Virgil had studied with the minutest care, uses the same simile with something of Thyrsis's ineptness (I, 1240–1249). Heracles, hearing the cry of Hylas, rushed forward like a woodland beast that hears the cry of well-penned sheep in the distance. The similes of Apollonius are generally most fresh, appropriate, and original, but for once he is infelicitous. Virgil may well have intended a correction of this very infelicity.

tains. But if, fair Lycidas, thou shalt visit me now and then, ash in the woods and pine in the gardens shall yield to thee." This again is pleasing and accurate description, which flashes little pictures in quick succession — dense woods, a formal Italian garden with its umbrella-pines, poplars fringing a stream, evergreens on the mountain-side; but it is flat to answer that Lycidas is better than any tree. That is enough of Thyrsis. From that day Corydon, Corydon is victor.

This eclogue, says Servius, comes almost entirely from Theocritus. Its numerous Theocritean echoes, indeed, put it among the *palliatae*. The scenery is Arcadian, flavored, in the poet's delicate way, with all that his native Mincio meant to him. It is curious that if his farm was at Carpenedolo, the little river Chiese (Clesis) nowhere appears in his poems. His familiar stream is none but the Mincio, to which he returns lovingly in the *Georgics*, with a reminiscence of the very lines of the present poem.[1]

Virgil echoes Theocritus, but his echoes, as ever, are set to new harmonies in the poet's own music. The exquisite simile, "softer than sleep," which Theocritus applies to fleeces,[2] or rugs,[3] acquires new depth and charm in the perfect line,

> muscosi fontes et somno mollior herba.

[1] *Georg.*, III, 14:
> propter aquam, tardis ingens ubi flexibus errat
> Mincius et tenera praetexit harundine ripas.

Ecl., VII, 12:
> hic viridis tenera praetexit harundine ripas
> Mincius.

[2] *Idylls*, V, 51.   [3] *Idylls*, XV, 125.

Tennyson, no stranger to this art of reverent emulation, challenges his masters in lines that they would applaud:

> Gray twilight pour'd
> On dewy pastures, dewy trees,
> Softer than sleep.[1]

One important detail does not come from Theocritus. The idealization of Arcady as the land of rural simplicity and delight, a fancy that ran riot in the pastoral literature of the Renaissance, is strangely absent from Theocritus; some Hellenistic tradition, though hidden from us today, probably was known to Virgil and his contemporaries. We have noticed it in Virgil as early as his *Copa*. More than this, the central idea of the eclogue is not found in Theocritus. The poem forms a companion-piece for the Third Eclogue. That illustrates the perfect, and this the unsuccessful amoebaean. In the Fifth Idyll of Theocritus, one of the shepherds wins, apparently because he knows how to provoke his rival to exhibitions of temper; Theocritus is an observer of his rustics' moods rather than a critic of their songs. It has taken readers some time to catch Virgil's meaning; Dr. Johnson fails to get it, but from Sainte-Beuve on it has become increasingly clear. Like the Third Eclogue, this is a lesson, an unobtrusive lesson, in good taste. Thyrsis successively shows himself arrogant, extravagant, choleric, inept, ridiculous, and insipid. His personal qualities pass into his style, — *abeunt studia in mores*, —

[1] *Palace of Art*, ll. 85-87.

whatever his accomplishment in the art of song. They are not Virgilian qualities.

Here the lure of allegory presents itself again. We are tempted to call the successful shepherd Virgil, especially when we note that Corydon's favorite is Alexis, as in the Second Eclogue. If Corydon is Virgil there, he is Virgil here. This apparently mathematical demonstration shivers on the fact of our poet's modesty. We know this if nothing else, that he would not end his poem by throwing up his cap and shouting, "Virgil, Virgil forever!" Thyrsis could not have made himself more conspicuous. Indeed it is more natural to conclude that since Corydon and Alexis do not stand for the poet and his favorite here, neither do they in the Second Eclogue. The master-poet here seems to be Codrus; in the Fifth Eclogue, Codrus comes in for abuse and the master is Amyntas. Starting from the meaning of the Fifth Eclogue, the advanced allegorists, whom Servius cannot accept, find the extremely incidental Daphnis here to be Julius Caesar, Corydon to be Virgil, and Thyrsis, one of his rivals, Bavius or Anser or Maevius. We might more plausibly see Virgil in Meliboeus, who modestly reports the contest of his betters in song. It is more profitable, however, not to follow any of these purposely defective clues to Virgil's allegorical maze, but to enjoy undisturbed the charm of pastoral art and the adumbrations of Virgil's literary ideals.

II

THE EIGHTH ECLOGUE

The poet announces a pastoral contest between Damon and Alphesiboeus, which, like the music of Orpheus, drew heifers from the field and lynxes from the wood, while the wondering rivers stopped in their courses. The poem is *palliata* with many reminiscences of the Greek poets. It is dedicated to some patron who at the moment was sailing past the rocks of Timavus or skirting the Illyrian coast. Who can this be but Pollio, back from his Dalmatian campaign in 39 B.C.? The hero is a man of letters, too, and in particular author of verse "worthy of Sophocles' buskin." This can hardly be Octavian or Antony. Maecenas tried his hand at poetry, including tragedy, but the less said of that the better. Horace, in a compliment at once valorous and discreet, says that his Maecenas is the man to sing of Augustus's exploits — in prose.[1] Horace also praises Pollio's tragedies in language recalling Virgil's lines.[2] Our poet further declares that his verse, undertaken at his patron's bidding, began and shall end with him — *a te principium*, *tibi desinet*. Though Virgil took orders from no man, it is true that Pollio had been his pastoral hero from the start. It is tempting, but by no means necessary, to suppose that the Eighth Eclogue is the concluding piece of a first volume of *Bucolics* specially dedicated to Pollio. In any case, the words *tibi desinet* denote the

[1] *Odes*, II, 12, 9.   [2] *Ibid.*, II, 1, 11.

poet's devotion to his friend. He begs him to twine a bit of pastoral ivy amid his own victorious bays. It is evidently the moment when Pollio is proceeding to Rome to celebrate his triumph over the Parthini in Dalmatia. As this triumph was held October 25, 39 B.C., the date of the eclogue is fairly certain.

Damon is the first singer. He fares afield in the early morning and, leaning on his olive-staff in an attitude suggesting the Marble Faun, pipes a melancholy song, which he declares is his last on earth, in protest against false Nysa, who breaking troth with him is now on this very day to become the bride of Mopsus. It is a fit wedlock, as fit as that of gryphons and horses, does and dogs. In imagination the shepherd sees the evening star arise, and the rites begin that unite this sorry pair. Does she despise a humble shepherd like himself? He thinks back to the day when first he saw her. She had come to his farm with her mother and he had proudly escorted them and helped them pick apples from the hedgerow trees. He was only a lad of twelve, and could barely reach the ends of the boughs, which would often break before he could seize the fruit — or, as Virgil has it, in a single line:

iam fragiles poteram ab terra contingere ramos.

This pretty picture comes from Theocritus,[1] though it is not quite the same, and even if it were, the beautiful Virgilian lines, which affected both Macaulay and Voltaire, would be their own justification. In Theocritus, Poly-

[1] *Idylls*, XI, 25.

phemus leads his sweetheart and his mother in a search
for hyacinths on the mountain-side. With his physical
handicap, the good ogre finds his mother a decided help
in his courting. Virgil by a neat use of the plural pronoun — *dux ego vester eram* — implies that the mother
was the girl's; perhaps it was a case of "daughter fairer
than thy mother fair." Had his own mother been present, the youngster might not have done the honors of
the place. At all events, that was the moment when
love's fury took away his senses. He knows now what a
rock-hearted monster Cupid is. It was he who drove
Medea to slay her children. A cruel mother she was!
Was the mother more cruel or that shameless lad?
Shameless was the lad; thou mother, too, wert cruel.
This is as far as the shepherd can get with the tragic
problem of the conflict of human wills and destiny.
Virgil has broached it before,[1] and will return to it in the
Fourth Book of the *Aeneid*. The lament ends with a re-
hearsal of the pastoral impossibilities which if Nysa be
wedded to Mopsus ought to come true; the wolf will flee
the sheep, narcissus bloom from the alder, owls will sing
sweeter than swans, and Tityrus, who generally is put to
menial tasks, will now rival Orpheus himself. Yes, let
the sea arise and cover all. This wish, which to certain
microscopic critics is proof that Virgil mistranslated
Theocritus,[2] is appropriate enough in the context of
absurdities, and not inappropriate in reality for one who

---

[1] See above, pp. 38, 48. [2] See above, p. 64.

lived in the marshy country of Mantua. With these last words, the shepherd prepares to leap down a high cliff into the waves.

The scene of this pastoral tragedy is difficult to locate. Apart from the deluged fields, if this is intended as a Mantuan detail, there are no suggestions of Mantua. Arcadia is again suggested as a part of the pastoral tradition. The song is accompanied by the refrain,

> Begin with me, my pipe, Maenalian verses.

There is also a description of Maenalus, the Arcadian mountain, with its whispering groves, and of piping Pan, to whom the shepherds confide their love-secrets. But Damon is not necessarily a shepherd of Arcady himself.

Alphesiboeus, in his answering song, takes the part of a maiden whom her lover Daphnis has abandoned. She tries by weaving various spells and by chanting this magic song to lure back her faithless swain. The scene and some, by no means all, of the details are suggested by the Second Idyll of Theocritus. The ending differs; the ashes on the altar blaze up spontaneously, and presto! Hylax is barking at the portal and Daphnis comes again. Virgil does not intend to rival Theocritus here; as Sainte-Beuve remarks,[1] he selects with good taste what suits his plan, later in the Fourth Book of the *Aeneid* taking ample revenge by the interpretation of a passion more tragic than that of the heroine of the

---

[1] "Théocrite," *Derniers Portraits*, Paris, 1854, p. 32.

Second Idyll. The incantation of Alphesiboeus is merely a bit of stately verse, making a fit companion-piece for Damon's lament and by its happy ending contrasting with it. Each piece has a refrain, appropriate in a lament or an incantation, as is apparent in the First and Second Idylls of Theocritus. Incantation is also suggested by the intentionally clumsy line: [1]

Limus ut hic durescit, et haec ut cera liquescit,

where the thumping rhyme seems to correspond to some act in the ceremony.[2] The two pieces in this eclogue are also alike in their dramatic character. Damon is apparently giving voice to his own sorrow, yet it is a contest after all; he is not really on the summit of a lonely crag, but singing with a fellow-shepherd to an audience composed of others, we should imagine, besides heifers and lynxes and brooks. The dramatic element in the song of Alphesiboeus is obvious enough. There have been touches of drama in the *Eclogues* before; in the Fifth, Alphesiboeus mimics the dancing satyrs — a versatile actor, if he is the same as our shepherd here. Theocritus's swains could play quite as elaborate rôles; in the Sixth Idyll, Daphnis addresses Polyphemus in imagination, to tell him that while he pipes Galatea is waiting to be wooed. Damoetas at once takes the cue and acts the part of Polyphemus. The dramatic material in the

[1] L. 80.
[2] Such rhyme is a natural accompaniment of incantation. Its presence in Anglo-Saxon charms has been pointed out by J. W. Rankin, *Publications of the Modern Language Association*, XXXVI (1921), 423.

Eighth Eclogue is arranged much as in Theocritus's idyll; with such models accessible, it is not surprising that a new literary variety, the Pastoral Drama, was developed in the Renaissance.

After the contest, the shepherds in Theocritus's idyll exchange kisses and gifts; it is stated that neither won but both remained invincible. The same is true of Virgil's singers, though never a word from the reticent poet after Alphesiboeus is done; heifers and lynxes and brooks, we infer, have listened to the end with all their might.

This poem is of an obviously Theocritean character, flavored, of course, with Virgil's own charm. One may wonder why he should give us this and nothing more after the new national note that rings in the Fifth Eclogue and the Fourth. Perhaps this very quality of reminiscence is part of the tribute to Pollio; the poet reverts to his earlier manner and to the first themes to which his friend had inspired him.

We are now ready for a poem in which Mantuan scenery is more definitely located than in Arcadia. The poet is speaking, in pastoral language, of the wrongs to which his fellow-townsfolk had been subjected.

III

THE NINTH ECLOGUE

The shepherds Moeris and Lycidas are on their way to town. The Fates have been cruel to Moeris. He has been thrust out of his little estate, and, crowning humili ation, is now taking some kids to the new master. Yes, it is true that Menalcas, by his power of song, had apparently won back everything — even from the point where the hills melt into the plain right down to the old beech trees and the water. But verses are hard to hear amidst the whistling javelins of Mars. Indeed, had it not been for the warning of a crow, neither Moeris nor Menalcas himself would have lived to tell the tale. "What infamy!" cries Lycidas. "What, should we lose the master-poet of us all? Who would be left to sing the nymphs? Or who could make such music as I overheard of late?

> Tityrus, till I return — my road is short —
> Feed thou my kids and drive them fed to water.
> But, Tityrus, as thou drivest, give wide berth
> To yon he-goat; he has an angry horn.

This is a straight translation from the Third Idyll of Theocritus.[1]

"Or better," says Moeris, "the lines in praise of Varus from a poem not yet finished:

> Varus, if only Mantua be spared —
> Poor town, to poor Cremona all too near —
> The chanting swans shall bear thy name on high.

The unfinished poem, it would appear, would deal with contemporary events; Menalcas, like Virgil, wrote pastorals of two sorts, Greek and Roman, foreign and national, *palliata* and *togata*. Lycidas remarks that the

[1] Ll. 3-5.

shepherds call him, too, a bard, though he will not believe them; rather he is but a cackling goose amid swans
like Varius and Cinna. Moeris now recalls another bit of
the master's verse:

> Come, Galatea, how can waves allure
> When here is purple spring, and round the brooks
> The earth heaps flowers and above the cave
> Hang poplars silvery, and drooping vines
> Weave us a flickering shade? Come here,
> And on the beach let mad waves break in vain.

Again a direct adaptation from Theocritus.[1] Lycidas can
cap these verses with those he heard Moeris singing on a
moonlit night. They are obviously Roman in character.

> Daphnis, why watch the ancient planets rise?
> For Dionaean Caesar's star comes forth
> And lo! the waving meadows laugh with corn
> And full grape-clusters flush on sunny hills.
> Daphnis, plant pears; thy sons shall cull the fruit.

Yes, Moeris remembers, though his powers are failing;
the days are past when he could sing till the bedtime of a
summer's sun. Now, his voice is gone. A wolf has
looked upon him first. Lycidas will take no such excuse;
they must go singing all the way to town. "Not so," rejoins the other. "Trudge on; we shall make better music
when the master is come."

One clue to the meaning of this poem is the Seventh
Idyll of Theocritus. There, three shepherds, one of
whom is the poet himself, though called Simichidas, are
journeying to a harvest-feast. They meet a fourth,

---

[1] Various lines from the Eleventh Idyll are here cleverly woven together.

Lycidas, who wears a shepherd's plaid and carries an olive-staff. This attire is as false as his name; he is a townsman, a poet in masquerade — his twinkling eye betrays him. On the way, Lycidas and Simichidas exchange songs, which are fully as elegiac as pastoral in character. Theocritus is illustrating — perhaps half quoting — the work of his brother-poets who sang of love; it is not like his own work, for it is perfumed with a delicate and somewhat sickly eroticism. Lycidas repeats his own verses; Simichidas tells of the loves of his friend Aratus. Aratus is evidently the well-known astronomer-poet. Other famous contemporaries, Sicelidas and Philetas, are also directly mentioned; Lycidas agrees to challenge the latter if frogs can sing against cicalas. Lycidas and the other names in the poem are, like Simichidas, pseudonyms for poets of the day. There is also a direct allusion to the celebrated literary quarrel in which Callimachus, a bit later, championed the new style of epic in the form of short legends against Apollonius, who clung to the lengthy affairs of the past — sky-scraping houses, as the poet calls them. This is an extraordinary amount of allegory for a poet whose other pastorals appear, or till recently have appeared, to contain none at all.

Virgil's Ninth Eclogue is, like the Seventh Idyll, concerned with the poetry, particularly the pastoral poetry, of his day. This, in fact, is the main theme of the eclogue — not the loss of the poet's estate, which merely serves as introduction. Nor is the riddle presented by the latter solved if, following Servius [1] and many subsequent commentators, we look to the First Eclogue for information. There we find a sorrowful shepherd, Meliboeus, who, like the irate farmer of the *Dirae*, is driven from his estate, and a happy shepherd, Tityrus, who thanks Octavian for confirming his tenure. Though Tityrus is addressed as an old man, Servius and his followers make him out to be Virgil, who, secure for the moment, later laments, in the Ninth Eclogue, that his songs are of no avail; he is therefore ejected for the second time. But the First Eclogue is not the first chronologically. Pollio was succeeded in the Transpadane region by Varus in 39, and the present poem is partly in the latter's honor; we still have no mention or suggestion of Octavian. If we can be sure that Menalcas is Virgil, we may infer that at the moment he was dispossessed, despite his previous appeal, which was made, however, not to Octavian, but to Pollio.

Where was his farm? Menalcas had saved by his songs "all the land from the point where the hills melt into the plain down to the old beech trees and the water." My friend Professor Conway, following the statement in the Life of Virgil transmitted under the name of that eminent scholar of Nero's day, Marcus Valerius Probus, locates the farm near Calvisano, thirty miles away from the city of Mantua on the road to

[1] See above, p. 74.

Brescia; in fact it lies today in Brescian territory. Inscriptional evidence is next called into play, and finally the nature of the landscape, which comports with that of the *Eclogues*. In fact, if we locate the farm at Carpenedolo, which is not far from Calvisano, — though, incidentally, it is not thirty miles from Mantua and no Virgilian inscriptions have been found there, — we can see the poet's hills in the ridge at Carpenedolo and note how they melt into the plain that slopes down to the river Chiese, the ancient Clesis — though, incidentally, the Clesis is not mentioned in Virgil's poems, while the Mincio, which flows by the city Mantua and by little Pietole where Dante and others before him thought Virgil was born, is a stream most beloved by the poet.

I have attempted in the little book called *In Quest of Virgil's Birthplace* to answer the arguments so attractively set forth by Conway, and will not resume them here. I merely would refer again to the remark in Virgil's commentator Servius that Octavius Musa, who, I think, is the Octavius to whom the boy Virgil dedicated his *Culex*, was commissioned by Octavian, when the land of Cremona did not suffice for his veterans, to measure off from it fifteen miles of Mantuan territory. I endeavored to show how this measuring was done and how the description of what Menalcas had saved by his songs best applies not to some particular farm, but, as is also suggested by Servius, to the whole sweep of the Man-

tuan district from the hills of the north down to the
waters of the Mincio:

omnia carminibus vestrum servasse Menalcan.[1]

It may be, as my friend Professor Nardi seeks to show,[2]
that the poem means his own farm after all and that the
description fitted then, though not now, the region of
Pietole. This may well be true, though I prefer, at least
for the moment, to think that Menalcas — whoever he
is — had won back by his songs and his petitions the
whole territory that Octavius Musa had measured off.

I have implied that it is not easy to make out that
Menalcas is Virgil, even though a writer so early as
Quintilian thought so.[3] Menalcas, like Virgil, writes
pastorals of two varieties, Theocritean and Roman; he
also worships Julius Caesar as the shepherd's god. He
is evidently the leader among a little group of poets, but
in the Fifth Eclogue, though Menalcas there comes near
to being Virgil, the master-poet is apparently Amyntas;
in the Seventh he is Codrus. Virgil might adopt a series
of pastoral names, but he would hardly change his part,

[1] See *In Quest of Virgil's Birthplace*, pp. 113 f., and Nardi's *The Youth of Virgil*, p. 135. Also important is Nardi's recent article "Nuove Ricerche sul Paese Natali di Virgilio," in *Virgiliana*, Mantua, 1930, n. 2, pp. 3–10. Gabriel Faure, *Au Pays de Virgile*, Paris, 1930 (pp. 16–18) is not won over by Conway's arguments.

[2] See *The Youth of Virgil*, pp. 129–135, and for an attractive presentation in popular form, Nardi's *Breve Guida al Paese Natio di Virgilio*, Mantua, 1930. The danger of talking about Mantuan scenery when one has not examined it at first hand is illustrated by J. Hubaux, *Le Réalisme dans les Bucoliques de Virgile* (see above, p. 79), who suggests (p. 86) that the calmed waters (*Ecl.*, IX, 57) may be those of Lake Garda (!).

[3] *Inst. Or.*, VIII, 6, 47.

now appearing as chief singer and now as subordinate. Furthermore, the rôle of chief singer is not one that he would voluntarily select — certainly he would not devote a whole eclogue to praising himself.

It were tempting to suppose that Pollio had written pastorals as well as tragedies, and that he is the Menalcas of the Ninth Eclogue; we noted this possibility in the Third Eclogue as well, where Pollio is pictured as a hero of the Golden Age and master of its miracles. He as well as the poet whom he befriended had been in danger and had been forced to leave. May we think of the moment when Pollio, by order of Octavian, was replaced as governor of the Transpadane district by Alfenus Varus? We may gather support for this suggestion from the enlarged form of Servius's commentary [1] or from Probus in the statement that Virgil's rescuer was his brother-poet Gallus, who surely might have effected a rescue by the art of song.[2] However, if Menalcas is either Pollio or Gallus, then Moeris is Virgil. But Virgil was not an old man whose voice was failing; no wolf had looked upon him first.

Lycidas has more of the Virgilian temperament; he is young and enthusiastic and modest. Moreover, the verses that set forth his humility are copied from Theocritus's Seventh Idyll,[3] where the contemporary poets Sicelidas and Philetas are directly named, as Varius and

---

[1] On *Ecl.*, IX, 11: '*Carmina' autem nonnulli quibus sibi Pollionem intercessorem apud Augustum conciliaverat accipiunt: quo fugato, rursus de praediis suis fuerat Vergilius expulsus.* Cf. on IX, 27: *sane blanditur Alfeno Varo, qui, Pollione fugato, legatus Transpadanis praepòsitus est ab Augusto.*

[2] See Thilo and Hagen, III, 2, 28.

[3] Ll. 37–41.

Cinna are here, and the simile of frog and cicala is the model for that of goose and swan. Now in Theocritus the verses refer to the poet himself. Does not Virgil have the same intention here? If so, we immediately wonder why he should select for himself the name Lycidas, which in Theocritus stands for some other poet than the author. Perhaps this very confusion would suggest that no definite allegory should be extracted from the poem. Virgil is not Lycidas or Menalcas or Moeris, but they all together symbolize the kind of pastoral that he and others were writing, their interest in Greek tradition, and their novel introduction of Roman atmosphere. The poem *Lydia*, apparently, gives evidence of other contemporary pastoral than Virgil's, suggesting in its spirit the delicate decadence of the later Hellenistic bucolics. This of course is not for Virgil, or not permanently for him. Impelled partly by his own temperament and partly by the call of Theocritus, he leads his generation back to saner feeling and more classic art.

As ever, then, in Virgil, the scent of allegory provokes the reader to search, but gives him nothing definite for his pains. For, again, this is a typical, not an autobiographical poem, and is hard to fix in place or time. The pastoral troubles pictured in the *Dirae*, the First Eclogue, and the Ninth began as early as 43,[1] and would arouse *saeva indignatio* in a local poet for four or five years to come. It would be a burning subject in the

[1] Cassius Dio, XLVII, 14.

year 39, when Varus was appointed governor of the Mantuan district. Virgil had perhaps made his acquaintance recently. In the present poem, he virtually promises him a panegyric if he will be as kind to Mantua as his predecessor has been. This promise is fulfilled, partly, at least, in the Sixth Eclogue.

IV

THE SIXTH ECLOGUE

The poet begins with an apology for not writing an epic in praise of Varus. He has been taught by experience; when he would sing of kings and wars, Apollo plucked his ear and reminded him that shepherds should feed sleek sheep but pipe a slender song. There will be others in plenty to herald the exploits of Varus. The shepherd-poet can at least make the woods ring with his hero's name, and honor his page by writing "Varus" at the top.

Now for the pastoral. The lads Chromis and Mnasyllus, abetted by Aegle, fairest of the Naiad-nymphs, steal up where Silenus, as ever, is sleeping off his yesterday's carouse, still clinging fondly to the well-worn handle of his bowl. They paint his face blood-red with mulberries. The color, appropriate to deities, was worn by a Roman general at his triumph, when he assumed the god; perhaps a mortal could more safely behold a god if he were so painted, or could work some spell upon him — or perhaps one should seek no ulterior motive in this boorish jest. Silenus, waking, laughs at the ruse and consents to give the lads the song for which they had often clamored. For the nymph there shall be other reward; knowing Silenus, we can guess what it will be.

As Silenus sings, fauns and beasts frolic in time to the music and stiff oaks nod their crests. For it is a song of universal marvels and metamorphoses. It begins in a Lucretian fashion to describe how the atoms of earth, air, fire, and water hurtle through the void until our world solidifies and is separated from the sea and the sky. Soon it is filled with life; forests begin to grow and beasts to wander over the strange hills. Thus far Lucretian science. But man cannot be explained by the atomic theory. Nothing is said of his creation, but he is re-created after the flood from the stones flung by Deucalion and Pyrrha. Then come the Saturnian Age and Prometheus's thefts that put an end to it. Next, the rape of Hylas; we are advancing chronologically to the days of Hercules. The story of Pasiphaë brings us closer still to history. It is an uncanny story, but Virgil somehow tells it in epic style, with a touch of shuddering pity that recalls the curious pathos of the *Ciris*. Not to be too chronological, the poet now reverts to Atalanta and the sisters of Phaëthon. Then, of a sudden, we find Gallus, wandering on Mount Helicon and greeted by the choir of the Muses, who present him with the pipes that they gave to Hesiod of old; with these he shall tell the story of the groves that Apollo loves best, the Grynean groves. Thereto the singer adds the legend of Nisus's Scylla, who,

> Girding with yelping monsters her fair loins,
> Tossed in deep pools the ships of Ithaca,
> Whose men were mangled by her sea-born hounds,

or the tale of Tereus's transformation, or the ghastly banquet that Philomel prepared,

> And how she sought the desert in her flight
> And hovered hapless over her own roof.

These passages with which the poet concludes are quoted almost to the word from the *Ciris*.[1] Such, then, he declares, were the themes of Silenus's song — all the strains of Phoebus that blest Eurotas heard and bade its laurels learn them. The valleys catch the music and toss it to the stars, until the shepherd lads are warned to drive their flocks home — for Vesper has come forth from the reluctant sky. The sky has been listening too.

This eclogue is in form a pastoral panegyric, in which Varus holds the ostensible place of honor. It begins with a eulogy of him, just as the Fourth Eclogue begins with a eulogy of Pollio. The tone, while sincere enough, is less enthusiastic. Epic is beyond the shepherd-poet, he pretends, but such verse as his humble Muse dictates shall be inscribed with the name of Varus. For Pollio, however, lowly shrubs and tamarisks had broken forth into a new song worthy of a consul. Varus is a minor hero for Virgil.

[1] Ll. 59-61, 50-51.

One touch of pastoral allegory appears in this introduction. The poet obviously means himself by Tityrus, the chore-boy among the shepherds, who rashly essayed to sing of kings and wars till Phoebus touched his trembling ear. The only autobiographical allegory in the *Eclogues* so definite as this is that which we have noted in the Fifth, where Menalcas is ready to give away the frail reed that had piped

and
> Formosum Corydon ardebat Alexim
>
> Cuium pecus, an Meliboei?

We may infer from both passages that Virgil puts a modest estimate on his own work and that he adopts different pastoral names. But we may not argue from the Fifth Eclogue that Menalcas is Virgil in the Ninth, or from the Sixth that Tityrus is Virgil in the First.

The purely pastoral part of the poem, the setting of Silenus's song, is as fresh and delightful as anything that Virgil has yet done, — or anything that Theocritus did, for that matter, — and that is saying a good deal. There is humor, moreover, in the description of the scared boys bent on mischief, of the fair and competent Aegle who directs the attack, and of the disreputable old god who even though sleeping is canny enough to cling to the handle — the well-worn handle — of his bowl, and, waking, appreciates the joke and dispenses condign rewards to everybody concerned. Ovid would need many more of his light-tripping verses to say as much. The charm of this world of fancy contrasts with the solemnity of the cosmic recital of Silenus, and that with the lyric enthusiasm of the closing verses. Joy in nature and joy in song are part of Virgil's temperament. It seems an accident that emotions so simple and so deep did not find expression in lyric verse.

The story of Silenus and his enforced song was taken by Virgil, Servius tells us, from the historian Theopompus. The latter recounted how two shepherds of Midas surprised the bibulous god, who regaled them, and their master too, with a musical discourse *de rebus naturalibus et antiquis*. Aelian [1] gives a summary of its contents. It is an informal sort of sermon on the things that are best for man, with a bit of moralized geography, a fable of two cities, "Reverent" and "Bellicose," and one of two rivers, that of Grief and that of Pleasure. In short, Theopompus had quite a different Satyr's song, and Cicero in his *Tusculan Disputations* [2] implies another still; the poet has filled in the traditional outlines to suit his purpose.

His song falls into three parts. First we have Lucretian science; Virgil has not forgotten his schooling in that doctrine or his reverence for the master who humanized it in verse. But Virgil had reacted from science; he was more penetrating than Lucretius in seeing that it did not satisfy all the demands of his nature. We pass next to a group of myths which continue, in a more or

[1] *Varia Historia*, III, 18.   [2] I, 114.

less chronological fashion, the history of the early years of the world. Servius, trying to make out Virgil a consistent Epicurean, thinks that the myths are employed, as in Lucretius, as a sugar-coating for unpalatable but wholesome truth. Nothing could be farther from Virgil's intention. He needs the myth as a supplement for science. The story of the world as it unrolls before him is a mixture of law and miracle. Metamorphosis in both the natural and the human order is its secret. The plan of Ovid's great poem was sketched by Virgil first. The title that Donatus gives this eclogue is μεταμορφώσεις; it was chosen either by Virgil himself or by somebody who knew exactly what the poem is about.

The third section brings us with a bound into contemporary history and a eulogy of Virgil's friend and fellow-poet Gallus, the last in the series of patrons who assisted him during the troubles at Mantua before his introduction to Octavian. The eulogy is less prominently placed in the poem than that of Varus, and is far more deeply felt. The fiction of the Muses' gift to Gallus is not extravagant. They had made the same to Hesiod before, and Gallus deserves it now, for he has done something worthy of Hesiod. As a passage in Propertius indicates,[1] he has turned from love-elegies to a larger theme — an epyllion on the Grynean grove in the manner of Euphorion, with didactic parts suggesting Hesiod.

After the little panegyric of Gallus, Silenus reverts to

[1] II, 10, 25.

his main theme, the metamorphosis, and ends with the stories of Scylla and of Philomel. In both, as we noticed, Virgil weaves in verses from his early poem, the *Ciris*, a practice which can be amply illustrated in his later works, and for which he had the authority of Theocritus. An eminent German scholar,[1] arguing that the verses from the *Ciris* are quoted from Gallus by way of compliment, infers that Gallus wrote the *Ciris* — an infallible conclusion if the minor premise is true. But there is no external evidence for that, and one detail is decidedly against it. The author of the *Ciris* takes pains, in the Alexandrian way, to show that he can tell the only true story of Scylla. She is the daughter of Nisus, and was transformed into the sea-bird; it never befell her to gird her fair loins with yelping monsters. But that is just what Virgil here asserts to be true. After his brief scientific period, he was not particularly concerned with mythological accuracy; he chooses the story of Scylla that fits his immediate purpose,[2] and in the present poem he rejects, with no qualms of conscience, what he had said before. Supposing, however, that he were quoting Gallus's verses, he would quote them straight and not burden them with petty quibblings about the real Scylla — least of all with a denial of what his friend had said. To make the quotation a compliment, we should have to suppose that after Virgil wrote his *Ciris*,

[1] F. Skutsch, *Aus Vergils Frühzeit*, 1901.
[2] See above, pp. 47 f.

Gallus told the Homeric story of Scylla the sea-monster, also identifying her with the daughter of Nisus; the language of the Sixth Eclogue would thus indicate a recantation on Virgil's part. But such speculation is not very profitable. There is compliment enough in calling Gallus the successor of Hesiod; we should not spoil the unity of the song with more allusion than this.

The chief purpose of the song of Silenus, then, is that underlying the story as Theopompus told it, however different the material. It gives a little outlook on life, in which not only Lucretian science, but poetry, friendship, and the sense of miracle, symbolized by the metamorphosis, have their place. It is a compact philosophy in a Satyr's song, wherein different elements, essentially unpastoral, have a unity of idea. Virgil is always pondering on the ultimate questions, and he speaks out on them here, as he will later in the Second Book of the *Georgics* and in the Sixth Book of the *Aeneid*, and as he had done when a lad of sixteen in the first of his poems.[1] At the end, the pastoral setting is instantly before us, and all is caught up, by Virgil's magic, into pastoral. Nemesian, in the third century, tells the story again, with no little charm and with more scrupulous observance of pastoral reality; his Satyr's song has as its theme the discovery of wine. Virgil attempts the harder task of combining the incongruous, and for all that is just as true to type.

[1] *Culex*, 58 ff.

Let us now descend from cosmic heights to local scenery. We are still on the search for Virgil's farm. We ought to find it, if anywhere, in the First Eclogue.

V

THE FIRST ECLOGUE

There is no doubt that this poem is in praise of Octavian. Tityrus, reclining comfortably under a spreading beech and piping of his Amaryllis, is accosted by Meliboeus, who has been ousted from his estate and his native town. Two types are at once set before us — the fortunate and contented and the ill-starred and sorrowful shepherd. Tityrus explains that a god has bestowed his happiness upon him; he will honor him as a god, at any rate, and offer the frequent sacrifice of a lamb on his rustic altar. Meliboeus is not moved to envy; he is a tender-hearted shepherd, to whom the sufferings of his herd are as painful as his own. He does not criticize; he is dumfounded, however, to see so radiant a bit of prosperity, when confusion reigns in all the countryside. Who can the god be? Tityrus postpones the answer. He is big with information about the mighty city Rome, which he once had fancied was something like the town to which the shepherds drove their flocks. But it differs in kind, not in degree; it is a proud cypress amongst the hawthorn bushes. We have here, as in the Twentieth Idyll of Theocritus, a new motive in the pastoral, a visit of the shepherd to town — an episode more elaborately treated by Calpurnius, and in the eighteenth century developed into a new species, the town eclogue.

Tityrus's motive in going to Rome was to secure his freedom. For freedom came to him, though late in time, after he was released from the thrall of his former mistress, Galatea, a young person of expensive tastes; she somehow absorbed the substantial earnings that accrued to the shepherd from his goodly flocks and their products. Tityrus is of the same class as Simylus, the hero of the *Moretum;* he has saved up enough money to invest in a little farm, as a slave might do, but could not, till now, quite raise the sum to ensure his freedom. Galatea out of the way, there is some prospect; for Amaryllis is a decent girl.

"So that's why Amaryllis was so doleful," says Meliboeus. "She missed you, Tityrus; so did the pines, the fountains, and the orchard trees." They, too, felt grief, as meadow, stream, and grove can in the pastoral; and they also needed attention. Virgil abruptly converts the "Pathetic Fallacy" into common sense.

"What could I do?" replies Tityrus. "I could not otherwise cast off my bondage, nor elsewhere find such present deities to help me." Tityrus goes to Rome with a double purpose. He has the funds to buy manumission, and is also going to appeal to some higher power to confirm him in the tenure of his estate. The first motive is plainly stated by the poet; the latter is suggested. At Rome, the shepherd saw that youthful god in whose honor his altar shall smoke, like that of the Lares, twelve times every year. For he made answer:

"Feed as before your kine, lads; rear your bulls."

This is all that the shepherd has to say of Rome. He leaves us to assume that he has obtained his freedom; for there was no doubt on that score. He now makes explicit what before he implied; the godlike youth favored his petition and the farm is secure. There is no confusion or incongruity in this picture, except that which some astygmatic critics have detected. The picture is composed exactly like that of the infant's smile at the end of the Fourth Eclogue, half expressed and half implied; Virgilian reticence allows neither excess nor defect. The poet is master of a sort of descriptive enthymeme; he suppresses the parts of the full description that a reader of artistic perceptions can take for granted."

"Happy old man," sighs Meliboeus. "So then thy farm is secure. Rocks may cover it and the marsh overspread the pasture with slimy rush. For all that, it is thine own, and free from contagious pest."

> Happy old man, thy fields are still thine own,
> Ample for thee, though bare rocks everywhere
> And swamps thy meadows coat with muddy reeds.
> No fodder strange shall tempt thy breeding ewes
> Nor plague infest them from a neighboring flock.
> Happy old man, here by familiar streams
> And springs divine thou 'lt court the cooling shade!
> There, as of old, the hedge along thy bounds
> That feeds the willow-flowers to Hybla's bees

Shall often summon sleep with whispers soft.
There the leaf-pruner by yon cliff shall sing
Into the breeze, while turtle-doves, thy pets,
Moan low unceasing in the aëry elm.

There is nothing in pastoral poetry more opulent than these verses. The closing passage in the Seventh Idyll of Theocritus, "Queen of the Eclogues," excels it in gorgeous, not to say extravagant, coloring, but does not surpass it in depth of feeling or felicity of expression. Familiar streams, sacred springs, sleep in the willow-hedge with its whispering bees, the leaf-gatherer on the hill singing into the breezes, the doves cooing in the aëry elm — this is the quintessence of pastoral joy in nature and in song set forth in exquisite verse that is carefully moulded to the sentiment. Somnolence itself is in the line

saepe levi somnum suadebit inire susurro

and Tennyson caught his "moan of doves in immemorial elms" from

nec gemere aëria cessabit turtur ab ulmo.

In gratitude for this pleasant vision, Tityrus swears by all the pastoral impossibilities conceivable that the image of his friend shall never fade from his heart. Meliboeus, who is altogether the better poet of the two, — Tityrus is somewhat smug in his contentment and his remarks are no longer than they have to be, — now paints the companion-picture, the desolation in store for his farm. Ah, shall he ever behold that little thatched cottage, that kingdom of his, after many harvests! Meanwhile some godless veteran will possess it. Just see the consequences of our civil strife! That's the sort of person that we sow our fields for; so plant your pear-trees, Meliboeus, rank your vines! This irony is as near as the gentle Meliboeus can come to cursing, in the fashion of the farmer in the *Dirae*. He sadly starts up his goats. No more the luxury of lying in the cave and spying them in the distance hanging from some cliff; no more pleasant fodder for them — and no more songs for him.

"At least," answers Tityrus, somewhat comfortably, "you might pass the night with me. I have no lack of mellow apples, soft chestnuts, and curdled milk. And look!

> "The topmost roofs of distant huts are smoking,
> And longer shadows fall from the high hills." [1]

These last words have the severe and culminating effect appropriate for the conclusion of an epic canto. Virgil has, in his fashion, seasoned the pastoral description in this eclogue with bits of Theocritus, but there is nothing in Theocritus like the cadence here. In theme, the eclogue is *togata*.

The scene of the poem is laid in Mantua. Says Maurice Hewlett in *The Road in Tuscany*:

"The cypresses begin to lift their heads, in groves by

---

[1] Et iam summa procul villarum culmina fumant,
maioresque cadunt altis de montibus umbrae.

the wayside, sable as night, or sparsely in the fields, one sooty flame striking up in a hedgerow:

quantum lenta solent inter viburna cypressi —

the Mantuan's image for a very Mantuan landscape."

There are other Mantuan bits in the description — the soaked and marshy pasture and the somnolent hedges with their whispering bees. This is what one finds at Pietole. But "bare rocks everywhere" indicates some other site. Carpenedolo is more appropriate — only that it has no marshes. Hills it has, — or one hill, — and Pietole today has none, but to find the poetry of Virgil's pastoral hills one must travel further than Carpenedolo or Calvisano. The scene, then, is Mantua, but the landscape is created by the poet in his magical way.

This fact may guide us in estimating the amount of direct personal allegory in the poem. As ever, it eludes us. Virgil or Virgil's family lost, or came near losing, the homestead in Mantua; of that we may be sure from the Eighth Poem of the *Catalepton*, from hints in the *Eclogues*, and from statements in the commentators. But the commentators are in places absurd and contradictory. Servius, seeing that the eclogue treats of the Mantuan affair, takes the chance to give his pet theory rein, and finds hidden meanings everywhere; pines represent the city Rome, fountains the eloquent senators, and orchard-trees the fruitful grammarians. Nor is Servius more trustworthy when he infers that Virgil was living at Mantua at the time when the troubles occurred and when the *Eclogues* were written. The *Eclogues* themselves, our most immediate source, give us clues but no goal. In the present poem, an offering of thanks to Octavian, Tityrus would seem to play the part of the grateful poet. But when we learn his history, particularly the history of his amours, and note his temperament, the supposition that Virgil meant himself by Tityrus becomes impossible. Meliboeus, the ejected shepherd, would make a better Virgil temperamentally — but in that case the poem is a hint, not a compliment.

In fine, as in every eclogue except the Fifth, where Julius Caesar is as good as mentioned, Virgil tantalizes us with a rare and impressionistic allegory; it is a light shining through the poetry, not an iron frame that confines it. Wishing to thank Octavian, but reluctant to sketch his own experience, he presents an imaginary though typical picture, with the darker as well as the lighter colorings. To Octavian be the praise for his mercy. But then, there is Meliboeus. Not all the wrongs of Mantua are righted yet. The poet offers his ruler the pathos of the afflicted no less than the joy of the rescued. This is no panegyric written at a monarch's command!

This poem, though the first in order, was nearly, if not actually, the last to be written. That is often the way with introductions. The Tenth Eclogue, in honor of Gallus, declares itself the last. We may so regard it, but not forget the possibility that Virgil put in the frontispiece after he had finished the colophon.

The First Eclogue also marks a turning-point in Virgil's career, in the history of his hero-worship. I have warned my readers on more than one occasion against an unduly Augustan interpretation of the *Bucolics*. The empire was not formally established or the name of Augustus conferred on Octavian till 27. The historian Tacitus [1] would not date until then the beginning of a reign of law and peace; in the twenty years preceding, he says, "neither custom nor right had existed." It is in the early part of this turbulent period that the *Bucolics* were written. From the start there hovered before the mind of the young poet the vision of a prince and savior, who should guide his people to a Golden Age of peace. Caesar was that monarch, but he met his death at the hands of envious men. Who should succeed him? Octavian was by no means the universal choice of monarchists at the moment. Virgil casts in his lot with his friend and patron Pollio, the trusted lieutenant of Antony, and sees in him the destined ruler. That is in the year 40. Virgil's other patrons at the period of the *Bucolics* are Varus, a minor hero, and his beloved brother-poet Gallus. While Pollio is off on his Dalmatian campaign, Virgil learns to know Maecenas. Now, thanks to him, a new champion has arisen, the godlike Octavian. Virgil will not abandon his former heroes; the tributes to them all are included in this volume of pastoral verse. But the volume is dedicated to Octavian.

[1] *Annales*, III, 28, 2 f.

CHAPTER V

VIRGIL'S ARCADIA

(ECLOGUE X)

W E HAVE had glimpses of Virgil's Arcadia in various of the eclogues already discussed; the Third, the Fourth, the Seventh, the Eighth, are particularly significant in this regard. On the whole, the epic note is more prominent in the earlier half of the *Bucolics*; the vision of Arcadia seems to possess the poet's mind more in the latter half. And in the last poem of the collection the entire scene is laid in Arcadia.

I

THE TENTH ECLOGUE

Grant this last song, O fountain Arethuse.

The last song is to honor Gallus, who knew himself to sing. It tells of his love, the while the snub-nosed goats crop the bushes and all the woods are listening. Where were ye then, Naiads, in what distant glades, when Gallus was dying of unrequited love? There was nothing to make you tarry on the heights of Parnassus or Pindus or by the spring of Helicon, while Gallus lay pining by a lonely rock in Arcady. The Muses should have left their haunts, Virgil means, and hastened to their poet's cry. The picture in Theocritus [1] at which Virgil glances, and

[1] *Idylls*, I, 66.

in Milton, who has both of the ancient models in mind, is the same; Virgil's compact description has tempted certain critics to suppose that the Muses are reproached, most infelicitously, for *not* being in their distant abodes on Parnassus or Pindus or Helicon.

In default of the Muses, laurels and tamarisks sympathize with Gallus, the sheep stand about him, shepherds and swineherds, among them Menalcas, dripping from his task of gathering acorns, cluster round—a homely group, but one with poets in fellow-feeling. "So disdain not thou the flocks, O poet divine." The pastoral god Apollo comes.

"Why let love craze thee, Gallus? Thy mistress Lycoris has followed another man through snows and shuddering scenes of war."

Silenus comes with nodding fennel and lilies for a crown. Comes Pan, ruddy with juice of elderberries on his face. "Have done," he says. "Love is a cruel god, and feeds on tears as bees on clover." This is the well-intended consolation of these pastoral friends; let Gallus return to sanity and throw off the thrall. He answers sadly that he knows Arcadia is a pleasant place; he would like to learn its music and tranquil joys, to keep a flock and prune a vine, to lie in the shade with Phyllis or Amyntas. How sweet! Phyllis would bind him wreaths and Amyntas sing for him. Yes, Gallus will yield to the charm. He will let love go, the love that racks and masters a man. He will flee real life and its turmoil of emotion. He will become a simple shepherd.

Here are chill springs, here softest grass — Lycoris.

Even as he utters the wish, the false loves of his pastoral dream vanish, and passion is with him again. Arcadia cannot be, unless Lycoris shares it. Ribbeck, Virgil's editor, takes the trouble to assume a lacuna and compose a lumbering hexameter to fill it —

o utinam hic esset potius mecum ipsa Lycoris.

But the poet makes his point in neater style than this.

So much for the pastoral dream; another succeeds it, a real and cruel vision. Lycoris cannot come to Arcady; Gallus is compelled, then, by his mad love to go in thought to the camps of Mars, far from country and home, to the chill Rhine and the Alpine snows which she must brave without him. What suffering for her — ah, may not the sharp ice cut her pretty feet! — It perhaps occurs to Gallus just then that another escort is looking out for that. "A truce, then!" he cries. "I will attune my lays of Euphorion to the measure of the Sicilian's reed." Gallus will become shepherd after all — not, however, that he returns to the pretty pastoral delights which had brought him no cheer before.

Ready am I mid woods and woodland lairs
To suffer gladly and my love to carve
On the young trees, which grow while grows my love.
I'll join the nymphs and roam through Arcady
Or hunt mad boars. No cold shall stay my hounds
Belting the upland glades of Parthenus.

Gallus would be a Hippolytus, rendering like service, however, to Aphrodite as to Artemis, and nursing his love as an ideal. It is a hard rôle to play.

> Not this the medicine my frenzy craves.
> That god does not relent for human woes.
> No more can woodland nymph or song itself
> Give me delight. Leave me again, ye woods!
> That god ne'er changes for our sternest toils.
> Not if we drink the stream of icy Thrace
> Or brave mid wintry storms the Scythian snow,
> Nor where the scorched bark shrivels on the elm
> We tend our flocks neath Africa's hot star.
> Love conquers all; let us bow down to love.

Such is the song that our shepherd has made for Gallus, as he sat weaving his humble pastoral basket. May the Muses sanctify the gift to his friend, for whom his love grows hourly as the green alder shoots up in the new spring.

> Now let us rise; 'tis shadow-time, and shade
> Works harm to shepherds' voices and great harm
> To junipers, and blights the crops. Go home,
> My pastured goats; for Hesper comes. Go home.

Servius remarks on line 46: "All these verses are from Gallus, taken from his own poems." How much "all these verses" includes we can only guess; they would be confined, we should imagine, to Gallus's speech, and not take up everything there. A modest amount of quotation makes a fit compliment, and Virgil may have found warrant for its use in the Seventh Idyll of Theocritus; we should assume in any case that he has not overworked the device. Yet even if the entire speech of Gallus is a cento from his poetry, the bits are cleverly fashioned into a consistent picture. Various critics have found an incongruity here, for Gallus now appears under an Arcadian rock and now is off at the wars. Skutsch [1] comes to the poet's rescue by admitting the infelicity, but merging it in the higher unity of what he calls "catalogue poetry," an unlovely species which consists in a series of quotations from an author's different works.[2] There is unity in the eclogue, but not of this kind. Nor is there any incongruity, if we brush aside the dust of modern comments and return to the ancient interpretation of verses 44–45; Gallus, not really off at the wars, but still lying under the rock, betakes himself in imagination to the camp where Lycoris is.[3] The poet sets before us the shifts and revulsions in his passion, his final resolution to remain true to it, or rather the discovery that he cannot escape it. There is nothing morbid in the sentiment here. The situation contrasts with that in the Eleventh Idyll of Theocritus, where Polyphemus finds the balm of love in song; Virgil has also, in the Second

[1] See above, p. 143.

[2] Another sort of catalogue poetry is illustrated by Hesiod in poems that are in essence lists of one thing or another or one kind of persons — beautiful women, for instance ('Hoîaı). Statius writes a catalogue poem to raise the works of Lucan (*Silvae*, II, 7). The Seventh Idyll of Theocritus contains illustrative quotations from the poets of the day. No catalogue poem in existence, to the best of my knowledge, is merely a mosaic or cento, as the present poem would be, in case it were consistently a catalogue poem.

[3] Servius: ex affectu amantis ibi se esse putat, ubi amica est, ut 'me' sit 'meum animum.'

Eclogue, interpreted the mastery of song over passion, and in general he is, like his Sicilian teacher, a foe of sentimentalism. But the present poem is a tribute — about as fine a tribute as one poet ever gave another — to the sincerity of Gallus's feeling, that is, to the abiding excellence of his elegiac poetry. We may also surmise, possibly, that Gallus had tried pastoral as well, turning from that to the form more adequate for deep emotion. If this is so, Virgil does not forget to commend his pastoral too.

Nor have thou shame of flocks, thou poet divine.[1]

Perhaps, then, Gallus was one of the little company of shepherd-poets of which we have had glimpses in various eclogues, particularly the Ninth, and in the *Lydia*. We are then brought round again to the possibility — we may not call it more than this — that Gallus is the master-poet celebrated under the name of Menalcas in the Ninth Eclogue.

From his boyhood, we have seen Virgil reaching out for friendship and pinning his hopes to one hero after another. He has not the aloofness of Lucretius, who could make the gift of friendship passionately and unreservedly, but only to one who could understand the mysteries that had been revealed to himself. Virgil has not the self-sufficiency of Horace, who loves to broach the Falernian and start a table-talk, but who gave the whole of himself to very few. Virgil, for all his shyness, devotes himself to his friends with the open and childlike tender-

[1] L. 17.

ness of Catullus, save that he does not merely yearn for human fellowships and *paulum quidlibet adlocutionis*; his friend must be his hero and the leader of his race.

It is impossible to attempt an exact dating of the poem from internal evidence; the allusion to the campaign in the Alps is too indefinite. But if we accept the statement of the ancient biographers that the *Eclogues* were done in three years and begun when the poet was twenty-eight, they are to be placed in the period 42–39; there is nothing in the poem to prevent our putting it late in 39.

After his song for Gallus, the poet stops weaving his osier basket and drives his goats to their stalls. It is all done quietly; we do not at first suspect that the flock is never to fare afield again — that Virgil has said good-bye to the pastoral. We might have expected the traditional prophecy of the poet's immortality, or the announcement, as in Ovid's farewell to the *Amores*, of a new and larger theme in prospect. But that is not Virgil's way; he makes such announcements at the beginning of a poem, in the form of a wish, not at the end in the form of an advertisement. Instead of saying, "From the lower level of pastoral I shall now ascend to epic or tragedy," he writes a panegyric of Gallus to show that the latter's love-poetry is deeper and richer than pastoral can be. It is the same Virgil who fled to the nearest doorway from the pointing fingers of the crowd. We also might have expected that the epic trumpet would wind a final blast, or at least that the rising of the evening star would be given a full line at the end. Not even that. The evening star is incidental. The shepherd sees it and knows it is time to go; he starts up his herd and trudges homeward.

II

The arrangement of the different poems in the *Bucolics* has been variously discussed. Some have pointed out that the odd-numbered pieces are monologues, the even-numbered dialogues. The only exception, the Eighth Eclogue, is of the kind that proves the rule; it consists of two monologues, which, though not related as question and answer, are the work of rival performers in a little pastoral drama, or rather pastoral *rappresentazione*. According to Professor Conway, in the odd-numbered eclogues the scenery is local, in the even-numbered it is foreign.[1] I have questioned the validity of such a principle as we have looked at the eclogues in turn, and will revert to it in a moment when we examine the scenery of the eclogues in general.

Further, it seems hard to believe that a poet of Virgil's temperament could have grouped his poems on any system of a mechanical sort. Let us rather imagine him, when all are finished, in the act of determining their positions one by one. The places of the Tenth and the First appoint themselves. The former he has declared the last, and the latter is the introduction to the series. Next,

[1] See above, pp. 89 f.

though an exact chronology is farthest from his mind, it becomes natural to put his earliest pieces, the Second and the Third, after the introduction, and somewhere after these the Fifth, which mentions them both as songs for the frail pipe that he now discards. But to break the precise order of sequence, he puts before the Fifth the Fourth, which with its epic tone makes the contrast of his former and his latter inspirations the more apparent; Virgil is a master of contrast and loses no chance to display it. Thus far the order is I, II, III, IV, V . . . X. What then? The last of the eclogues in honor of Pollio, the Eighth, is next in order of time, and for that very reason he will postpone it. The eclogues in honor, or partly in honor, of Varus are in chronological order IX, VI. The Sixth, with its tribute to Gallus, may not come too near to the Tenth. Here are two reasons, then, for inverting the order of these two pieces — and let us put the Eighth between them. There remains just one, whenever it was written, the Theocritean piece, the Seventh. Let it stand before VIII, which in character it resembles, and let us set VI and IX on either side. This arrangement will keep VIII as remote as possible from III and IV, which likewise mention Pollio. Some such considerations, proceeding from the twofold desire to associate the similar for unity and to separate them for contrast, would account for the order of every eclogue from I to X. Far be it from us to declare how Virgil must have proceeded. Certain it is that he was guided in his arrangement of the eclogues by principles of art and not of classification.

III

As Virgil ended his *Georgics*, some seven years later, he looked back, with an amused affection, to what he calls the youthful hazard of his *Bucolics* —

> carmina qui lusi pastorum audaxque iuventa
> Tityre te patulae cecini sub tegmine fagi.

The *Bucolics* are indeed hazardous for anybody save a magician like Virgil. Many critics since Boccaccio regard the infusion of allegory to be Virgil's contribution, a dubious contribution, to the development of the pastoral. Unlike Theocritus, as Boccaccio [1] puts it, Virgil hid much under the bark of his verse; or, in the words of John Addington Symonds,[2] Virgil, "with Roman bad taste, commits the capital crime of allegorizing." Bad taste or not, both Boccaccio and Symonds would be surprised to know how much scholars have recently found under the bark of Theocritus. At least the Seventh Idyll contains both extensive allegory and pastoral masquerade. Simichidas and Lycidas, as we saw, are not real shepherds, but Alexandrian poets who discuss literary conditions of the day. They suggest, in their alternating songs, it may well be with incidental quotation, the kind of subjects that Theocritus's contemporaries were treating; in fact,

[1] *Le Lettere*, Ed. F. Corazzini, 1877, p. 267.
[2] *Studies of the Greek Poets*, Amer. ed., II, p. 267.

as we have seen, one might discover "catalogue poetry" there. We need not go farther afield with those scholars who have found an amazing amount of allegory in other, apparently simple, poems of Theocritus. We may rest the case with the Seventh Idyll, which served Virgil as a model in both his Ninth and his Tenth Eclogues.

Personal allegory so definite as that in the Seventh Idyll appears only once in Virgil; in his Fifth Eclogue we cannot escape the conclusion that Daphnis is not the simple shepherd lad, but the risen Caesar. Elsewhere, as we have seen, Virgil either mentions contemporary characters outright, as Gallus and Varus and Pollio; or he alludes to them unmistakably, though without either pastoral or actual designation, as to Octavian; or else he employs a baffling and impressionistic kind of personal allegory that eludes explanation the moment it is observed. This is not "confusion," but deliberate and delicate art. It is an innovation, clearly, which at once adds to Theocritean allegory and subtracts from it; less in actual amount, the allegory is more pervasive. It is a bold device, managed with an artist's skill by Virgil, not repeated, so far as I am aware, in subsequent pastoral poetry, and not understood by many of Virgil's critics.

Moreover, there is a yet more dangerous innovation. Though the pastoral names are not consistently allegorical in any eclogue save the Fifth and thus do not actually set either the poet or his friends before us, the

Bucolics do present, in the First and the Ninth Eclogues, a larger allegory, a contemporary situation, the troubles of the ejected tenants of Mantua; though the portraiture is incomplete, one thinks of Virgil and Octavian. If the *Dirae* is Virgil's work, we may see by its help that the poet was not merely seeking to enliven the pastoral by filling it with alien matter. Rather, he started with a contemporary event that greatly concerned him, and choosing an appropriate form in which to make his protest, the pastoral curse, he later found the pastoral itself a natural medium for the same theme. Even if the *Dirae* is not Virgil's, it might have shown him the way. At all events, the theme is prominent in the two eclogues in which it appears (the First and the Ninth), fused with traditional bucolic scenes; it is treated, that is, exactly as real persons are treated in the *Eclogues*, being reflected hazily in a pastoral atmosphere rather than precisely described. Virgil could absorb and harmonize the incongruous in a setting of his own creation; but for many a Virgilian imitator this rash design was fraught with disaster. He alone has the magician's skill.[1]

IV

The scenery in Virgil's *Bucolics* is just as tantalizing, and to the prosaic critic just as incongruous, as the epi-

[1] My idea of the nature of allegory in the *Bucolics* agrees essentially, I am glad to find, with that of Funaioli in his article "Allegorie Virgiliane," *Rassegna Italiana*, II (1920), 155–190. See also H. Bennett, "Vergil and Pollio," *Amer. Journ. Philol.*, LI (1930), 324–342. Pollio is coming into his own.

sodes are. Virgil was a "landscape-lover," as well as a "lord of language," in Tennyson's phrase. Sainte-Beuve finds in the *Bucolics* a "continuous and perfect observation of rural details, faithful portraiture of nature, and a delicate and expressive art." [1] Moreover, Virgil's feeling for nature was not confined to a placid admiration of smooth lawns and slipping streams. With no touch of romantic sentimentality, rather with that wholesome revelry of the senses which makes him akin to George Meredith, he exults in country sights and sounds. The "Pathetic Fallacy" is a part of the pastoral convention, and was carried to absurd lengths by the later Hellenistic poets; Virgil either reduces it to common sense, or exalts it into epic. Nor do the wilder aspects of nature make a less powerful appeal to him. Gallus, pining by his Arcadian rock, shudders as he dramatically should at the thought of Lycoris braving the Alpine snows; a panegyric of the grandeur of the Alps, which some modern readers evidently miss here, would be singularly inept. Virgil keeps his scenery pastoral. But Aeneas, when he goes forth at last against Turnus, joys in the combat and clashes his thundering arms,

> Looming like Athos or like Eryx' height,
> Or like our mighty father Appennine
> What time he roars with all his quivering oaks
> And shakes his snowy locks exultantly
> Into the winds.[2]

[1] (*Nouveaux Lundis*, XI, p. 191): "Une continuelle et parfaite observation rurale, d'une peinture fidèle, prise sur nature, et du *rendu* le plus délicat."
[2] *Aen.*, XII, 701.

Nature has become glorified and heroic in justice to the epic setting. To be sure, Virgil can also make his woods a worthy background for a consul, and at the vision of the translated Daphnis can catch the song of the un-shorn mountains as they call it aloud to the stars. His Muses are not domestic or courtly deities, but have their homes on far-off mountain-peaks. And even his humble shepherd, like the despondent lovers in Roman elegy, turns naturally for sympathy to pathless woods and hills. Lucretius, too, could hear the distant music of a pipe   In pastoral wilds, realms of unearthly calm.[1]

Like him, Virgil can enter into this longing for the soli-tudes, but with no trace of the Romanticist's excess or absurdities.

Virgil loved his native town, and wove many Man-tuan bits into his pastoral scenery. But Keightley, an editor of Virgil more expert in agriculture than in poetry, cast a critical eye over Mantua, and discovered to his indignation that the scenery of the *Bucolics* does not everywhere match it. Conway comes to the poet's rescue by moving his farm to a spot where the scenery fits that of the *Eclogues*.

But does it? And should it? Virgil did not, perhaps could not, intend that it should. He had already trav-elled far in the realms of gold. With his own impres-sions of actual Italian sites, Mantuan and others too, he

---

[1] V, 1387: per loca pastorum deserta atque otia dia.

had stowed away in the "deep well" a host of literary reminiscences, touches of traditional scenery, which imagination had made no less real to him than actualities; thus he created out of nature and of art an ideal Arcadia, a land with its own laws, which to the prosaic seem a welter of confusion.

Shelley was not blind to the iridescent and impressionistic character of Virgil's art. In his *A Defense of Poetry* he declares,[1] "Lucretius is in the highest, and Virgil in a very high sense, a creator. The chosen delicacy of expressions of the latter are as a mist of light which conceals from us the intense and exceeding truth of his conceptions of nature."

As we come down the centuries, we find a new Arcadia, fashioned by Sannazaro and his successors. They took all their principles, though perhaps not fully aware of the fact, from Virgil and his contemporaries, with possibly, though not surely, some stray suggestions from the Greek romances. The actual Arcadia is hardly mentioned in the Greek bucolic poetry known to us. The poets of the Renaissance, who knew no more of Hellenistic literature than we, built on no earlier descriptions than what they found in the Romans; whether consciously or unconsciously, they also appropriated from Virgil the design of constructing Arcadias of their own. These novel creations are very different from Virgil's; they represent an inferior type of imagination. Virgil

[1] *The Prose Works*, ed. H. B. Forman, London, 1880, III, p. 121.

also differs from his models. His Alexandrian precursors, whoever they were, could hardly have combined the diverse elements, certainly not the Roman elements, of which Virgil constructed his pastoral Fairyland.

V

Here, then, is another striking difference between Virgil and Theocritus. The *Idylls* of Theocritus, perennially fresh and delightful, have seemed to others besides Austin Dobson to enshrine a Golden Age.

> O singer of the field and fold,
> THEOCRITUS! Pan's pipe was thine, —
> Thine was the happier age of gold.
>
> .   .   .   .
>
> Alas for us! Our songs are cold;
> Our Northern suns too sadly shine:—
> O singer of the field and fold,
> Thine was the happier Age of Gold!

Perhaps the very reason why Theocritus can offer to the world-weary modern a retreat into the Golden Age is that his own vision is centred on the immediate present. Shepherds' songs had doubtless existed in Sicily from the time that there were shepherds to sing; they may perhaps have been turned into a literary form by Stesichorus at the end of the seventh century, as the good people of Catania have recorded in no uncertain terms on their poet's monument today.[1] Whatever the varieties of the pastoral before Theocritus, his is an outgrowth of the

---

[1] "La poesia pastorale inventò."

realistic tendencies of his day; it is a special kind of that cross-section of the comedy of manners, the mime. The bucolic poet finds his themes in the country instead of the town; his sketches are shepherd-mimes. This is perhaps the most essential clue to an understanding of Theocritus, though it breaks down if we imagine that the realism of Theocritus is of the lowly and photographic sort that appears in the mimes of Herodas. Theocritus is a great observer. Enough types and incidents appear in his *Idylls* to make the fortune of an ordinary playwright. Not all of his subjects are pastoral; he can write the town-mime too, and retell epic stories in brief compass. He belongs with those who take all the human comedy, in its mirth and its pathos, as their province — he is a comrade for Horace, Balzac, and Shakespeare. The *Idylls* are more deeply human and more worldly-wise than Virgil's *Bucolics*, even though the *Bucolics* are not a work of youth. But Theocritus is too broad and creative to be merely realistic; he remembers his debt to the poets of the past. He has passages which the Virgiliomastix would call literary or artificial if only Virgil had written them. Indeed one may distinguish two classes in the pastoral *Idylls*, the idealizing and the realistic. Of the latter, the Fourth, Fifth, and Tenth are admirable specimens; with the former, the idylls devoted to the woes of Polyphemus, the Sixth and the Eleventh, surely belong. These and others of the same category do not lack the vital contact with Mother

Earth; we merely wonder whether such delightful rustics existed in reality any more than Polyphemus, who is as real as any creature alive.

For Virgil, the classes of idealizing and realistic do not exist. We have detected two other classes instead, *togatae* and *palliatae*. But whether he works with Greek or with Roman incident, Virgil's craftsmanship is of a piece. There was plenty of material in Italian life for new pastoral of the realistic sort. Varro prosaically sets forth some of it.[1] The author of the *Moretum* puts a true episode into delightful verse, and later, under Nero, Calpurnius has the good sense not to trespass in the Virgilian Arcadia but to cultivate a humbler and more genuinely rustic plot. But Virgil is a dreamer of no ordinary dream.

VI

Virgil also differs from Theocritus in his treatment of pastoral love. It is a necessary theme, one of the three chief themes for which the shepherd calls.

> Mopsus, begin, if aught thou hast to tell
> Of fire for Phyllis or for Alcon praise
> Or hot dispute with Codrus.[2]

The Second and the Eighth Eclogues are primarily concerned with the sorrows of love, and the Tenth is a tribute to the love-poetry of Gallus. There are incidental allusions in most of the other eclogues, but love plays al-

---

[1] *Res Rusticae*, II, 10, on shepherds. See also the delightful book of Fairfax Harrison, *Roman Farm Management*, New York, 1913.
[2] *Ecl.*, V, 10.

together a minor rôle in Virgil as compared with Theocritus. A French scholar, the author of one of the best short accounts of Virgil's pastoral poetry ever written,[1] cleverly remarks that Tityrus in the First Eclogue recalls his liaisons with Galatea and Amaryllis merely for the purpose of verifying a date, nor is it a date with Amaryllis. The later Greek pastoral joined hands with the elegy and perished in a surfeit of sentimentalism. Virgil reacted from this encroachment of the neurotic to which the author of the *Lydia* succumbed.

VII

Panegyric is another element in Virgil's pastoral, and, like love, one of the important traditional themes. It is natural enough for a shepherd to praise his master or some fellow-singer, as in the Fourth Idyll of Theocritus. Praise of the ruling prince is another affair. Theocritus has incidental bits of such panegyric, but not in his pastoral idylls.[2] He also devotes entire poems [3] to eulogies. It was easy for Virgil, with the volume, or volumes, of Theocritus before him, to introduce political panegyric into the pastoral itself. He was inclined, from the start, to epic and to hero-worship. Making an early attempt at epic and finding his powers not matured for it, he had turned to the *Bucolics*. In the simple Theocritean pas-

---

[1] P. Laignel, in the introduction to the translation of the *Bucolics* by Fabre des Essarts, Paris, 1901, p. 18. "Tityre ne rappelle ses liaisons avec Galatée et Amaryllis qu'afin de fixer une date."
[2] *Idylls*, XIV, XV.
[3] *Idylls*, XVI, XVII.

torals with which he began he deviates from his Greek models by introducing a touch of incidental panegyric in honor of Pollio. Then something occurred that impelled the poet to another innovation; it was the deification of the murdered Caesar, following the apparition of his comet, an event that must have stirred his imagination powerfully. Virgil boldly made Caesar the hero of a pastoral poem; the novelty consists not in the use of allegory, but in the infusion of elaborate panegyric. The result is a new literary form, the panegyric-pastoral.

The Fourth Eclogue, which followed soon, belongs to the same variety; it is, besides, a pastoral prophecy, possibly, though not necessarily, taking part of its imagery from the Messianic visions of the Old Testament. The Tenth Eclogue is a panegyric of a poet; the First, a most artistically constructed eulogy of Virgil's latest hero, to whom he dedicates his volume. The Sixth and the Eighth, like the Fourth, have an introductory dedication; Theocritus has several such dedications, but panegyric is not prominent in them. Incidental eulogy occurs in the Sixth and the Ninth Eclogues; only the Second and the Seventh are free from this element, unless the name Iollas in the former poem is meant to suggest Pollio.

This is a startling amount of panegyric, a pastoral novelty indeed, for which Virgil's hero-worship is responsible. It is natural for him; the exuberance of his devotion can buoy it up. Nor should we, with the potent examples of Pindar and Isocrates in view, regard pane-gyric as more germane to the Roman spirit than to the Greek. Let us not call it another of those instances of Roman bad taste. For all this, I would not obscure the fact that panegyric was destined later to sink the Roman pastoral, as the elegy had sunk the Greek. Calpurnius announces a ponderous Golden Age in honor of that ponderous shepherd, Nero, and constructs a novel amoe-baean in which the subject is always the same. Instead of a variety of pastoral themes in which one shepherd leads and the other matches him, the poet presents one central and imperial figure, the immovable Nero, on whom different pastoral stage-lights are played.

The reason why Calpurnius and other pastoral pane-gyricists come to utter failure is that they have no breath of the epic spirit which exalts Virgil's *Bucolics* and distinguishes them from any production of the Alexandrian Age. Not all the eclogues are epic through-out; their tone varies, as in any music, to suit the mo-ment. Virgil, as Calpurnius aptly said,[1] could make his oaten reed resound with the music of the lyre. But he never seizes the lyre and throws the reed away. His music is always pastoral. Dr. Johnson, as we have seen,[2] implies that Virgil has injured the heritage of Theocritus. Milton was of other mind, else he would not have followed Virgil's daring lead and, reckless of the proprieties, attained a similar success.

[1] See above, p. 8.   [2] See above, p. 113.

Audax iuventa. The *Bucolics* are indeed full of haz-
ards, in their novel allegory, their scenery, their mixture of realistic and literary elements, their panegyric
and their heroic style. The keenest critics, like Sainte-
Beuve, are aware of the triumph in the face of heavy
odds. The elements are most incongruous; the hazard
lies in the mixing of them. But the harmonious mind
may harmonize anything; the mind is its own place.
Anatole France, while serving against his country's foe
in 1870, had time one day to read the Sixth Eclogue with
a comrade of like tastes.[1]

Whilst the Prussian batteries sent white clouds of smoke
afloat upon the hills on the horizon of the gray and bare
country, we two, seated on the river bank, near the piled
rifles, our heads leaning over a copy of Bliss's little "Virgil,"
which I have yet, and which is dear to me, were making comments upon that cosmogony, which the poet, by a delightful
caprice, enshrined in an idyll.

The critic, if he have the harmonious mind, will not
merely analyze the *Bucolics*, but note their harmony.
To quote again from that fine little essay by Laignel:

The sovereign art of the poet has accomplished this miracle,
that the *Bucolics* are in turn rustic idyll, love-elegy, mythological fable, mystic dream, without ever ceasing to be eclogues. . . . This perfect accord of inspirations so diverse,
this supreme unity in a variety so complex, has been realized
by Virgil through the delicacy of his taste, by that exquisite
sense of measure which seems to be the privilege of the great
Classic artists.

[1] *La Vie Littéraire*, deuxième série (*Œuvres Complètes*, Paris, 1926, VI,
p. 611), translated by A. W. Evans, London, 1914.

Such, then, is Virgil's venturesome creation, his magic Arcadia, the revery of a youthful shepherd to whom all things were possible. It is a Golden Age, not dreamed of as a distant past or future, but boldly set before us now. It is a fairyland of young hopes with a climate of perpetual spring.

Nunc frondent silvae, nunc formosissimus annus.

CHAPTER VI

WORKS AND DAYS—A CHALLENGE TO HESIOD

IN VIRGIL'S *Bucolics*, the poet's temperament becomes clear and harmonious after the turmoil of his youthful attempts to find his true nature and the apt means of its expression. Still, there is as much prophecy as finality in this achievement. The sure and unforgettable notes that sound in this poetry are, first, the sheer joy of the country and of a perpetual and Arcadian spring, and, no less clear, the deeper tones of epic. Virgil's epic pastoral is a magical harmony and not an artificial incongruity just because he must create it to do justice to this twofold aspect of his nature. He is not trying for something novel or bizarre; he is expressing himself. For this expression, he studies, with the most patient care, his predecessors in bucolic verse, particularly Theocritus, that he may at once identify himself with the proper tradition and attest his originality by transforming it.

I

With the *Bucolics* before us, we seem to see the *Georgics* growing from that fertile soil as naturally as a plant develops from its seed. This is an ultimately false view of any art, no more than a half-truth, at any rate; for at every step in its progress the creative act of human will has intervened. Still, at the end, the vista seems continuous; first the blade, then the ear, then the full corn in the ear. At all events, no external intervention can explain Virgil's success — no order from Augustus or Maecenas. When the poet declares that he is but following out the "stern commands"[1] of his patron, he speaks with an inevitable courtesy, and with a delicate Socratic irony that Maecenas would be the first to understand. A simple consideration of the historical background should deter us from imagining the *Georgics* a paid advertisement of Augustus's agricultural programme. As we have already noted,[2] the Augustan Age, strictly speaking, does not begin till the title of Augustus was conferred upon Octavian and his reign of law and peace began. The poem was written, according to the ancient biographer,[3] in seven years. The seventh year after the completion of the *Bucolics* would be 31 or perhaps 30 B.C. The introduction to the Third Book presupposes the victory at Actium in 31, and the last half of the Fourth, in its present form, was written after the disgrace and suicide of Gallus in 26. These passages represent the last stage in the composition of the work, and perhaps first appeared in its second edition. The preliminary plan must have been formed, and indeed the poem in its first shape virtually finished, at a time when Octavian's mind was set on things vastly different from agricultural conditions in Italy; his immediate objective could

---

[1] *Georg.*, III, 41: tua, Maecenas, haud mollia iussa.
[2] See above, p. 152.   [3] Brummer, p. 16, l. 89.

hardly have been more than the settling of Antony's business. In such a period of commotion, Maecenas, with whom Virgil had become intimate at least as early as the year 37, might well have suggested, after reading the *Bucolics*, some sort of a panegyric of country life in the interests of peace, precisely in the sense in which Pollio inspired the *Bucolics*.[1] Further than this "stern commands" could not have gone. The poet's own temperament impelled him to a larger and more general treatment of the theme that he had made his own, even as Ovid wrote, largely in the vein of parody, to be sure, a complete *Art of Love* after the preliminary essays of his *Amores*. The new venture at once offered Virgil the freedom of familiar ground and allured him to extend the scope of his ever-strengthening passion for epic.

II

The form of the new poem, determined by its theme, was obviously didactic. It immediately became Virgil's task to consider the methods of his predecessors — to be original in the most difficult way. The classic poet, in any period of literary history, starts with his own idea. It must be both contemporary and universal, else it would neither have appealed to his own generation nor have descended to ours. To be thus immortal, the plan of the work must show genius and its very lines and phrases must glow with life and color, the charm of all the Muses

[1] See above, p. 123.

flowering in a lonely word. But beyond these obvious requisites, the poet must survey the achievements of his predecessors in the same field. He must catch the torch of tradition from them, kindle it with his own light, and hand it on. He is not merely a creator, forming a new world from the elements of chaos. That were the easier task. It is his to accept the design, to submit himself to law, and, working within it, make it a fresh and free expression of his own purpose and his own art. A young poet today (or perhaps a young poet in any age — young Virgil, for instance, according to Pope) feels himself above tradition and the critic's law; his ambition is to express himself and be different. But ignorant of what he is to be different from, he sometimes proves very much the same. The poet of the classic turn in any age schools himself in the masterpieces of old and from his very compliance with the norm is bound to interpret it in his own way if he possesses any poetic life whatsoever. Virgil was forever engaged in a decent worship of poetic convention and a fervid revolt against it.

As Virgil turned to the past, he found a mass of writers on didactic subjects, but just two masters, so far as we can gather from the fragmentary condition of ancient literature, to whom a special homage was due and to whose works he devoted *lungo studio* and *lungo amore*. These two masters were Hesiod and Lucretius. From the Alexandrians, Virgil took bits of information and details of technique. Eratosthenes, the distinguished librarian and geographer of the third century, supplies, in his poem called Ἑρμῆς, a model for the account of the zones in the First Georgic. From Nicander of Colophon, a writer of the second century, come the title *Georgics* and part, certainly, of the matter of the story of the bees in the Fourth Book. Nicander's Γεωργικά and Μελισσουργικά are unfortunately lost, but judging from the manner of two of his didactic poems that are preserved, one on the remedies against the wounds inflicted by dangerous animals, Θηριακά, and one on antidotes to poison, Ἀλεξιφαρμακά, we may infer that Virgil would have welcomed, and not feared, a comparison with the poems most nearly related in subject to his own. Nicander was a poet of some distinction, as we learn from Cicero; he chose farming for a subject not because he was a practical farmer himself but because it appealed to him as apt for poetry.[1]

Another Alexandrian, of higher poetic quality, is Aratus, the friend of Theocritus, who made a metaphrase of the astronomical prose work of Eudoxus, the Φαινόμενα, with an appendage on the signs of the weather, Διοσημίαι. Aratus is one of the poets whom St. Paul has in mind when in his sermon on Mars' Hill he quotes a half-verse to show that the ancient Greeks were not altogether bound in the shackles of idolatry: "For we, too, are his offspring." The words τοῦ γὰρ καὶ

[1] *De Oratore*, I, 69: constat . . . de rebus rusticis hominem ab agro remotissimum Nicandrum Colophonium poetica quadam facultate, non rustica, scripsisse praeclare.

γένος ἐσμέν occur in the invocation of Aratus's poem, in a passage expressive of a beautiful and tender pantheism. Cicero exercised his powers, which in mere technique were considerable, in the translation of this work into Latin hexameters. It thus had a certain eminence in Virgil's time. But again, imitation for Virgil is a sign, not of submission, but of challenge. Aratus, describing the indications of weather furnished by the moon, says

πάντα δ'ἐρευθομένη δοκέειν ἀνέμοιο κελεύθους.[1]

When Virgil turns this into the exquisite verses,

at si virgineum suffuderit ore ruborem,
ventus erit; vento semper rubet aurea Phoebe,[2]

he obviously wishes the reader to observe first what Aratus did, and then what he might have done.

It was a more audacious undertaking to transcend Hesiod and Lucretius, but that, too, is Virgil's ambition. All of his works are conceived in a spirit of adventure and high emprise that seemed to the poet himself well-nigh bravado.[3] We cannot appreciate the hardihood of the task until we examine the literary background on which the poet sought to project a new and startling pic-

[1] L. 803:
"If the moon redden, know that then the wind
Is on its path."

[2] I, 430:
But if the virgin blush, a wind will rise;
For golden Phoebe blushes in the wind.

[3] On his *Eclogues*, see *Georg.*, IV, 565: audaxque iuventa. On his *Georgics*, see *Georg.*, I, 40: audacibus adnue coeptis. On the *Aeneid*, see his letter to Augustus (Macrobius, *Saturnalia*, I, 24, 11): tanta inchoata res est ut paene vitio mentis tantum opus ingressus mihi videar.

ture, and note the vastly incongruous matters which, by his art of magic, were caught up harmoniously into his poetic design. We must inquire into the laws of didactic poetry and consider the nature of two didactic works that Virgil evidently regarded as supreme — the poems of Hesiod and Lucretius.

III

Hesiod's *Works and Days* has suffered almost as much as Homer himself from the disintegrating analysis of the last century. It is only of late that the reader has been allowed to brush aside the dust of hypercriticism, assume the unity of the poem, and find its purpose. Virgil labored under no such handicap. He read the *Works and Days* early in his boyhood, and he read it straight. He saw its meaning then, and he incorporated it in the *Georgics* in a way that should help us back to it today. To him the poem of Hesiod was not an incoherent mass of scraps, primitive in thought and naïf in sentiment, but a consciously literary product, the work of a writer who observed, as he himself observed, the established laws of his art. He was a writer, moreover, who had pondered life as a moral satirist ponders it, and who knew, as the youthful author of the *Culex* observed, how to absorb peaceful drafts of it into his own tranquillity,

securam placido traducit pectore vitam.[1]

Hesiod's poem is addressed to his indolent brother Perses, who after exhausting his substance tried by

[1] *Culex*, 97.

bribing unjust judges to dispossess Hesiod of his share of their father's inheritance. After an invocation to the Muses, — and to Perses, — the poet discourses in a general fashion (vv. 11–46) on Ἔρις, or strife. There are two kinds of strife, an evil kind which involves men in wars and feuds and in which Perses is now engaged, and a good kind, competition, which is the clue to wealth and to which Perses is invited to turn his attention. Perses is endeavoring by a resort to corruption to get something out of nothing. The right way is to limit desire, to know that the half is better than the whole, and by honest toil Perses should settle his affair privately, as Zeus and Justice shall direct. This poem is founded on four main principles, more or less explicitly mentioned in this introduction — Justice, Contentment, Industry, and Religion.

Why cannot men see what their true utility is? Zeus has hidden this knowledge from them, doubtless in anger at the wiles of Prometheus, who was responsible for most of the ills of mankind. The poet tells the story of Prometheus, with borrowings from his earlier account in the *Theogony*. To enforce the point, he turns to another myth, the Ages of Man. There has been a steady degeneracy from the Age of Gold to that of Iron, and one more dreadful yet is in store, when Wrong shall rule at large and Reverence and Righteous Retribution shall leave the world once and for all.

This sounds like undiluted pessimism, but Hesiod's prophecy, like the prophecies of the Old Testament, is not so much a revelation of historical events as a warning against moral consequences. For his purpose, he has introduced a striking novelty into the Golden Age. The story had doubtless been told from time immemorial before him, and was repeated by countless writers after him. It is they who kept the traditional features, and Hesiod who innovated. For him, the life of primeval man was one of industry. He admires the piety and simplicity of that happy time, and has no desire for unnecessary toil and pain. But he is far from sentimentalizing the past, or indulging in the tired peasant's dream of a perpetual holiday, in the fields of No-Work, as our Anglo-Saxon forefathers, on one interpretation of their word (Neorxnawong), called Paradise. To Hesiod, life without work would not be a Golden Age; the subsequent epochs erred not in laboring more, but in introducing short cuts for labor, such as war and the arts of deceit.

This myth is likewise a parable, pointed with special reference to Perses. The poet completes this section of his work (vv. 47–212), with a brief fable addressed to the judges. It is the story of a gentle nightingale, struggling in the talons of a greedy hawk. No moral is drawn, nor need be. The judges would understand. Written before the trial, these words of the poet bespeak a mind master of itself and serenely disdainful of consequences.

Next comes a passage (vv. 213–285) so different in coloring from the preceding that at first glance one might imagine one's self in the presence of another poet. But it is the same Hesiod, returning to the gnomic manner of the passage on Strife which preceded the fables. He is expounding their meaning unmistakably, if Perses has ears to hear. The first lesson is the sovereign need of justice. "O Perses," he cries, "give ear to justice, and foster not insolent transgression." This is one of the burdens of the song of the ages, and justice is one of the four principles announced at the beginning of the poem. The passage consists of maxims strung together somewhat loosely, yet having as much unity as a chapter in Proverbs or a section in Theognis dealing with a general theme. The morality is of that effective and Horatian sort that does not belabor the iniquity of the offender, but, rather, shows him his lack of intelligence. For "justice is better than transgression for those who follow it to the end, and the fool finds this out by experience." The poet addresses the judges before he finishes this part of his theme, and ends it with a final appeal to Perses.

Another gnomic passage succeeds (286–382), devoted to another of the central ideas of the poem, industry. "I will speak to you with good intent," says the poet, "O foolish Perses. Vice is easy and virtue hard; the gods have put sweat in front of it. But though the start is rough, the path is smooth at the end. The gods require the industrious man and punish the sluggard. Work,

then, Perses, scion of the gods. If then your heart is
set on wealth, so do; and work you work upon work":

ἔργον ἐπ' ἔργῳ ἐργάζεσθαι.

Industry has rarely been proclaimed, even in these in-
dustrial days of ours, with such a vigor.

The little discourse on Industry is now made specific.
The poet reviews the chief labors that engage the farmer
(383–617). This is the part of the work that, some may
think, is most intimately associated with Virgil's poem.
Important coincidences in detail occur, but more important still, in its likeness and its difference, is the
setting. For the precepts on farming are incidental.
They are involved in the larger theme of industry as the
only avenue to wealth. It is a Gospel of Work in general,
and, specifically, it is a Gospel of Work for Perses.
Hesiod's art of farming is not purely didactic and technical, but didactic, gnomic, and personal at one and the
same time. With Hesiod before him, Virgil could not
possibly have limited his scope to a simple treatise on
agriculture.

Hesiod begins his story with the task of reaping at the
rising of the Pleiades and presents in a kind of farmer's
almanac the labors of the year in the order of occurrence. He by no means covers everything that the
farmer needs to know; his object, as ever, is to induce
Perses to work. With touches of quaint humor, genial
ridicule, and sound common sense, he points the consequences of both the observance and the neglect of his

wholesome maxims. Hesiod knows the farm; his hands have felt the soil. But, once more, he is not writing a manual of agriculture; farming is incidental and illustrative; his subject is the moral attitude of the farmer. The following passages are typical:

Now first get a house and a wife and a plough-ox. Do not put off till the morrow, for procrastination, as surely as idleness, leads to ruin. The first cry of the crane is the sign for ploughing to begin. If you have your oxen and plough all ready, you can begin. See that you have them. Try not to borrow, for you will be refused, nor think, like the man whose wealth is in imagining, that you can make your plough then; for a plough is not made overnight. So have it ready, and then to work with you, you and all your men. With a prayer to Zeus Chthonios and to Demeter, duly begin the ploughing, with a small boy to sow behind you and make trouble for the birds by hiding well the seeds. For order is the first law of the farm. Obey it and, Zeus willing, you can garner full sheaves and get the cobwebs out of your bins. Thus you will not look to others, but others will look to you.

But the Boeotian farmer must know something about the sea. A brief passage, therefore, is devoted to this art (618–694):

At the setting of the Pleiades tempt not the sea, but proceed to work your soil as I instruct you. Beach your boat, carry the tackling home, and hang up your rudder above the smoke. Wait for good weather and then start out with a cargo and make money on it, as our father used to do, you foolish Perses. For he came all the way here from Cyme in Aeolis, fleeing penury, and got him a habitation in the miserable little town of Ascra. So, Perses, mind all works in their season, and especially sailing. Commend a little boat and put your cargo in a big one.

Perses's neighbor might be induced by such commendation to put his wares in a little boat and hence take less to market. These instructions on sailing are no more technical — in fact they are much less minute — than those on farming. But they contain useful hints for the moral improvement of Perses.

There follows a passage (695–764) which contains a miscellaneous array of maxims on man's social and religious conduct. The poet begins with marriage. There has already been mention of a wife, together with a good plough-ox and other necessities of the farm, but now her qualities are described. Other maxims on friendship follow, and then comes a series of religious injunctions and taboos; it ends with a line or two on Rumor, which one may avoid by observing these precepts of the gods. By works, ἔργα, we see, Hesiod means "deeds," "principles of conduct," as well as the operations of farming. These religious precepts, further, illustrate one of the four principles suggested at the beginning. Various pious utterances have appeared before, but here is a definite collection of maxims devoted to religion.

The last of the main sections of the poem is that on Days (765–825). The keynote is set in the opening line. "The Days that come from Zeus keep well, and duly tell them to your servants." The precepts are religious, like those in the latter half of the preceding section. Those prescribe what deeds should or should not be done; these tell when certain deeds are best done. Taken together, they illustrate the idea of religious duty. The passage on Farming has something of the chronological nature of the present part, for it considers works in the order of the calendar. But here the treatment is more minute; each day of the month is lucky or unlucky for some special thing. Thus Hesiod gave instructions before about the general time for sowing, but now adds that the thirteenth day of the month is a bad day to begin the sowing, though excellent for setting out plants. Similarly, "the eleventh and the twelfth are good for shearing sheep, the sixth is a kindly time for building a pen, the fourth for taking a wife to your home; and few know that the twenty-seventh is the time for broaching a jar and yoking up your beasts of burden and launching your boat." These superstitions appear to be part and parcel of the farmer's life, altogether as important as an intimate acquaintance with the make-up of a plough. Agriculture was still the handmaid of theology; only a theologian could really plough. If Hesiod set about to give his brother, I will not say complete, but even sufficient instruction in the art of successfully managing a farm, he could not, with his deeply religious temperament, omit these precepts.

No more appropriate title could be devised for this poem than *Works and Days*. It falls into the following five parts: General Precepts on Justice, Industry, and Economy; Precepts on Farming; on Sailing; Social and Religious Precepts; Days. I cannot conceive that the scheme would be complete with any one of those gone. The main principles on which the poet bases his appeal are stated at the beginning, and all but one are elaborated in special sections. The one principle not thus treated, Contentment, is incidentally involved in all the others. Another subject, Social Duties, is only vaguely suggested at the beginning, but receives occasional treatment in various of the main passages and occupies part of the passage preceding that on Days. It develops naturally out of the passage on Work, with its specific illustrations, for ἔργα means not only Tasks, but Deeds, or Principles. As in all artistic creation, the poem avoids at once a loose irrelevancy in construction and a too mathematical rigidity. The plan is completed by an admirable summary in just three lines at the end:

"So a man becomes happy and wealthy who knowing all these things works, blameless in the sight of the immortals, minding their omens, and eschewing transgressions."

This is the life of a man who steers his course by Contentment, Work, Justice, and Religion. These verses bind beginning, middle, and end into one consistent whole. There is roughness at the junctures of the main parts and lack of sequence in the details of the gnomic passages, but a central idea with subordinate ideas has been planned and successfully set forth.

Such, then, is the poem with which Hesiod answers his brother, and which perhaps was read at some gathering of the people before the trial came off; at any rate, it was composed before that event. Under the circumstances, the kind of retaliation that Hesiod made for his brother's wrong-dealing bespeaks a calm and lofty mind. Hesiod's temperament is rich in moods, but is not for that reason disordered. He has moments of prophetic fervor, of sturdy hopes and sturdy despair, but such a poem could have been written at such a time only by a man who, master of himself and of his future, could treat his antagonists with the placidity of an Horatian satirist. In the "miserable little town of Ascra," far back in the history of Greek letters, we find the same genial raillery and worldly wisdom, the same moral earnestness, too, that later shed their pleasant light upon the Sabine farm.

If we may now make a final attempt at definition, we cannot call the poem technically didactic, though it contains technical elements; it has likewise gnomic and personal and narrative elements. Its main object is to present to Hesiod's erring brother, in the abstract and the concrete, those principles that lead to a happy and successful life. It suggests a philosophical essay, something like Seneca's *De Vita Beata*, or Cicero's *De Senectute*, in which latter work the part on agriculture occupies about the same relation to the whole that the passage on the same subject does in the *Works and Days*. The nearest analogue in poetry to our work is moral satire; no single one of Horace's satires is closely parallel, but you can extract from all of Horace's works bits that are closely akin — perhaps we should say that Horace has been gathering crumbs from Hesiod's table. Hesiod was perhaps not aware that he was writing moral satire. If he reflected on literary types, — and the *Theogony* shows that he had a wholesome reverence at least for the epic tradition and the epic vocabulary, — he might have regarded the present work as catalogue poetry, of which, according to antiquity, he wrote numerous specimens. This is the implication of the wholly admirable title, *Works and Days.*

Hesiod's poem, written perhaps about 800 B.C., primarily with a moral rather than a didactic purpose, inevitably served as a pattern for all who later essayed more technical and strictly didactic themes. For such themes could not be poetically presented in exactly the form appropriate for a manual of the subject. The poet must diversify his treatment, provide it with shiftings of the scene, and exalt his theme into higher regions of thought and emotional appeal. In short, he must humanize it; for he wrote not so much for craftsmen as for all mankind. Thus Aratus, whose subject was astronomy and whose facts and the very order of their presentation were borrowed, lightens his scientific material sometimes with expressions of a tender religious sentiment, as in the invocation of the poem, and sometimes with touches of mythology. He, too, tells the story of the Ages, though with quite a different purpose from that of Hesiod.

IV

In the same way Lucretius, Virgil's other master, whose purpose is anything but mythological, resorts to the myth, so strong was the force of tradition upon him, as an accepted device for lifting his theme into another sphere. He may treat the myth with allegory, for which, against the tendencies of his school, he had a curious predilection, or he may shrivel it with the blast of scornful criticism. But in the telling of it his keen imagination can make it live. Though a poet *malgré lui*, Lucretius is intensely a poet. And after all, though he would deny the charge with vehemence and contempt, the myth is true to certain depths of his own temperament, which made him, as I believe Macaulay declared, the most religious of the Romans. He further effects the lifting of his theme by passages of vivid moral feeling and poetical charm, which in spirit resemble the choral odes of Greek tragedy and are found at the beginning of books or turning-points in the argument. These give Lucretius's nearest approach to divinity — and he approaches very near. They offer the necessary relief after stretches of didactic exposition, and close philosophic reasoning, though these, too, have their beauties. High levels of retrospect are reached by long ascents; we better enjoy the view if we have climbed to it. Sometimes the outlook is from the ivory tower of a satirist, who looks down with a complacent mastery on the world of foibles from which he is free. Hesiod's vein of moral satire, with none of its lighter and Horatian elements, is more prominent still in Lucretius. Passage after passage reveals a kind of satire in the grand style, to which the rhetorical Juvenal aspired in vain, and which the wise Horace did not try to reproduce in poems that were first of all "conversations" — *sermones*; he rivals this spirit, as nearly as he can, in his odes.

Lucretius is a philosopher above everything else. He runs eagerly with the pack that craves to drag the truth from its lair. He is intent on all branches of philosophic search. Epicurus starts with ethics, and dabbles sufficiently in psychology, physics, and metaphysics to make his cosmos safe for the tranquillity of the sage — ἀταραξία. Lucretius admires the outcome of this philosophy, and exalts its founder to godhead. But he wants to know all the steps of the way. Nevertheless, though the philosophic interest is the keynote to Lucretius's character, the immediate purpose of his poem is ethical and national. Like Hesiod, he is not merely explaining the details of an art or a philosophical system. He would benefit his countrymen by saving them from superstition and, in particular, from the idle fears concerning the life to come. He addresses a patron, and apologizes for distracting the attention of the great man from affairs of state. But he believes that his message means not only the salvation of philosophy but the salvation of Rome.

Virgil's masters are preëminently Hesiod and Lucretius. He found in their works the chief principles of didactic poetry as it had been practised by Greek and Roman writers before his day, and he studied these great models until they became with him a kind of second nature. He took his facts from various sources. The agricultural treatises of Mago the Carthaginian, Cato the Elder, and especially Varro,[1] related works of Xenophon, Aristotle, Theophrastus, and the inevitable Posidonius, may have furnished him with information to supplement his own practical experience with the life of the farm. The question of source in the use of such material is of exceedingly small significance. His subject was not "Improvements in Agricultural Method"; he was not "introducing" the latest crooked plough. He sought to make the business of the farmer appeal to the imagination. If country life as he sets it forth at once smells of earth and fuses naturally with poetry and imagination, the creator has accomplished his task; it matters not whether he sings of his own handling of the plough or imparts a new life into some typical or technical account of that operation.

The sources of the *Georgics* — what a word! The poet's only source, his spring, is his own mind, whence his fancies flow. The stream that issues is the wine of his own genius, flavored with this and with that. Let us speak of the material that the poet's mind absorbs as matter, or ingredients, or chemical substances, or what

[1] The importance of Varro for Virgil is well brought out by Fairfax Harrison, *Roman Farm Management*, pp. 14-18.

you will — anything to disturb the smug satisfaction of the hunter of sources, who confuses the tracking down of themes or imagery with the explanation of the poet's art. "Models" is the word that we were seeking; it applies both to the works and to their authors who helped to mould the poet's mind, but never can account for the informing genius of his creation. The critic who analyzes the poet's composition into its elements sometimes imagines that he thereby disproves its originality. He deals with "sources," influences, and deadly parallels; his mind is set on the discovery of coincidences, whereas his proper concern is with diversities and with the act of magic, if it exist, that has combined the discordant and the prosaic into harmonious poetry. These acts of magic strew the pages of Virgil. The critic will find plenty to do simply recording them all. The awesome magician into which the romantic fancy of the Middle Ages transformed our poet must bow, rather clumsily, to the actual man, as to a master in his own art.

V

The *Georgics* comprises in its general plan topics that are germane enough to the theme. The First Book treats of soils, tools, and signs of weather; the Second of trees and vines; the Third of the animals of the farm and their diseases; the Fourth of bees and how to create a new supply of them. Nothing could be more practical; the farmer will find something useful on every page. Yet

upon this subsoil of information Virgil grows an astonishing garden of fancy, as different from the facts of his
subject as flowers are from soil, yet springing just as
naturally from their midst. Art and nature, alternating,
contrasting, and forever merging, in poetry that never
ceases to be real — that is the charm of the *Georgics*.

THE FIRST GEORGIC

The poet, addressing his patron Maecenas, begins
with a succinct statement of the subjects of his four
books. The details are matter-of-fact, but by one of his
touches of magic he boldly suggests, to a reader who
knows his Homer, that it is an epic theme. "From such
a cycle comes my song" — *hinc canere incipiam*; this is
his announcement, like that of Homer at the beginning
of his Odyssey — τῶν ἁμόθεν γε θεά. Like Homer, and
like didactic poets from Hesiod on — for even Lucretius, as we saw, cannot escape the tradition — Virgil
now invokes the deities who best can help him. He calls
on Sun and Moon, Bacchus and Ceres, Italian fauns and
Grecian dryads, Neptune who created the horse, Aristaeus to whom was revealed the art of making bees, the
pastoral Pan, guardian of flocks and herds, Minerva
who gave man the olive, Triptolemus, the inventor of
the crooked plough, old Silvanus from the forest primeval, and then, lest some god take umbrage at the absence
of his name, the poet displays the customary Roman
caution and adds an appeal to all gods and goddesses

who protect the fields, send rain from heaven, and bring forth unwonted crops from never any seed at all. *Non ullo semine iacto* — just a phrase, but Virgil needs only a phrase to paint another dominant coloring into his theme. Farming is not only epic; there is a bit of magic about it, and this magic is in the hands of the kindly gods whose favor may be sought in prayer. This dwelling on the mystery of Nature bridges the gap — it is a large one — to the final appeal. He invokes Caesar Octavian, the last and the greatest in Virgil's line of heroes, goddess-born and lord of the waves, master of the wide empire of Rome, soon, all too soon, to join the gods in the starry firmament, and already a god on earth, if he will but learn the call of his worshippers. Farmers need his compassion and the poet his help in what he knows is a "venturesome emprise."

This introduction to the work does something more than state the subject and invoke the necessary gods. It envelops the theme with suggestions of the higher levels into which it is destined to rise — epic dignity, religious mysticism, and national aspiration. It is, further, a declaration of loyalty to his hero, whose cult, not formally established in Italy at the time, Virgil has anticipated. He has found, like Lucretius, a human god, a Roman savior, but one who will establish the state on principles far more lasting than those of Epicurus. The worship declared in the First Eclogue acquires a new significance:

A god he is forever in mine eyes,
And at his shrine I'll offer many a lamb.[1]

The farmer's business starts in spring. The moment
the soil is loose, he harnesses his oxen and drives his
plough in the furrow till the share glistens. Land will not
respond unless it has twice been upturned to summer
heat and twice to winter's frost; only spend this energy
on it, and your barns will be filled to bursting. Before
you start, however, you must know the conditions of
farming, the temper of winds and sky, and those eternal
characteristics that nature has ordained for different
climates. You must know how to treat a soil. Now and
then it must lie fallow, or submit to a rotation of crops
— a method that has sometimes been vaunted as a discovery of the nineteenth century. Peas burn the land,
but if they are followed by vetch or lupine, which are
turned in and make admirable manure, it will recover
its strength. Soak it with manure — a precept that, as
Cicero points out, the "practical" Hesiod had neg-
lected to include.[2] Scatter dirty ashes over it. Get
dirty yourself; the real farmer is never shamed to merge
with his soil. Burning the stubble will help, and so will
constant harrowing of the lazy clods. Work your land
and golden Ceres will smile on you from high Olympus;

---

[1] *Ecl.*, I, 7:
    namque erit ille mihi semper deus, illius aram
      saepe tener nostris ab ovilibus imbuet agnus.

[2] *De Senectute*, 54: Quid de utilitate loquar stercorandi? . . . de qua
doctus Hesiodus ne verbum quidem fecit, cum de cultura agri scriberet.

the farmer must be pious, but piety without work will raise no crops; heaven helps those who help themselves; success is his who gives the earth an incessant drilling, and lords it over the fields. (Ll. 43–99.)

The gods will hear a prayer for rain. Pray for a wet midsummer and a cloudless winter; thus will the meadows laugh and sing and Mount Ida wonder at its own harvests. But if prayer is not answered, irrigation remains. After throwing your missiles of seed, get to close quarters with the soil, and undermine the heaps of sticky earth; dry cultivation will accomplish something. But in a drouth the farmer will dig a channel for the water over the brow of a hill. There you are! See it come tumbling down with a raucous murmur and gushing with its grateful relief over the parched fields. You must similarly check too rapid and luxuriant a growth. Sometimes sheep or horses are called in to crop the tender blades and thus strengthen the stalk, and if the soil is too rich and moist it may be drained by an admixture of sand, especially if the river turns into a freshet, and, as is frequent enough in Mantua today, leaves the ground cluttered with smoking pools. (100–117.)

But do not imagine that thoughtful planning and strenuous execution are the whole story. After you have done all that reason could demand, there remains the perverse and irrational contest with the pests — bane of the farmer's existence. The saucy goose will promptly put in an appearance, likewise the crane, who is distinguished with the heroic epithet "Strymonian." Perhaps this is epic dignity; perhaps the cursed thing comes from Strymon after all; an experienced farmer must expect anything. Besides, the bitter chicory will twine its fibres round the growing plants, and a shady tree, by which you sowed before the leaves were out, will blight the rows beneath it. For the Father did not intend that the way of the cultivator should be easy. He sharpened men's wits by turning agriculture from a pastime into a science. No reign of lethargy for him! Before Jove's time, tillage was needless and fences were not allowed. Men garnered for the common store and earth gave forth her bounties gratis. It was Jove who devised the snake to mar this paradise. He let loose the prowling wolves, stirred up the placid sea, knocked off the honey from the leaves, took fire away, and checked the free-flowing streams of wine, that man might discover the arts by experience and expect crops only in the furrows he had made. Thus thrown on their own resources, our fathers hollowed trees into boats and named the stars, —

Pleiadas, Hyadas, claramque Lycaonis Arcton, —

caught birds and beasts in traps, and fish with line and net. They added the use of the saw to that of the prime-val wedge. They found the various arts. Labor conquered all things, insatiate, under the stress of pinching poverty. (118–146.)

Almost before the reader is aware, Virgil has lifted his rural theme to one of the higher levels to which, as we

saw from the poet's precursors, it should ever have ac-
cess. It is the Myth of the Ages again, which Hesiod
and Aratus had differently used, and which our poet
applies to his own purpose. Unlike Hesiod, he follows
the traditional conception; the Age of Saturn is a time
of reposeful inactivity. Jupiter is the innovator, and his
innovation, though ruthless, is good for mankind. We
cannot have comforts thrust upon us; we must win them
in the struggle for existence, through inventions stimu-
lated by our needs. But though the myth is differently
interpreted, its spirit is still that of Hesiod's Gospel of
Work —   ἔργον ἐπ' ἔργῳ ἐργάζεσθαι —

which Virgil has implied from the start and which he
here vigorously proclaims. It is a more sturdy gospel
than that in Lucretius's story of the ages, which go ringing down a groove of degeneracy till the world is dissolved into atoms anew. It is a far-flung challenge to the
hardships of life, the spirit that exults in the conflict and
recklessly — aye, impudently — beats out a victory:

> Labor omnia vincit
> Improbus.

This energetic and dynamic view of life, which would
accord well with evolutionary theories held today, may
seem an advance over the mystical and youthful dream
of a Golden Age in Virgil's Messianic eclogue. But we
must examine more of the present poem before we are in
a position to compare.

For inventions in agriculture, Ceres first deserves the farmer's thanks, for she taught him about better crops than the primeval acorns of Dodona. But the grain of Ceres does not spring up spontaneously, in the style of the Golden Age, and it is subject to diseases and pests. Mildew blights it, thistles choke it, weeds replace it, and birds devour it, unless you wield the hoe, scare the invaders away, and offer prayers for rain. The lazy farmer will look wistfully on his neighbor's high-piled sheaves, and solace his own hunger by shaking what he can, in the good old-fashioned way, from a woodland oak. (147–159.)

In this new agriculture, the farmer must be equipped with elaborate tools, or rather weapons; for, once more, as Octavian's veterans might be interested to know, he arms himself for a hard battle with the soil. Virgil knows them all and exults in their utility. What poetry could he have made out of modern agricultural machines! They would have aroused his awe, not his contempt as symbols of a mechanical age — a hay-cutter driven by electricity, a thresher in Kansas fields, pouring a fountain of golden grain into a swelling heap. These tools are extraordinary in another way. They are the adjuncts of a religious rite. They are called no common names, but rather "the slow-rolling wains of our Lady of Eleusis, the baskets of Celeus, her priest, and Bacchus's mystic winnowing-fan." Every line in the description is as useful to the farmer as the notices in a seedman's catalogue;

and every line has epic dignity. Few epic poets could make a verse out of harrows and drays and heavy hoes with the stately resonance of

> tribulaque traheaeque et iniquo pondere rastri,

and the account of the building of the crooked plough, which thanks to the spirited comment of our "Virginia farmer" [1] we can read with more intelligence than before, sounds, without a touch of bombast, like an epic deed. Such, then, are the farmer's weapons, which he must have in readiness, if he would know the divinity of meadow, stream, and grove —

> si te digna manet divini gloria ruris.

Hard work before you and heaven lying all about — such is the cost and such the gain of farming. (160–175.)

Now for a few precepts of the ancients. Make your threshing-floor of solid concrete, so that pests cannot break through and steal your wares. For the tiny mouse builds his granary there, or the blind mole, or the toad, — who here hops into classical poetry for the first and last time, — or the countless other strange creatures of the earth, like the weevil and the ant. Then, too, observe the wild almond. If its blossoms set well, thus promising a heavy crop of fruit, you will also have a good stand of corn, but if it is covered all in leaves your sheaves will abound mainly in chaff. It is a good practice

---

[1] Fairfax Harrison, "The Crooked Plough," in *The Classical Journal*, XI (1916), 323.

to medicate seeds in soda and dregs of oil. Plants will degenerate unless you keep the stock true by seed-selection. Fate will always set us back, like the man in the row-boat pulling upstream; if he rest on his oars, the current will quickly spin him downward —

> si bracchia forte remisit
> atque illum praeceps prono rapit alveus amni.

These precepts do not closely cohere. Virgil would suggest, without too lengthy an imitation, the disjointed manner of the gnomic sections in Hesiod. There is a special purpose in calling Hesiod to mind just here. The philosophical sentiment at the close of the passage likewise marks the close of the first half of the book. The part following the invocation up to the present place, lines 43 to 403, relates strictly to "Works," with a lusty call to "Work" echoing everywhere. It closes, not with an explicit exhortation, as in Hesiod, but more artistically and more powerfully, with the picture of the lazy man swept down the river. Horace, for the same reason, often ends his odes with pictures; the reader is the more impressed with a moral which he himself is left to draw.

The second main part of the book, beginning with verse 204 and ending it is hard to say just where, corresponds to Hesiod's "Days," with infusions of Aratus's "Signs and Seasons." Virgil's own phrase for this two-fold aspect of this book is *arvorum cultus et sidera caeli*, which he uses in recapitulation at the beginning of the next book.

To know the proper times, the farmer no less than the sailor must watch the stars. The autumnal equinox will tell him to plough and to sow barley, flax, and poppies. Beans come in spring, with clover, and millet, when the Bull opens the year with his golden horns. For wheat and corn, you must wait till the morning setting of the Pleiades in November. It is with an eye to the farmer that the sun traverses his yearly path through the signs of the Zodiac over the zones, and also belts the earth daily, lighting, too, it may be, the Antipodes beneath our feet in the hours when the hosts of the stars are flashing in our heavens. The heavenly lights, therefore, mark the years and seasons for mankind, and also determine for the farmer the time to reap and to sow, to trust his bark to the faithless sea, and to cut the matured pine in the forest. (204–258.)

Even rainy days have their use. The farmer can sharpen the blunted ploughshare, or hollow a boat from a tree-trunk, or brand his cattle, or label his sacks of corn. Props and forks and fastenings may be made for the vine, baskets woven of briar-wood, and corn ground and parched. Yes, even on holy days he may cannily take advantage of the subtle distinction between offensive and defensive operations; the latter are allowed. He may drain a pool that threatens to spoil his crops, or fence in his corn-land against trespassing men or beasts, set traps for birds, burn brambles, and bathe a flock of really suffering sheep. Evidently a little knowledge of casuistry would not hurt the farmer who wants to utilize a saint's day. It is something like the question of where pruning leaves off and weeding begins in Milton's Garden of Eden. In any event, the farmer can go to market on a feast-day, loading his slow-stepping donkey with oil and cheap fruits and returning with a millstone or a lump of pitch. (259–275.)

The days of the month have their different meanings. The fifth is a bad day; Orcus and the Furies were born on it; so were the giants, who made a huge ladder of Pelion, Ossa, and Olympus, and would have taken heaven by storm had not our Father with the stroke of his lightning laid the mountains in ruin. Virgil pauses long enough over this detail to color the whole passage with epic; the lines could be taken from the present context and set, without change, into epic. The seventeenth day is a lucky one for setting out vines, breaking in oxen, and starting a new web. The ninth is propitious for running away, as masters of slaves should notice, but not so good for thieving; let us hope no runaway took a hint from these lines to secrete his stolen goods the day before. Again the flavor of this passage, as Servius observes, is Hesiodic.[1] Virgil does not give us an exhaustive calendar, nor does he agree with Hesiod in all his items. He is painting a bit of Hesiodic coloring into his picture, which, when finished, will be neither that of Hesiod nor of anybody else. (276–286.)

[1] See his comment on ll. 276, 277.

The Virgilian farmer has work for the evening as well as the day. He does not resort to a padded daily paper or the movies, but finds his recreation in a change of employment. The dewy evening is a good time for cutting stubble, or within, by the pleasant fire, he sharpens his pine torches. No radio beguiles his toil, but he has better music, the song of his wife as she throws the shuttle across the woof or cheerfully boils down the unfermented grape-juice into wine. But for reaping and threshing the grain of ruddy Ceres, the hot mid-day is the time. Put your whole self into the task.

Nudus ara, sere nudus —

strip to plough, and strip to sow. Winter, not summer, is the farmer's holiday. We may not forget the Gospel of Work; like a theme in a symphony, it has run through its own movement, but occasionally is echoed later in the piece. Some diversion there must be, and winter is the season for it. Then comes the interchange of banquets and birthday cheer; sweet is pleasure after pain. Winter is the haven into which the tired farmer pulls, and crowns the good ship with garlands. For all that, a Virgilian holiday is never sheer idleness. There are things to do in winter — picking acorns, laurel-berries, and olives, setting traps for cranes, and nets for deer. And one may hunt in the depth of winter, when snow lies deep and rivers chafe against their coats of ice. As the creatures make less headway, you can better stalk them, shoot at better range, and feel distinctly epic as you give the air "the hempen lashing of a Spanish sling" —

stuppea torquentem Balearis verbera fundae. (297–310.)

Every season has its character and its problems. What of autumn and the autumn storms, its lessened heat and shorter days? The farmer must fit his needs to these conditions. There are freshets in spring and thunder-showers at harvest time — yes, just when the field is ready for the reapers. There is a boisterous battle of the winds, that tears the heavy grain up from its roots and carries it on high in a tempest, like so much straw. Often a countless host of waters advances from the sky, the clouds assemble darkly for a mighty downpour, high heaven falls, pelting rain descends on the rich fields, the product of the oxen's toil, and sweeps it all away. The ditches fill, the hollow rivers swell and roar, and the sea surges and seethes with hissing waves. Almighty Jove, amid the night of clouds, wields his flashing bolts, at whose sending the earth quakes, beasts flee, and mortal hearts throughout the world sink in prostrate terror. Our lord hurtles his burning weapon on Athos or Rhodope or lofty Ceraunia, and smites them with a crash. The blasts from the south and the beating rain redouble their fury. Now the woods and now the shores moan in the mighty wind. (311–334.)

There are few storms in poetry, or in nature, like this. No translation or description can give an adequate idea of it, for the reason that each syllable and each pause in the verse contributes something to the effect. Our poet has started with a splendid storm in Lucretius,[1] but he lets it loose with no whit of its vigor lost, and with an unapproachably superior art.

"The elaborate splendor of these lines," observes Kennedy,[2] "is surpassed by no other descriptive passage in Virgil. . . . The pause at *dextra* marks the calmness of conscious strength; at *tremit* breathless terror; at *pavor* prostrate expectation. The following *ille*, and the thrice-repeated *aut*, express the majestic ease of omnipotence; at *deicit* falls the sudden crash of the bolt; in the words which follow is heard the rushing, struggling, moaning tempest."

This description, the best with which I have met, hits some, at least, of the noteworthy elements in the metre. It would take a long chapter to do justice to them all. Instead, I will print the lines with indication of what seem to me the chief pauses in each, leaving the reader to study this sample of Virgil's many devices for diversifying his effects, with trisected, and variously trisected, as well as bisected lines, with the halt at a diaeresis as well as a caesura, and with every word in the place that

[1] I, 271:

> principio venti vis verberat incita pontum
> ingentisque ruit navis et nubila differt
> interdum rapido percurrens turbine campos
> arboribus magnis sternit montisque supremos
> silvifragis vexat flabris: ita perfurit acri
> cum fremitu saevitque minaci murmure ventus.

[2] B. H. Kennedy, *The Works of Virgil* (London, 1879[2]), p. 350.

its importance demands. The passage deserves some consideration by those who would belittle the importance of caesura in ancient poetry.

Saepe etiam immensum / caelo venit agmen aquarum,
et foedam glomerant / tempestatem imbribus atris
collectae ex alto nubes; / ruit arduus aether,
et pluvia ingenti / sata laeta boumque labores
diluit; / implentur / fossae et cava flumina crescunt
cum sonitu / fervetque fretis / spirantibus aequor.
Ipse Pater media / nimborum in nocte corusca
fulmina molitur dextra: / quo maxima motu
terra tremit; / fugere ferae et / mortalia corda
per gentes humilis / stravit pavor: / ille flagranti
aut Athon aut Rhodopen / aut alta Ceraunia telo
deicit; / ingeminant / Austri et densissimus imber:
nunc nemora ingenti / vento / nunc litora plangunt.

In the presence of the sublime cataclysms of Nature, which are part of the yearly round, there is no place for man's self-esteem. The farmer watches the signs of the stars with all his might, and venerates the gods. He pays the due rites to Ceres at the opening of spring, when lambs are fat and wine is mellow, when sleep is sweet, and shadows gather on the hills. In a pleasant rustic ceremony, he conducts the victim thrice about the unreaped fields, with his men chanting the praise of the goddess, and then, binding their brows with oak leaves in her honor, clatter in the rude dance and sing the harvest-hymn. Even the verse catches the spirit of the performance and in a quite un-Virgilian way hops and stumbles in time with the country clowns:

det motus incompositos et carmina dicat (350).

How arid and sordid is the life of many a farmer today, horny-eyed as well as horny-handed, with his improved machinery, his cheap diversions, and his dull religion, or dull scepticism, if any religion or scepticism he have at all!

Once more, then, a study of the moods of nature is part of the farmer's art. Jupiter forewarns him of heat and rain and winds and cold by certain signs. If a windstorm brews, the waves of the sea begin to swell, a dry crash is heard on the hills and a moaning in the woods. And it will be a bad time for the boat on the waves when gulls fly squawking to the beach, coots play on the sand, and the heron, leaving his pools, flies high above the clouds. Sometimes you will see stars shooting through the sky, with white flames in their wake, or fallen leaves begin to dance, or feathers flutter over ponds. If a thunder-storm is gathering, with a concert of all the winds of heaven, and freshets in the ditches, and a downpour at sea that makes the mariner furl his soggy sails, there is always warning for him who can read the signs. The cranes of the air take refuge in the valleys, the heifer snuffs the breeze, the twittering swallow makes the circuit of the pond, and the frogs in the marsh intone their old complaint. Often, when the rainbow is sucking up moisture, the ant, wearing a narrow path, brings out her eggs from her secret abode. She really is bringing them home, scientists have now informed us. At any rate, when her act is observed, remarks a care-

ful observer of nature,[1] who thinks Virgil better informed than some of his commentators, "though there
be not a cloud in the sky, your walk or drive must be
postponed." The crows will likewise give you warning,
when they leave the meadows in mass-formation with
flapping wings; or watch the Asian birds on the banks of
the Cayster, as they lustily splash the water on their
shoulders, duck in the stream, and skim along the waves,
aimlessly fluttering in the transport of the bath. Then
the pert raven calls full-throated for the rain, and stalks
in stately solitude over the sandy strand. A delicious
couplet, with humor in the metre as well as in the allit-
erative words, does justice to the solitary majesty of the
raven, and his sense of responsibility, equal to that of
Rostand's chanticleer, for the appearance of the storm:

> Tum cornix, plena pluviam vocat improba voce
> et sola in sicca secum spatiatur harena.

Finally, there is a household sign as well, when maids at
their evening task see the oil sputter in the lamp, or
snuff gather on its surface. (335–392.)

Conversely, you can prophesy good weather in the
midst of bad. The light of the stars is no longer dimmed,
and the moon's radiance is bright enough to be her own
and not the mere reflection of her brother's rays. No
flecks of down scud across the sky, nor do the kingfishers,

[1] John Burroughs, *Signs and Seasons* (Boston and New York [1914]),
p. 9. See also, E. S. McCartney, "An Animal Weather Bureau," *The Classical
Weekly*, XIV (1920/21), 92.

beloved of Thetis, spread their wings to the mild sun on the beach; they are on the deep again, certain of the calm. And filthy swine no longer root in their straw and toss it with their snouts. The clouds sink to lower levels and lie over the fields, and the screech-owl on the roof-top practises with vain omen her evening song. The osprey and the ciris, preserving the natures that once were Nisus and Scylla, are at their perennial battle in the air. Both the words and the metre describe with a delicate humor how the big bird pounces fiercely from above, and the little one, just in time, sails gracefully out of his clutches:

> Apparet liquido sublimis in aëre Nisus,
> et pro purpureo poenas dat Scylla capillo:
> quacumque illa levem fugiens secat aethera pennis,
> ecce inimicus atrox magno stridore per auras
> insequitur Nisus; qua se fert Nisus ad auras,
> illa levem fugiens raptim secat aethera pennis.

The inevitableness of the pursuit and its perpetual failure are skilfully suggested by the repetition of the verse that describes the liquid and triumphant flight of the little bird. The passage is Virgilian if anything is. We have seen it before at the end of the *Ciris*. Virgil, with Hesiod, among others, for authority, has reached back for one of the good things in his earlier work. He plunders his *Ciris*, which he felt that he had outgrown, as the Venetians plundered some ruin of antiquity, to give a fine fragment a setting of new splendor.

The ravens are quite as happy as the other birds.

They raise their clear, thin-throated cries, or rustle in their high-swung beds, full of some sweet unwonted joy —

nescio qua praeter solitum dulcedine laeti.

For after the storm they can pay a new visit to their tiny brood in the pleasant nest. Is all this a sign that these dumb creatures are divinely endowed with intelligence and the prophetic sense? The poet thinks not, but, as befits a former member of the school of Siro and Lucretius, he reasons that successive condensations or rarefactions of the atmosphere affect the sensory organs of the birds, their "inner aspects," which have but the semblance of a mind — *species animorum*. It is mere reflex action — or behaviorism, shall we say? — that prompts the chorus of birds in the fields, the glad cries of the flocks, and the ravens' full-throated cheer. (393–423.)

Where else in literature can one find the naturalist's clear sense of cause so charmingly combined with the poet's delight in the sounds and movements of all living things? Where else is such a sympathy, the true sympathy that includes both pathos and humor, with the life of dumb animals? There is more poetry in Virgil's science than in the romantic sentimentality that attributes human traits to birds and beasts. He understands their "happy insensibility," their irresponsible and automatic joys untroubled by *humana ratio* or a New England conscience, but he does not, like Keats, moralize this theme. He sings of "too happy, happy farmers," but not "too happy, happy trees." Like Homer, he has as keen a relish for nature, he can merge our very being as intimately with it as any of our modern poets, despite their supposed discovery of a new insight into the natural world. Nor does Virgil ever, like Wordsworth, in Pater's happy phrase, see nature from the steeple of a church.

We now proceed to the more majestic and more reliable signs given by sun and moon. When the new moon is dim and the outline of the rest of her orb obscure, farmers and sailors may expect a downpour of rain. But if a blush spreads her face, a wind will rise; for golden Phoebe always blushes in the wind. If at her fourth rising — this is the surest sign — her light is clear and the tips of her horns distinct, the next day and every other till the end of the month will be free from wind and rain, and rescued mariners will pay their vows on the strand to the gods of the sea. (424–437.)

The sun gives omens both at his rising and at his setting. If he rises all dappled with spots and shrinks into a cloud, suspect a shower from the deep. When he shoots out his rays from behind a mass of clouds, or when the dawn is pale, then your vine-leaves will be slight protection for your grapes, for you will hear a hail-storm dance and clatter on the roof. Likewise, when he has measured his daily course, he will turn blue to announce a rain, or fire-red for a wind, and if a

mottled red, then look for clouds and winds in a general
mêlée. On such a night as that, nobody could tempt me
to loose cable and put out to sea. But if both at the
birth and at the burial of the day his orb shines clear,
then fear no clouds, for the woods will toss in a clear
north wind. (438–460.)

Such is the sun's true prophecy of rains and clouds.
Who indeed would dare call him false? He likewise gives
warning of tumults, treasons, and secret insurrections.
Aye, at the death of Caesar he veiled his face in pity of
Rome, and the impious world feared everlasting night:

> impiaque aeternam timuerunt saecula noctem.

This epic verse, of the type that Dryden called golden,
is a kind of weather-sign itself of the following mood.
Other portents attended the disaster of Caesar's death,
omens of land and sea and beasts and birds. Aetna
burst the Cyclops' forges and deluged the plain with a
molten stream. Germany heard the clash of arms in the
sky, and the Alps felt unwonted quakings. A mighty
voice was heard in still groves, and pallid ghosts came
forth at night. Cattle spake, rivers stopped, the earth
gaped open, and the gods' statues broke out with sweat.
Eridanus, the king of streams, rose madly to a freshet,
— and the verse comes in a freshet, too, — tore forests
down, and carried off flocks and herds with their very
stalls. The soothsayers found ominous fibres in the entrails, wells flowed with blood, and city streets rang at

night with the howl of wolves. Never did such lightning flash from the blue or such dire comets gleam — Caesar's death plays havoc even with Epicurean science!

Such the omen; and its fulfilment was another clash of Roman arms that Philippi saw, when the gods on high thought it no outrage that the plains of Thrace should twice batten with our blood. Aye, the time will come when the husbandman working the soil with the crooked plough will turn up rusty spears, or with his hoe strike helmets, empty now, and wonder at the mighty bones that he digs from their sepulchres. It is an awesome, not to say gruesome picture, into which Virgil paints a reminiscential bit from an utterly different setting; here again is that same crooked plough which we noted before in a much more cheerful context. This transfer of significant details from one context to its opposite for the sake of contrast is a device rare in modern poetry, so far as I have observed, but familiar to Virgil and other ancients.

"Gods of our fathers," the poet ends, "gods of our land, Romulus and mother Vesta, that guardest Tuscan Tiber and Roman Palatine, hinder ye not this youth at least from rescuing a world overthrown. Long since have we made due atonement by our blood for the false oaths of Trojan Laomedon. Long since, O Caesar, doth the palace of the sky begrudge thee to us, and mourn that thou dost care for human triumphs, triumphs of earth, where right and wrong are interchanged; so many wars in the world, crime in so many forms, no worthy honor paid the plough, fields lying waste, with none to till them, and the curved pruning-hook forged to a stiff sword. Here Euphrates, there Germany awakens war, and neighbor cities, breaking their compacts, rush to arms; Mars storms in godless conflict over all the world, even as chariots that have burst the barriers speed round and round the course; the driver, vainly pulling at the curb, is swept on by his steeds; the car heeds not the reins."

There is no more splendid expression of impassioned patriotism in Roman verse than this. The epic poet is speaking in Virgil as never before. Didactic poetry like that in Aratus or Hesiod is caught up into a loftier atmosphere. Virgil has fulfilled the laws under which the classic poet must work. The theme is immediate and contemporary; he elaborates it with imagination and with art; and also, as the highest sort of originality, pays homage to the masters who have handed a sacred tradition to him.

VI

Virgil's chief model in this book is Hesiod; as the structure of the book has already shown us, he has planned a new *Works and Days*. He intends, like Hesiod, not to write a manual of agriculture, but to invest the life of the farm with poetic charm and to make thereby an appeal to certain ideals. These, in Hesiod, were the principles of Justice, Industry, Contentment, and Religion. Of these, Industry and Religion are prominent enough in the First Georgic; the farmer should see here, no less clearly than in Hesiod, that for him happiness will derive from two main sources — hard work and reverent worship. The joy of such a life, the joy of any life spent in communion with nature, is implicit in many a line, but this theme is not deliberately developed; still, the poem is not yet done. Nor is Hesiod's idea of Justice particularly enforced; here is the point where Virgil deviates from his master in his essential plan. The motive that immediately prompted Hesiod to write, his sense of the injustice of his brother's conduct, gives place to a larger idea. Virgil's animating purpose is the need of his country at the moment, its need of peace, well typified by the simplicity of rural life. He would recall his country from war, as Hesiod his brother from greed and injustice. Virgil thus takes Hesiod's theme of rural simplicity and the Gospel of Work and inserts it in a considerably more majestic setting. Our standard editor of Virgil[1] comments on "how little Virgil understood of his author's genius or his own when he spoke of himself as singing the song of Ascra through the

[1] Conington, on *Georg.*, II, 176; see *The Works of Virgil with a Commentary* by John Conington and Henry Nettleship, Vol. I (revised by F. Haverfield, London, 1898), p. 142. A similar judgment is delivered by a high authority, von Wilamowitz-Moellendorff (*Hesiodos, Erga*, Berlin, 1928, p. 160): "Nur den Lehrer der Landwirtschaft zieht Vergil heran, weil es eben ein Klassiker war, auf den hier und da mit einen Worte hinzuweisen den Beifall des Kenners eintrug. Stil und Ton sind ganz anders, eher aratisch; von Hesiods Humor haben alle beide [i. e., Virgil and Aratus] nichts." For those who can see humor as well as discourse on it (*ibid.*, p. 154), the passage discussed above (p. 215) is, among others, of some significance.

towns of Rome." Virgil, I am sure, shows better understanding of Hesiod than Conington shows of Virgil or
of the problems in imitation and originality with which
a classic poet is concerned. Virgil's declaration is true
to both his ambition and to his success; he has made the
Works and Days a Roman poem:

> Ascraeumque canit Romana per oppida carmen.

With his other great master, Lucretius, there is nothing in the theme that invites comparison. There is a
challenge in some of the description, notably that of the
storm, and there is a challenge in every line of the dac-
tylic hexameter. Virgil had learned the art of this verse
from Lucretius, who had smoothed away, whenever he
cared to descend to art, many of the crudities of Ennius,
and other predecessors. But the inner secrets of this
verse, its sweet graces and its majestic strength, its
subtle harmonies contrived by variation of pause and
the interplay of word-accent and verse-ictus, were
known to Virgil alone. There is also, despite the naturalistic interpretation of the moods of animals, a protest against Lucretius and the science that he professed,
in the tender piety and fervent faith that the poet com-
mends not only to the farmer but to the citizen who
wishes well of Rome.

There is a touch of something like Lucretian pessimism in Virgil's picture of the Thracian farmer who turns
up in the field the mighty bones of the men of an earlier
and a better day. This rustic has been compared to

Lucretius's ploughman, "gloomy planter of the withered vine," [1] who sighs for the good old times, not comprehending the philosophic solace of the inevitable law of cosmic degeneracy. Lucretius's ultimate cosmology is not pessimistic; the prospect of ceaseless annihilation and recomposition with an eternity of unconsciousness for the individual has for him the value of an exuberant optimism. He is ready at any moment to merge his little existence in the cosmos. "Come, Chaos, I have seen the best." But the strength of many a passage in Lucretius's poetry comes from what to those less sure of the cosmic outlook seems a deep and sombre view of the immediate moment. The slow decline of civilization will induce, for most of us, a mood of gloom at our present lot rather than one of elation at the prospect of an ultimate liberation of the atoms. We need not yet examine what Virgil's philosophy may have been, but our reading thus far has revealed a spirit living intensely in the present, which despite the sins of humanity and its wrongs is big with hope and guided by a hero. But the immediate moment is poignant, and the final note in this book is one of despair.

It would seem, then, that Virgil's political outlook is less exuberant than when he wrote his Messianic eclogue. His devotion to his hero — a new hero now — is no less intense, but grim events have occurred. His mood is nearer to the gloom of Horace's Sixteenth

[1] II, 1168–1174.

Epode, or to Horace's milder forebodings on the destiny
of the Ship of State;[1] as the Fourth Eclogue was intended to answer Horace's pessimism, the present passage sounds like a recantation. We may also detect the
flavor of Theocritus's lament on the decay of poetry —
and the inadequate compensation of the poet — in the
days of Hiero after the devastation of Sicily at the hands
of the Carthaginians.[2] The moment is the same, —
like that through which our world has lately passed, —
and Virgil reverts inevitably to a great and typical protest of art against the barbarities of war, though of
course not suggesting the curiously naïf commercialism
of Theocritus; he does not threaten to leave for a court
where poets are better paid. The introduction to the
book is of course more buoyant; it might well have been
wrought into its final form after the battle of Actium.
But the final mood is sombre. The poet will not blink
evils. A reformer does not proclaim that there is nothing
to reform.

VII

The structure of this book shows several distinct
parts put together with consummate felicity; the chariot
of state may career through chaos, but not the poet's
art. The introduction (1–42), with its invocation of the
deities, is epic in tone. The body of the work (43–463) is
didactic, or, specifically, georgic. The form, whatever
the emotional or material contents, is always dignified,

---

[1] *Odes*, I, 14.   [2] *Idylls*, XVI.

and passages occur that, despite the subject, are thoroughly epic in treatment. There are, further, two descriptions which I would not call by the name of set-pieces, if I knew a better term — the passage on the Gospel of Work (118–147 or 159), and that on the harvest-storm (311–334). They occur at approximately equal intervals from the beginning and the end of the stretch of georgic narrative, and have the value of a lift, or change of scene. If the greater part of either, say verses 121 to 146 or 322 to 334, were separately quoted, — as they frequently are, — and if the reader were unfamiliar with the context, he would scarcely divine the nature and the subject of the poem from which they come. And yet they are no mere purple patches. So naturally does the poet glide into them, and so naturally does he glide away, that the reader is transported into a new atmosphere and back without realizing that he has ever left the subject; and editors will differ as to where the new scene begins and where it ends. It is a kind of aviation; the poet can soar almost imperceptibly between widely different levels, but it is all the same flight.

The art of gradual development is conspicuous not only in the set-pieces but in the composition of the whole book. Beginning with the formally Hesiodic description of lucky and unlucky days (276), the georgic matter is subtly varied and infused with a spirit that does not seem altogether georgic — a kind of premonitory stirring of the breeze before it blows in full strength. The

pleasant winter-scene, almost pastoral in character, like
that in the Seventh Eclogue, is succeeded by the storm,
with its exuberant joy in the wild powers of nature.
Then we pass to the tranquil beauty of spring, the peasant's cheerful worship and his lively harvest-home. In
the account of the weather-signs, we are taken not so
much with their value as with the poet's delicate and
humorous portraiture of a numerous company of birds
and beasts — the automatic but self-important prophets
of changing atmospheres. Then come the more certain
and majestic warnings given by sun and moon, not only
signs of weather, but signs of great events, like those
which prophesied, and mourned, the death of Caesar.
At this magic touch, the tone changes instantly from the
rural and the didactic to the national and epic, and so
continues to the end of the book. As we read the closing
lines, we feel that we have travelled far from rotation of
crops and irrigation and the crooked plough. Yet we
cannot lay finger on any point in the development where
the poet ceases to be relevant. And look again! The
plough is not forgotten after all — its slighted honor is
one of the crimes of war:

> non ullus aratro
> dignus honor, squalent abductis arva colonis.

This is georgic enough. Virgil manages his effects with
the power of a musician, conducting one and the same
theme through harmonies of varying mood with an artful crescendo to a final crash. Such music can be trans-

lated into our own or other language if Beethoven's music can. "The poetry of this book," observed Dryden, "is more sublime than any part of Virgil, if I have any taste."[1] Many readers will agree, at least while occupied with this and not with certain other parts of Virgil.

[1] In his *Notes and Observations on Virgil's Works in English* (*The Poetical Works of John Dryden*, the Cambridge Edition, G. R. Noyes, Boston and New York, 1908), p. 701.

CHAPTER VII

THE PHILOSOPHY OF VINE AND TREE
A CHALLENGE TO HESIOD AND TO LUCRETIUS

I

THE Second Book will be in praise of Bacchus, and will likewise treat of woodlands and the olive-tree. So, come, Father Lenaeus, the fields are flowering and the vintage is all in the vats. Doff thy buskins, and plunge thy bare legs with me into the new must. (1–8.)

This is a tantalizing introduction. Bacchus is invited, somewhat audaciously, to join the Italian peasants in the merry task of treading the grapes, and the reader is invited to the bowl. Who would not step up to see what the poet has for him? But instead of offering the cup at once, the poet treats us to a technical account of arboriculture. It is a cruel sort of dramatic suspense.

Listen, he says, and learn the modes of rearing trees. Some spring up of themselves in the broad meadows or along winding streams, like the osier and the broom, the poplar and the willow, hoary with shimmering leaves. Others, like the chestnut and the oak, come from the seeds they drop. Cherries and elms grow a thicket from their roots; thus the little Parnassian bay pokes its way up into its mother's shade. But these primitive modes of reproduction have been helpfully supplemented by the inventions of experience. We have learned to transplant suckers or sets or slips or shoots, to bend a layer into the ground, and even — wonderful to relate — to get new olive trees from bits carved from the trunk. Again, there is an art which can change the branches of one tree unharmed to those of another, making the pear produce apples and the sloe blush with cherries. After all, the raising of trees is full of excitement and metamorphoses. The expectation of miracles ought to allay our thirsting for the bowl. (9–34.)

So come, ye farmers, learn your arts after their kind, improve your varieties by cultivation, and let not your land lie idle. Some high achievement calls you to a new pleasure — planting the Thracian mountain with vines, or covering the heights of Samnium with olives. "And thou, my glorious patron, set sail with me, Maecenas, on the broad deep. My powers are slight for my song. We will go cautiously, hugging the shore. And I will not delay you with a long preface to some fictitious lay." No fairy tales for Virgil! His theme is real and plain, like that of Lucretius and those Alexandrians who revolted against the outworn fables and stale conventions of mythological epic. This poem is a practical affair! (35–46.)

Whatever rises self-prompted into the coasts of light bears little fruit, but is strong and lusty with nature's power under it in the soil. Yet by man's cultivation the natural growth will lay aside its sylvan character and quickly respond to artificial culture. The sterile shoots whose productivity is checked by the shade of the mother-tree will thrive if transplanted in rows in the open field. A tree will grow from seed, but your grandsons will be the first to get any shade from it, its fruit will lack the original savor, and the grape-clusters will be good for nothing but plunder for the birds. Here we see Virgil's "reticent" description again; one imagines from the first part of the sentence that he is speaking only of trees, but the closing words show that the principle applies also to vines. The moral of it all is that you must expend toil on everything; no profit without cultivation. The verse that says this is as rugged as the sentiment:

> Scilicet omnibus est labor impendendus, et omnes
> cogendae in sulcum ac multa mercede domandae.

With diaereses after the first and the second feet, — the latter a great rarity in Virgil, the combination still more rare, — and a vigorous word-accent on the emphatic word *labor*, the first line is well-nigh prose; the second is guttural and grating, though sweetened with liquids when it suggests the reward. Virgil, our horny-handed poet, has cast aside his toga for a tussle with the soil. There are many methods to learn. For propagating olives, use truncheons; for vines, layers; for myrtles, sets. Hazels and ashes and poplars and oaks are best grown from suckers, and so the palm, and the pine that is destined to the life of the sea — or, as John Burroughs calls it,[1] that "symmetrical tree, tapering, columnar, shaped as in a lathe, the preordained mast of ships." (47–68.)

The art of grafting will work wonders. The wild strawberry tree will bear walnuts; the plane tree, apple boughs; the beech tree, chestnuts. The ash will be covered with the white blossoms of the pear, and pigs munch acorns under elms. Could Burbank do better than that! Donald Grant Mitchell, in his delightful *Wet Days at Edgewood*,[2] an indispensable commentary on our poem, speaks of the miraculous achievements chronicled by Palladius and the author of *Geoponica*, and asks, "Is it remotely possible that these old gentlemen understood the physiology of plants better than we?" We must believe Virgil, at any rate, for this is no *carmen fictum*. Miracles are possible, if you will only work hard enough for them, and master the niceties of the art. For there are different sorts of grafting. Now you make a slit just below the place where the bud bursts the light tunic of its bark, and now you insert the shoot in an opening made with a wedge in the smooth trunk. Use the right method, and before long the tree will send up lusty branches to the sky, and wonder at its new leaves and fruitage not its own.

Coming to each species, we have numerous sorts to

---

[1] *Signs and Seasons*, p. 45.   [2] New York, 1884, p. 51.

learn. There are different shapes of olives, impressive enough to deserve an epic line,

> orchades et radii et amara pausia baca,

"orchid and spindles and pausia of the bitter fruit." So with apples, including the variety that King Alcinous grew, and pears —

> Crustumiis Syriisque piris gravibusque volaemis.

These names mean little to us, even after consulting the Dictionary of Classical Antiquities, but to the contemporaries of Virgil they had the succulence of

> Cool juicy Sheldons and Boscs, small Seckels and corpulent Bartletts.

And who can number all the brands of wine? The vintage of Lesbos or Thasos, white Mareotic, which Cleopatra appreciated only too well, the vines of rich or lighter soil, the Psithian grapes good at least for raisins, and that subtle Lagean brand, seemingly innocent but destined

> To trip the legs, some day, and tie the tongue —
>
> Temptatura pedes olim vincturaque linguam.

What of red Precian, and O Tyrol wine, how sing thy praise? Still, better not enter the lists with old Falernian! The Aminean is a stalwart brand, for whom Mount Tmolus of Lydia and royal Phanae, port of Chios, will stand attention — or, as we might say,

> O wine of Asti, potent draft, to whom
> The Rhineland and the Kings of Rheims bow low.

Virgil cannot count all the varieties, or the sand on the seashore, nor can I repeat all those of which he sings. Who else could turn a vintner's catalogue into high and seductive poetry, that despite the unfamiliar names will bring longing to an American heart and tears to his eyes? The poet has passed us the bowl sooner than we had thought. (83–108.)

We may return to trees. They, too, have their different soils and climates; for all lands cannot bear all things. Again, this is no Golden Age, like that pictured in the Fourth Eclogue, in which

omnis feret omnia tellus;

rather, there are fixed conditions, which Lucretius had described,[1] and which the husbandman must know. Willows and alders grow by water, ashes in the mountain, myrtles on the beach. The vine likes sunny hills, and yews a northern exposure. Look abroad to the farthermost districts of the earth, the lands of Arabs or the tattoed Scythians; you will find that each has its native trees. Black ebony is peculiar to India, and spice to Sheba, where balsam sweats from branches, and gum from the acanthus tree. Aethiopians can pick wool, — as Virgil picturesquely calls cotton, — and the Chinese comb a fine fleece from leaves. By the ocean of India, in the farthest limit of earth, no archer can speed an arrow to the top of the tallest trees. Media is rich in pungent savors, and the lingering flavor of the blessed citron, an-

[1] I, 166.

tidote for the poison that some fiendish stepmother may have brewed. The tree is tall, and like a laurel — yes, you would call it a laurel, were it not for its fragrance, which the Medes apply to their breaths or old men's asthma. (109–135.)

But neither the woods of wealthy Media, nor the land of the fair Ganges, nor Lydian Hermus with its mud of gold, nor Panchaia, rich with all the odors of Araby, can challenge the praise of Italy. Here is a land that no fire-breathing bulls upturned for seed of dragons' teeth and a crop of armed warriors. It teems in grain, and Massic vines, groves of olives and lusty herds. No myths here, no Golden Age, but abounding nature, helped by man's toil. It gives the war-horse, proudly pawing the fields. It gives the white oxen of Clitumnus and the bulls that often have led a Roman triumph to the temples of the gods. This is the land of perpetual spring and summer in alien months, twice blest with the offspring of cattle and twice with the produce of fruit trees. We pause a moment in wonder, for the poet seems to be straying from natural science and Lucretius, who declared that crops cannot flourish in "alien seasons of the year." [1] No tigers are here, continues Virgil, no baleful brood of lions, no poisonous aconite deceives the unhappy gatherers, no scaly snake hurries endless circles along the ground or gathers his long stretches into a monstrous coil. We must pause again. For this description is as-

[1] I, 181.

suredly pastoral rather than georgic; after all, we have been inveigled into the Golden Age. Let us not quibble over the size of the snake, though we shall meet a rather large one before finishing the poem, but we may protest that aconite was found in Italy, and refuse the desperate defence of Servius, who would have Virgil mean that Italians were so familiar with aconite that they were never beguiled into gathering it. Servius might have stuck by his description of this passage as an encomium of Italy, constructed after the accepted "rhetorical principle of asserting that the object of your praise possesses all good things and lacks all bad ones." [1]

But we turn from nature to the work of man in Italy — its splendid cities, its little hill towns, which rejoice the traveller today, "piled by hand on jutting crags," its rivers, gliding at the base of ancient walls. There are its seas, the Adriatic above, the Tuscan below; its lakes, mighty Como and Garda, surging with waves that have the roar of Ocean:

> Te Lari maxume teque
> fluctibus et fremitu assurgens Benace marino.

These gifts of nature have been helped by the genius of man, who fenced in the Lucrine Lake, opened it on the one side to the chafing sea, on the other to the dread Avernus, and thus turned into the Julian Harbor what once had been the entrance to Hell. Our land also has

[1] On *Georg.*, II, 136: iam incipit laus Italiae, quam exsequitur secundum praecepta rhetorica: nam dicit eam et habere bona omnia et carere malis universis.

its streams of silver, and quarries of bronze and flowing veins of gold; for such, means the poet, is the value of Roman commerce. But more than these things, Italy has brought forth sturdy men, Marsians and Sabines, Ligurians and Volscians; and leaders of men, a Decius, a Marius, a Scipio, and, greatest of its heroes, thee, O mighty Caesar, who now in the far coasts of Asia leadest the humbled Indians to the citadels of Rome.

> Hail, mighty mother of crops, Saturnian land,
> Mighty of men! Thy deeds of ancient praise,
> Thine arts I tell, and dare to open free
> The Muses' sacred fountains, while I sing
> A song of Ascra through the towns of Rome —
>
> Ascraeumque cano Romana per oppida carmen.

This set-piece is one of the great passages in the poem, and, like those of the First Book, no purple patch. It occurs at about the same place as the first set-piece in the First Book. That is the Praise of Work, and this is the Praise of the Italian Farmer's Country — both legitimate themes, and both introduced without a break. The poet leads up in a powerful crescendo from crops to towns and from the works of men to the men themselves, the older heroes and the hero of the age, in which the golden days of Saturn have come again. The theme has surged into epic with the same strength and inevitability as at the close of the First Book. And it is at this exalted moment that Virgil defines the purpose of the poem; it is a new *Works and Days*, with a national and contemporary meaning. There is a break at the end, but it is the sudden breaking from the epic tone back to the subject of the work; it is not an interruption, but an effective mode of transition.

The passage has appealed to many readers. The "rich Virgilian rustic measure of Lari Maxume" came to Tennyson as he wandered by Lake Como, and he catches it up in "The Daisy." Palgrave, in his admirable little work on *Landscape in Poetry from Homer to Tennyson*, quotes lines of similar cadence from the First Book (356 ff.) and adds: "I quote these lines, remembering how Tennyson would read them to me in the days that are no more, saying that from the magnificent music of the Vergilian hexameter, as here exemplified, he believed Milton caught (or recognized) his own splendid blank verse movement in the *Paradise*." [1] Goethe, too, was wakened by his journey about Lake Garda to the truth to nature displayed by the splendid verse

fluctibus et fremitu assurgens Benace marino. [2]

Would that his *Italienische Reise* had included a similar topographical setting of other descriptions in Virgil. It might have led to the gradual perception of many things worth his notice.

We have been brought back abruptly to the work of the farm. It is the same subject from which we deviated — the proper soils for different trees. The passage on

---

[1] London, 1897, p. 51.

[2] *Italienische Reise*, Torbole, Sept. 12, 1786: "der erste lateinische Vers, dessen Inhalt lebendig vor mir steht." Even so, the verse is quoted imperfectly, with a tame *resonans* for *assurgens*.

Italy is a splendid improvisation into which the poet was impelled by the passion of the moment; despite his proclamation of a matter-of-fact treatment of plain things, the love of his country has opened the door for myth again; we are at once in the reign of Caesar Octavian and in the Golden Age. Yet somehow these things are of a piece. So back to our soils. A poor soil with much clay and gravel is just the thing for olives; you can tell it from the presence of the wild olive. A soil rich in grass and loam, like that formed in the cup of a mountain-valley, where the blessed silt accumulates, or a slope towards the south, rich in those ferns that the crooked plough abominates — that is the land for growing vines; that is where you will raise a crop for Father Bacchus, to pour libations from golden bowls when the portly Tuscan plays his pipes at the altar and you offer the entrails in deep platters. We have returned to practical farming! Who but a farmer would call mud blessed, or curse the picturesque fern? (177–194.)

If you want soil for pasturing cattle or sheep or the destructive goat, then make for the glades of Tarentum, or the fields that poor Mantua lost, where snowy swans feed by the sedgy stream, and the grass is so lush that what the herds crop by day the cool dew of night restores. We will not stop to inquire whether we are in Italy, or the blue-grass region of Kentucky, or California, or the Golden Age, but will pass quickly on. Rich, black, crumbling soil, the kind that is artificially pro-

duced by ploughing, is best for grain; many heavily
laden wains return from such a field. Likewise efficient
is the virgin soil which the irate farmer has cleared of an
ancient grove, overthrowing the ancestral abodes of
birds to their lowest foundations. They, leaving their
nests, soar to the sky, but the untried soil gleams with
the driving share. No time for a sentimental tear over
the fate of the poor birds! They will look out for themselves. We cannot think of them when the farmer has
won a field. The only sentiment for him is anger —
anger at the cursed stump, irrationally and tenaciously
in the way. Be ye angry and sin not; anger is a good
agricultural asset if applied at the other end of a plough.

A thin gravelly soil will scarce supply your bees with
casia and rosemary. Scabrous tufa gives notice to ser-
pents that no other ground can better furnish them sweet
food and winding lairs. A porous soil, quick to imbibe
moisture and exude it again, clothed with green herbage and free from salt rust, will twine your elms with
joyous vines or bear you oil. Try it, for it is easy for
your beasts to work. Such is the land round wealthy
Capua or the Campanian plain by Mount Vesuvius.
(195–225.)

There are methods for testing the kind of soil. If you
wish a heavy soil for grass or a light one for vines, sink a
pit in the ground, put back the earth and trample it down.
If there is not enough to fill the pit, the soil is light,
good for pasturing or raising grapes. If not all the earth

will go back, it is thick; expect reluctant clods and hilly lumps, and hitch your stoutest oxen to the plough. The salty or bitter soil, which, inauspicious for crops, unreformable by the plough, reduces all your nice varieties of grapes or fruits to one dead level, may be thus tested. Fill a thick-meshed basket with it, and pour in fresh water. The drops will work their way through the soil, and will tell its nature to the taste, for if it is bitter it will pucker the face. Test a rich soil by rolling it in the hands; it will not crumble, but will stick like pitch. A wet soil is rank with herbage; it tempts a crop to a premature growth. Heaviness and lightness of soil are indicated by the weight. Your eyes will show you the black or any other color. But to find the accursed cold soil — ah, there's the rub! It furnishes another worthy cause of agricultural wrath. You plant in it unwittingly, and later learn that it is good only for pitch-pine or baneful yew or trailing ivy. (226–258.)

Now for setting out the vines. First you must dry out the plot into which they are to go, by furrowing the hillsides with trenches and exposing the sods to the north wind. To get a good crumbling soil, you need the action of the wind and of the frost and of — the energetic ploughman. Further, if you are going into the niceties of the art, you will select a spot in the field of the same sort as that in which the vines are grown, indicating the points of the compass on the bark, so that they shall not feel the change in Mother Earth; for great is the force of habit with tender growing things. If you are planting in a fertile plain, put the vines close together, but if on a hillside, be generous with the rows, though making the paths exactly square with the cross-ways. Your vines should be formed like the cohorts of a legion, when the earth quivers with the gleam of bronze before the horrid fray begins, and Mars hovers uncertainly between the lines. This nice and military disposition of your vines is not intended to feed the idle satisfaction of the beholder, but to provide equal opportunity of growth for every plant. Here speaks the practical farmer again, with a rebuke that most of us deserve; I well remember the pleasure of seeing a battalion of vines marching up a hill of Pistoia in quincunx order. But this is a sentiment that farmers and generals abhor. It is especially interesting to find the practical Virgil involve in his condemnation the aesthetic Lucretius, who confesses a sense of delight at watching the trim rows of trees bounding farm from farm with an alternation of colors.[1] I fear that even Virgil himself is not blind to the incidental beauty of well-spaced vines, or of a well-ordered description of them in his verse. (259–287.)

As to the depth of your pits, a small furrow suffices for the vine; for the tree you must dig deeper, especially for the oak, which sinks its roots as deeply toward Tartarus as its branches mount to the skies. That is why winds and storms cannot stir it, but it stays, outliving your

[1] V, 1376.

sons and your grandsons — aye, many generations of men, —

> multa virum volvens durando saecula vincit, —

and stretching widely its strong boughs encompasses a mighty shade. This is fine verse, which Virgil thought good enough to repeat in the Fourth Book of the *Aeneid*.[1] Is the passage too good for the present context? One who has transplanted trees and made the natural error of not setting them deep enough will find this description useful as well as ornamental. (288–297.)

Do not let your vineyard slope to the setting sun, nor plant hazel, whose roots injure the vines. Do not take your cuttings from the extremities of the shoots, for that is too far away from Mother Earth. Do not cut them with a blunt knife. Do not try grafting olive on wild-olive stock. For a fire may break out, hiding covertly beneath the bark, then, rushing up to the leaves with a roar that fills the skies, and darting along the boughs, reign in the summits and, wrapping the grove in flames, roll a black cloud of pitch to the skies — all the more if a storm settle on the woods and a wind drive the fire in a rolling mass. The result is that, as the engrafted olive cannot grow again after you have cut back the stocks, the miserable wild olive with its bitter leaves reigns in its stead. This passage consists of a Hesiodic medley of principles, some on vines and some on trees, that lead the

[1] Ll. 441–446.

way, in the fashion illustrated in the First Book, to an impressive and harmonious picture. (298–314.)

Do not suffer some "expert" to advise you to plant in winter, when Boreas blows and the ground is stiff and the seed cannot fix a well-developed root in the soil. One might not imagine this advice necessary, but the expert in farming is ubiquitous, and a certain type of agricultural mind is fascinated by advice in proportion to its improbability. But heed it not! The best time to plant is the glowing spring, when comes the radiant bird that snakes detest, or at the cool end of autumn when Sol has not yet driven to winter, but summer has passed. But spring is the time of times. Then the forests turn to green, and the earth swells and calls for the birth-giving seeds. Then the almighty Father Aether descends in fecund showers into the bosom of his joyous spouse and the mighty mingling of their mighty frames brings forth all nature's offspring.

These lines are a lesson in imitation. Lucretius, in expounding the law of the conservation of energy, speaks of the rains perishing, for the moment,

> ubi eos pater Aether
> in gremium matris Terrai praecipitavit [1] —

vigorous verses, but with even too much vigor in *praecipitavit*, suggesting a rattling hail-storm rather than a fructifying spring rain. We might also cavil at the rather domestic *Pater Aether* and *Mater Terra* — one

[1] I, 250 f.

such title is enough. Virgil replaces these rough verses with lines of exquisite tenderness and grace, with far more sensuous delight and quite as much power:

> tum pater omnipotens fecundis imbribus Aether
> coniugis in gremium laetae descendit, et omnes
> magnus alit magno commixtus corpore fetus.

In spring, the poet continues, the thickets ring with the songs of birds, the cattle feel the call of love, the kindly fields give birth, as the quivering breezes of the Zephyr relax their folds. The tender sap mounts in growing things, and the grass ventures out and up into the new sunlight, nor does the vine fear the rising wind of the south, or a storm driven down from the north, but pushes out its buds and displays its leaves. No other days than these could have shone at the birth of the world. It was spring throughout creation, when the first cattle drank in the light and the earth-born race rose from the hardy earth, and beasts were set in the woods and stars in the sky. Nor could the tender things bear the stress of life, were not the seasons of heat and cold relieved by such a time of calm and heavenly indulgence. (315-345.)

At the beginning of this passage, it looked as if the second half of the book, like that of the First Book, were to be devoted to "Days," but Virgil always has his surprises. He gives instead another of the set-pieces, lines born to decorate anthologies, but, like the similar passages in Lucretius, best appreciated in their context.

There is no mawkish sentiment in the description, such as spring poems frequently breed, but the sympathy with the growing things of nature is quite as intense as that which the poet has already manifested for birds and beasts. In both regards, Lucretius has shown him the way; and both these poets need considerable attention from those who talk of an intimate delight in nature as a prerogative of modern times. Virgil in turn was studied by a later poet, the author of one of the most gorgeously beautiful works in Latin verse, the *Pervigilium Veneris*. The description there of the birth of the world in spring harks back to the present passage, which it intensifies with brilliant coloring, mystic emotion, and lyric poignancy; but it is less perfect art, well on the road to eroticism and decadence.

Virgil glides gracefully back from his flight, as ever; he meant no panegyric of spring; he was merely pointing out its utility as a kind of resting-time in the strenuous existence of crops. He passes easily from what seemed, at least to the reader, a joyous and exalted vision of spring, to the topic of manuring the earth. If this is not audacity, let Pope try the like without soiling his hands! Manure is indispensable. Dig it in deep, and mulch your plants with a scattering of gravel or ground shells; the water soaks in at the pores, the thin exhalation rises through them, and the plants lift up their hearts. Some experts will protect them with flat stones or potsherds, a defence both against excessive showers and against the heat with which the Dog Star parches the summer fields. (346–353).

After the vines are set, they need frequent cultivation. Ply the hard grub-hoe, or drill the soil with the plough, and in the very vineyard curb your tugging bullocks. Then you must set up smooth shafts of peeled rods, ashen frames, and stout forks on which the vines may learn to scorn the winds and climb from story to story to the tiptop of the elms. Here we shall miss Virgil's picture, and his sympathetic humor, if we imagine vines mounting to the top of some lofty New England elm. They are wedded to very diminutive trees, as we have seen before.[1] One should follow the career of the vine, however, not by looking down on it from our elevated station, but by taking its own point of view, appreciating its long journey, the grateful help of the support, the growing audacity of the plant, and its final security at the very top of what to it was an elm of some dimensions. (354–361.)

While the vine is young, while it is joyously driving with full-flung reins into the blue, use the sharp sickle sparingly and pluck the leaves now and then with thumb and finger. But when it has embraced the elm with a sturdy stalk, then clip its locks and lop its arms; wield a stern sovereignty and keep its flowing branches within bounds. (362–370.)

[1] See above, p. 70, and Varro, *Res Rusticae*, I, 8 (F. Harrison, *Roman Farm Management*, pp. 85–88).

Here again Virgil has boldly seized a striking bit of Lucretius's imagery and, I will not say improves it, but recreates it in his fashion. Lucretius, in describing the early days of the world, speaks of the trees, still lusty with the marvellous new life, as racing to the heavens with full-flung reins —

> arboribusque datumst variis exinde per auras
> crescendi magnum immissis certamen habenis.[1]

There is less force in Virgil's picture; he cannot assume the miraculous growth that Lucretius makes natual enough for the starting of life upon earth, but he replaces these qualities by a joyous sympathy and felicitous description; the reins get a new meaning when we think of the tendrils of the vine —

> dum se laetus ad auras
> palmes agit laxis per purum immissis habenis.

Virgil can hang his picture beside that of Lucretius, sure that we shall see the likeness and the difference and know that both are great.

Fence your vineyard in while the plants are young. They have enough to suffer from beating storms and burning suns without exposing them to buffaloes and wandering goats and sheep and greedy heifers. How often buffaloes strayed into Italian vineyards we need not imagine; they probably came with the Strymonian cranes. The farmer should expect them, or anything

[1] V, 786 f.

else in the way of pests. For neither cold nor frost nor the heat of summer beating on the parching rocks can harm a vine like the poisonous scar left on the plant by a beast's hard tooth. The goat is worst of all, and that is why the Greeks sacrificed him to Bacchus, performing in town and country the time-honored plays, when rustic wit was spurred by the hope of prizes, and the country folk danced merrily on oiled wine-skins. And we Italians, who trace our lineage to Troy, know the sport of uncouth verses, hearty laughs, and awful masks of bark. We chant thy praises, Bacchus, and hang thy swaying images on the pine, that vineyards may teem and glades and valleys be filled with increase wherever the god may turn his honest face. It is meet and right, therefore, to praise our Bacchus with the ancestral rite, to bring him cakes and platters, to lead the accursed goat to the altar, and toast the entrails on hazel spits; the hazel, too, as we saw, was an enemy of the vine, and likewise deserves its punishment. (371–396.)

It is hard to decide whether this passage is a set-piece. It is not very long, and it is immediately related to the theme, since religious veneration, for Virgil as for Hesiod, is a part of farming. At the same time, farming has been lifted, if only for a moment, to one of the higher levels — a pleasant retrospect of the pious rites of primeval Italy, a glimpse, too, of the ultimate origin of the nation and of a sister-country outside its bounds.

The care of the full-grown vine brings another round

of toil that knows no end. Three or four times a year you must tear up the soil and beat out the clods everlastingly — *aeternum frangenda* — with a good full sweep of the grub-hoe. Your vineyard grows like mad into a regular forest, and you must keep pace with the pruning. The farmer's life is one long chore; his year revolves along the same old trodden paths. Aye, when the vine has doffed its last leaves and the cold blasts have stripped the woods of their glories, even then there is no let-up for the poor rustic; he must get after the remnant of the vines with his sickle—called "Saturn's curved tooth" as an ironical reminder of a Golden Age of rest — and prune them into shape. Be the first to stow the poles indoors, but the last to garner. These are the farmer's laws; Virgil expresses them in legal language, and there is no escape. Prune and weed, weed and prune! The shade becomes a nuisance twice a year, and twice a year the plants are cluttered with a thick briarage of weeds. Two calls to hard work! Praise big estates and cultivate a small one. Here Virgil has made over an epigram of Hesiod [1] into one of his own, worthy to be inscribed in letters of gold on every country-place.

"As I return to Virgil," writes Mitchell,[2] "and slip along the dulcet lines, I come upon this cracking laconism, in which is compacted as much wholesome advice as a loose farm-writer would spread over a page:

---

[1] *Works and Days*, l. 643: "Commend a little boat and put your cargo in a big one." See above, pp. 187 f.

[2] *Wet Days at Edgewood*, p. 52.

laudato ingentia rura,
exiguum colito.

'Praise big farms; stick to little ones.'"

But there is more trouble still for the vine-grower. He must cut the broom in the woods and the reed by the river with which to tie his vines; yes, the willow, which nature somehow ought to tend to, calls for his care. Then when the vines are all tied, and the pruning is all done, and the vine-dresser sings in triumph at his finished rows, even then you have to stir the earth and beat it into dust that covers and protects the grapes from sun and shower. After all that, when they are nicely ripened, you still should fear the pouring rain of Jove. (397–419.)

Servius, with an acuteness not imitated by modern commentators, calls this section a *vituperatio vitium*, "an execration of the vine." An execration is the opposite of an encomium; we might call it a set-piece, if the theme for a moment left the ground. Instead, it pictures a morose and exasperated farmer, who continually thinks that the plaguy task is finished and continually finds that it is not. There is a little book, written by James Beresford at the beginning of the last century, called *The Miseries of Human Life*, the spirit of which would be appreciated by Virgil's farmer. He could make up a telling "misery" from his own experience. "After you have raised and trained and cultivated your vines through the hot summer, and after you have followed the law of 'First to prune and carry off the clippings, first to tie up the clusters to the sunlight,' and then have banged the clods with the grub-hoe again and showered the grapes — and yourself — with protecting dust, according to the latest theory of scientific *occatio*, and then have obeyed the law of 'Last to garner,' and watched your neighbor get his grapes in, while you reflected how much better yours would be for the few extra days of sun and air, *then* to have an equinoctial storm descend and spoil the entire crop." Along with practical rules and flights to higher levels, Virgil has incidentally described the agricultural temperament, with its varying moods of joy, energy, anger, and now — exasperation. Any farmer has felt them all; the poet, with humor and good sense, hides none of them. Perhaps this does not make the best campaign document for Augustus's programme of "back to the country," or perhaps, as I have intimated, this programme had not yet been formulated. In any case, Virgil writes around and above it.

The olive, it is a relief to know, needs little treatment — no pruning, no cultivating, when once it has a firm hold on the soil. Plough the ground but once when you set out the young trees, and once again at bearing-time; Mother Earth will supply the needful moisture. So then, cultivate the olive, a worthy berry and an emblem of peace. (420–425.)

Fruit trees, too, when they gain their normal strength,

shoot upwards by their own power without our help. The forests also are a natural growth and the untended aviaries of the woods blush with crimson berries. Clover gives food for cattle, and the woods supply torches that start our fires and give us evening light. With all this natural output, why should men hesitate to add their bit of care? The farmer's mood has changed from exasperation to the lust of work.

But why, asks the poet, should he follow the more epic theme of forest trees? The willows and the humble broom offer leaves to the flock, shade to the shepherd, a fence for the crops, and food to the honey-bee. What joy — again the mood changes — to look on Cytorus waving with box and on the Bruttian grove of pitch-pine, to see the fields that owe no debt to rakes or any care of man. It is the call of the wild, which came, I repeat, as frequently to the ancient as to the modern man. Even the barren forests on the crest of Caucasus, where the east winds forever clash and crash, —

quas animosi Euri assidue franguntque feruntque, —

have their own produce. The pines give beams for ships, and cypress and cedar furnish timber for houses. Of these, farmers make spokes and drum-wheels and keels for boats. Willows are rich in twigs, elms in leaves, myrtle and cherry are good for spears, and the yew of Palestine makes fine bows. Linden and box can be fashioned by lathe and knife into diverse shapes. The alder may be scooped out into a boat that will safely swim the torrent of the Po, and even a rotten oak tree provides a serviceable home for bees.

Tree wins after all in the contest with Vine that has run on through this book! What can the bounties of Bacchus show of equal note? Aye, Bacchus deserves our blame. It was he who brought the mad Centaurs to their death, — Rhoetus and Pholus and Hylaeus, — threatening the Lapithae with his big bowl. No carouse for us after all! Instead, it is something of a *vituperatio vini*, in the spirit of Horace's encomium of Bacchus with an afterthought,[1] or Oliver Wendell Holmes's convivial ode with emendations by a teetotaller. It is only a mood — a passing mood, we somehow prophesy; but for the moment the trees have won. They have their poetry, too, and what is of even more account in this practical poem, their greater utility. (426–457.)

O happy husbandmen, if they but knew their blessings! Far from the tumult of war, they gain a ready sustenance from the equitable earth. They may not own a proud palace that disgorges from its portals a wave of morning guests — for such is the emetic with which receptions end; they may not gape in wonder at lintels inlaid with tortoise-shell or at gowns tricked out with gold or at Corinthian bronzes; they may not stain white wool with drugs of Assyria or spoil good olive-oil with perfumed cassia. No pernicious sugar in their coffee! But sure repose is theirs, and a life innocent of deceit. They

[1] *Odes*, I, 18.

have the real luxuries, and the real peace of broad estates, caverns of the woods, and living lakes — not the
dead ponds artificially piped with water on the rich
man's place. Valleys cool as Tempe are theirs, and lowing kine, and sweet sleep under the trees. It is a somnolent line,

> mugitusque boum mollesque sub arbore somni,

which Victor Hugo applied to a rapturous and romantic
interpretation of Virgil's theme. In the country, too, are
glades and lairs of beasts. And there is young manhood,
patient of toil and used to little. There are the rites of
the gods and reverence of elders. Justice had her last
foothold there, when she left the earth at the end of
the Golden Age. (458–474.)

The reader feels at once that the theme is lifted again,
without ceasing to be agricultural, to one of the higher
levels of more general thought. It is an encomium of the
theme itself, the praise of country life. Soon we see that
it will be the epilogue of the book, and the focus of the
entire work. In character, this poetry is moral satire,
like that which we have seen in Hesiod and Lucretius.
It is of course its own justification, but it is further intended as a tribute to tradition, a sign that Virgil is
aware of the various flavors in the poetry of his predecessors. Echoes of Lucretius appear in the phrases, and the
spirit of the whole is true to both these masters. It is a
formal declaration of allegiance to one of the four main

principles, that of Contentment, on which we found the
poem of Hesiod to be based, and which Virgil, once
more, recognized even in his boyhood. He had learned
the delights of simplicity, in part, surely, from the shepherd of Ascra, who, to repeat his words once more,

securam placido traducit pectore vitam.

Virgil continues with a more intimate confession of
faith; it is a moment of outlook over the essential things
of life, such as we saw in the Sixth Eclogue. It is his
philosophy. First and foremost, he declares, he would
be the priest of the Muses, loyal to their worship, enrap-
tured with their love, "smit with the love of sacred
song." It is not a mere revelry in the emotions; emotion,
as in the lyric intellect of George Meredith, joins hands
with reflection. The Muses will lead him in the paths of
science, will show him the courses of the stars of heaven,
the failings of the sun, the travails of the moon, earth-
quakes and storms at sea, the reason why the winter sun
hastens to its dip in ocean, and why the nights are re-
tarded in their course. This is a programme of Epicurean, or Lucretian, science, to which Virgil had devoted
several years of his youth, and which, despite his rever-
sion from abstract philosophy to poetry, never ceased to
command his enthusiasm and his respect. But science is
not for all. If the secrets of nature, he continues, are a
closed book to me, if my brain is murky with penumbral
fogs, why then I can resign myself to the inglorious love
of meadow, stream, and grove. I hear the call of far-off

fields, Spercheos and Taygeta, where Spartan maidens revel wild and free; I am summoned by the chill valleys of Mount Haemus and the broad-branching trees of its woods. This nature for which the poet longs is not that of a picture by Watteau. He lays his scenes in desolate and distant places, like Thracian Haemus, or a spot like Taygeta, *virginibus bacchata Lacaenis*, suggestive of Dionysiac orgies, which, I suspect, were nearer to the untamed heart of nature than anything that modern poets have dreamed or that exotic young ladies engaging in what are courteously called "Greek dances" have portrayed.

But is the love of nature a mere *pis aller*, a consolation for wits? In answer come the startling words, with the clearness of a trumpet-call, —

> Happy the man who knows the cause of things
> And sets his foot on fears and ruthless fate
> And stills the roar of greedy Acheron.
> But lucky he who knows the country gods,
> Pan, and old Silvan and the sister Nymphs.[1]

These lines make one of the great challenges of history; Virgil, whose change of heart has been implied in his work, now openly and by word of mouth flings the gauntlet down before his master Lucretius. He does not need to name Lucretius in verses which are skilfully

[1] L. 490:
> Felix qui potuit rerum cognoscere causas
> atque metus omnis et inexorabile fatum
> subiecit pedibus strepitumque Acherontis avari.
> Fortunatus et ille deos qui novit agrestes
> Panaque Silvanumque senem Nymphasque sorores.

composed from fragments of his poetry, and which describe the animating purpose of the *De Rerum Natura*. The statement, to be sure, is modest in form; the emphasis is inverted; it is perhaps the supreme example of Virgil's "reticence." Virgil, once more, does not relinquish his devotion to science; least of all does he abandon himself to sentiment. But he insists that the world of Lucretius is a half-world; it is untrue to experience in its exclusion of religious faith, the faith professed by country folk, and symbolic of their true simplicity.

This brings us again to the encomium of country life. Even that theme has been raised to a level of higher thought and intenser feeling. The countryman, continues Virgil, has no thought of political agitation, whether it benefit the rabble or the ruler, or of civic strife, or of the league of invaders from the Danube, or of the "Roman question," or of kingdoms doomed to wane. He has no pity of the poor or envy of the wealthy.

We must pause a moment to make sure that the rustic is neither unphilanthropic, as our standard editor of Virgil declares, nor, as Servius would have it, a Stoic sage, icy to all the πάθη of emotion that so easily beset the ordinary man. The rustic is really a philosopher, but not one whose virtue is, in the words of Pope, "fix'd as in a frost." The writer of the supplementary note in Servius, who may well have derived his comment from Donatus, neatly remarks that the poet "is not bringing on his stage a cruel rustic, in that he has no compassion on the poor, but since he knows that poverty is no evil, he does not lament the poor man's lot; in the same way, he does not envy the rich, because he knows that there is nothing inherently good in riches."[1] This is a good deal for Virgil to say in so few words, but it is all there. William Blake makes a devil reply to a satisfied angel who has been singing of mercy, pity, and peace that

> "Mercy could be no more,
>   If there was nobody poor,
> And pity no more could be,
>   If all were as happy as ye."
> At his curse the sun went down,
>   And the heavens gave a frown.

There is no discernible reason why the heavens should have frowned. In Virgil's rustic world, at least, they continue to smile. For it is a world of Hesiodic contentment, in which — as it might in our own world today, if we could only learn the lesson — the distinction of rich and poor absolutely ceases to be. It follows inexorably that both pity and envy have likewise taken flight.

This happy condition seems appropriate for a Golden Age, and the rest of the picture is in keeping. The countryman plucks fruit that boughs bear spontaneously. He knows nothing of iron laws; nothing of the crazy Forum, with its surging mobs, shouting orators, and crafty brokers; nothing of the Public Record Office, with

---

[1] On *Georg.*, II, 499: *non crudelem rusticum inducit, qui inopis non misereatur, sed qui sciens paupertatem malum non esse, pauperis non doleat sortem: et ideo adiecit 'aut invidet habenti,' quia non invidet, sciens divitias bonas non esse.*

its careful files of historical error and their solemn custodians. Others may stir the unseen ocean with their oars, rush on the spear-point, or work their way up to the antechamber of the King. One lays siege to some unhappy town that he may drink from gems and sleep on Sarran purple. One broods over his buried hoard of gold. One drinks in an orator's eloquence in rapt bewilderment, while the orator lists attentive to his own applause as it goes rattling through the auditorium, caught up by nobles and commoners alike. Some enjoy staining themselves with their brothers' blood, and change their pleasant homes for a land beneath an alien sun. The farmer's life is to stir the soil with the crooked plough. This is his yearly task; by this he supports his ancestral home, his children, his flocks and herds, and the bullocks that well have won their recompense. There is no intermission in the bounties of the year. It teems with fruit, or offspring of the flock, or sheaves of Ceres' grain, loading his furrows with increase and bursting his granaries. In winter, the olive is crushed in the press; the swine return sleek and lusty after their feeding in the woods; autumn exhibits its varied stores; and high on sunny rocks the luscious vintage mellows —

> mitis in apricis coquitur vindemia saxis.

There is no reproof of Vine in this comfortable picture — perhaps Tree is not victor yet! To brighten the farmer's toil, his sweet children hang about his lips; purity stands guardian of his house; his cows come back to the barn with full udders; and plump kids tussle in the glad meadows. My lord himself keeps holiday, and, outstretched in the grass while his companions light a fire and crown the bowl, he makes libation to Father Lenaeus and arranges games; an oak is marked for a target, or the hardened rustics strip for a wrestling match. That is the life that the Sabines led of old; that is how Romulus and Remus and brave Etruria grew, and Rome became the loveliest city of earth and encompassed her seven citadels in one wall. Aye, such was man's life before the reign of Jove, before the impious race that banqueted on slaughtered bullocks; so golden Saturn lived on earth, before trumpets were blown or swords rang on the anvil.

"But we have crossed a boundless stretch of plain," — so run the last lines of the book, — "and now it is time to unloose the necks of our foaming steeds":

Sed nos immensum spatiis confecimus aequor
et iam tempus equum fumantia solvere colla.

II

This has indeed been a boundless stretch of plain, and we have driven in a chariot and four, not in an ox-cart; the concluding couplet is epic in tone, and appropriate enough. The preceding passage, the epilogue to the book, contains a whole philosophy of life. The country teaches Virgil, as Menander, virtue and freedom:

ἆρ' ἐστὶν ἀρετῆς καὶ βίου διδάσκαλος
ἐλευθέρου τοῖς πᾶσιν ἀνθρώποις ἀγρός.[1]

[1] *Menander. The Principal Fragments with an English Translation*, by F. G. Allinson, London and New York, 1921, p. 432.

But Virgil's philosophy is more inclusive than this. It draws its spirit mainly from Hesiod, and contains a challenge to Lucretius; it is a philosophical interpretation of Contentment, one of the main ideas in the *Works and Days*. This book pays in full, and more than pays, the poet's debt to Hesiod. We saw what in the First Book Virgil made of the theme of "Days," how he started with an apparently technical reproduction of it, and in a few moments transformed it to a vision of nature, and with an ever-increasing intensity and majesty, into a national appeal. The method is different here. Hesiod at first does not appear, except for the poet's utterance of his name in the passage in praise of Italy — the proud declaration that he has achieved his ambition of doing for the Augustan Age what Hesiod did for his generation. There are few Hesiodic details in this book as compared with the First Book, but the tribute to Hesiod's ideas and the new creation of them is none the less impressive. In the First Book, the idea particularly emphasized was Industry; here it is Contentment. Both books, incidentally, and none the less effectively, make it as clear as Hesiod does that Religion is part and parcel of the farmer's life. If Octavian had so early as this formulated his plan of the revival of the ancient rites, Virgil is expeditiously killing two birds with one stone; he is at once fulfilling the demands of tradition and applying this heritage to a need of the immediate present. Nor is the twofold aspect of his accomplishment the less conspicuous in case we agree, as I think we must, that only vague suggestions could have come to Virgil at this time from either Octavian or Maecenas; the contemporary need is none the less real if he himself discovered it. And what setting could be devised more impressive than this for the attack on Lucretius? It is not merely a question of theory or individual outlook; the life of the nation is at stake. The prophet of science had torn down; the prophet of faith will build again.

The Contentment pictured in the epilogue is found only in a Golden Age, in which the difference between rich and poor has ceased to be. Has Virgil become blinded to reality? Has the matter-of-fact farmer so much in evidence in the early part of this book and in the First Book, where he explicitly excludes the Golden Age from his sturdy exhortation to toil, suddenly lapsed into the dreamy romanticism that critics have found in his youthful work, the Fourth Eclogue? I have taken pains to show that there is nothing sentimental or, in the bad sense of the word, romantic in that earlier piece. Youthful we may call it, — though the poet was thirty years old at the time, — for it is full of the spirit of youthful confidence; but it is not immature or lacking in worldly wisdom. Nor have we a different Virgil here. His hope is not less for having passed through the critical and disheartening events that succeeded the peace of Brundisium. His purpose in the First Book is not to let us know that with the wisdom of increasing years he has ceased to believe in his earlier vision, but to shake into the farmer an intense realization of the necessity of hard work. The Golden Age, to which he here returns, is precisely that which Hesiod, innovating, had set forth; work is a part of its essence. Scan this pleasant picture again; you will note the presence of toil in the background. The crooked plough fails not; crops come from furrows — which do not make themselves; the luscious vintage mellows, not promiscuously, but on those sunny hillsides which the farmer, following Virgil's manual, has prepared for it. The farmer's happiness, his round of feasts and games, are not his daily occupation; they are the rewards of work; sweet is pleasure after pain. In this manner, Virgil ends the book with Hesiod.

III

The composition of the book suggests that of the First, with the inevitable differences that an artist is bound to arrange. The introduction and the invocation both are brief, and immediately georgic in character. Both should be contrasted with the openings of Lucretius's books. After his First Book, in which a special invocation is necessary, Lucretius follows the same pattern everywhere; first comes an introduction of some length, in which he is apt to strike the higher levels of his poetry; then there is a brief recapitulation of his treatment thus far, and then a brief statement of the subject of the coming book. Lucretius does not care.

He is writing philosophy, not poetry; he casts us a few sugar-coated pills, gives an orderly table of contents, proceeds about his business, and, despite his best intent, burns through the stubble of his facts by the fire of his genius. Virgil, intending art as well as philosophy, must banish the monotonous and the prosaic.

The introduction to the Second Book of the *Georgics*, therefore, is different from that of the First Book. It does not stand out. It is merged in a purely georgic setting, which extends to the final passage in praise of country life. It contains, like the First Book, two set-pieces, growing easily out of the context, though differing, in the first of these, from the mode of transition employed in the corresponding piece in the First Book. We may also note that passage on the cheerful festivals of primitive Greece and Rome, which almost but not quite stands out as a separate picture; there is no effect quite like this in the First Book. The subject of this georgic part is likewise differently treated. In the First Book, it is evenly divided between Work and Days. In the Second, a double subject, Vine and Tree, is announced, and the two themes are started on a kind of race throughout the whole passage, now one and now the other forging ahead, till in the end the victory is the Tree's. A further interest of the strictly georgic part, if any part is strictly georgic, is the development, more noticeable than in the First Book, of agricultural moods, aspects of the farmer's temperament — anger and exasperation, as well as delight; all these moods, honestly confessed, merge in the larger and permanent satisfaction that attends the life of toil.

The book has a closing passage of imposing length and grandeur, like that in the First Book. In essence it is not epic, like that, but moral satire, sanctioned for a work of this sort by the examples of Hesiod and Lucretius, and raised to the same level of reflection and dignity that they had reached. Dryden, on the strength of a far less impressive passage in the rustic billingsgate of the Third Eclogue, declared that Virgil might have been the prince of Roman satirists, had he chosen.[1] In the vein of Lucretian satire, which, as I have said, Horace avoided and Juvenal failed to attain, Virgil lacks his master's powerful scorn, but is his peer in elevation of thought, and, as ever, more than his peer in the art of verse.

The finale differs from that of the First Book in other respects besides its general tone. Instead of rushing precipitously to the goal, it mounts at the start to a high but placid stretch; rises in the proclamation of the poet's ultimate views of life, with its challenge to his master; descends again to the calm level at which it had started; and so continues to the end, where the poet suddenly draws in rein, much in the fashion of the epic closes, say, of the First and the Seventh of his pastorals. The substance of the epilogue is not epic, if I may again define epic as poetic narrative ennobled; it is not narra-

[1] See above, pp. 83 f.

tive, but reflective satire. But the manner of this is noble; the poet makes us feel that a life of perfect simplicity is an epic deed.

The epilogue is likewise introduced in a fashion different from that in the First Book. There Virgil planned an elaborate climax, obvious not only in the passage itself, but in all that leads up to it. Here the new theme is abruptly introduced. Abruptness is one kind of transition, as Virgil has already illustrated, and the effect here remains abrupt, even though Servius properly adds that the praise of country life is related to what has preceded.[1] There is another sort of abruptness within the passage. It contains two surprises, which are flung at us like bolts from the blue. One is the challenge to Lucretius. When once it has come, we remember certain prophecies of it by the way, bits of Lucretian coloring, and an occasional rivalry in descriptive effect — faint rumblings in the sky, which we, not versed in the science of signs, did not recognize as the precursor of a storm. Its coming is all the more tremendous.

The other surprise is the return to the Golden Age. One may more easily suspect this *dénouement* than the first surprise, yet it is so strange a pass to travel that the reader hardly ventures to guess the goal before he actually has reached it. For we started in the First Book with the rejection of Saturnian fancies for Hesiod's

[1] On *Georg.*, II, 458: non est abruptus transitus ad laudem vitae rusticae, nam ad superiora pertinet.

Gospel of Work. We begin the Second Book in the same practical mood, leaping into the wine-vat, swinging the grub-hoe, pruning the vine, and manuring the soil. But the poem is full of contradictions. Now we have the real crops and soils of nature in a land that boasts no miracles; now some little miracle appears and seems quite at home. We are gradually aware that we are in an idealized Italy, in an idealized spring, and are even told that the country is Saturnian. With these warnings, we should know what to expect, and when the poet leads us step by step to his conclusion we cannot protest. For, as a final surprise, we discover that it is a novel Golden Age — novel to all but Hesiod — to which we have returned.

The two finales differ in yet another point, in which is involved the main purpose of the poem, the ideal object most vitally present to the poet's desire. That, we saw, was not, as for Hesiod, Justice, though Justice of course has returned in Virgil's Golden Age, but Peace. At these two points of vantage in his work Virgil hangs two pictures for us to contemplate. The first is of the chaos of a world at war; Mars is on the throne, and the placid art of farming perishes unobserved. In the second picture peace is restored; the life of the country, with its simple enjoyments and its hard work, becomes the model for all the occupations of men. The poet does not propose to abandon other pursuits, but he does show,

with a merciless truth, that the more sophisticated operations of man are cluttered with vanities. For war there
is surely no place. Anvils still ring, but no longer with
the forging of a sword. The sword is beaten into a
pruning-hook in this new Golden Age of work.

CHAPTER VIII

THE ANIMALS OF THE FARM
A CHALLENGE TO LUCRETIUS AND TO
ENNIUS

SERVIUS declares that the theme of the *Georgics* is
finished with the Second Book, since the Third and
the Fourth Books are pastoral. This remark is etymo-
logically sound. The working of the soil and the raising of
crops therefrom are finished, and we now are to hear of
acts of the shepherd, the feeder of flocks and herds, and
the keeper of bees. It is almost, says Servius, as though
we were beginning a new work — pastoral, that is —
after the completion of the georgic part.[1] We will later[2]
examine the significance of this remark.

I

THE THIRD BOOK

The introduction contains one of Virgil's surprises,
the announcement of a rash venture. He begins with an
appropriate invocation of Pales and Apollo, both of
them pastoral divinities, and he prays to nature, too —
the woods and streams of Arcadia. Servius is not wholly

[1] On l. 1: Sane non est mirandum, usum esse eum prooemio, sicut est usus
in primo: nam aliud quodammodo inchoaturus est carmen, pastorale scilicet,
post completum georgicum.

[2] See below, p. 337.

to blame for thinking that a pastoral is to follow. The kind of poetry, Virgil declares, that fascinates idle minds has become a shallow convention. Mythological wonders, like the gigantic deeds of Hercules, the rape of Hylas by the nymphs, the floating island of Delos, the ivory shoulder of Pelops, are mouthed by every poet and charm no reader of sense. We now expect the poet to assert, as he had done in the preceding book, that his subject is new and practical — unattempted yet in prose or rhyme, and useful to the present generation. A passage of this kind — it is a familiar Alexandrian device, as we saw from *Culex* and *Ciris* and *Aetna* — occurs in the First Book of Lucretius, and is used again by that poet, who was apparently running short of introductions, at the beginning of his Fourth Book. Virgil might well select the present place, relatively as far along as that in Lucretius's poem, for an expression of the same sentiment. But he cuts it short with a surprise. I, too, must essay a path, he declares, whereby I may rise above the earth and float victorious on the lips of men:

> Temptanda via est quo me quoque possim
> Tollere humo victorque virum volitare per ora.

No Roman reader would fail to observe the new challenge. The final phrase is taken bodily from the famous epitaph of Ennius, who asked for no lamentation at his death, seeing that his fame would be immortal:

> Nemo me dacrumis decoret nec funera fletu
> Faxit. Cur? Volito vivos per ora virum.

I must scale the same heights of immortality, declares Virgil. My fame, too, must flit from lip to lip! But why this rivalry with Ennius? Had not that poet, freethinker that he was, sung a certain amount of myth in his epic of Rome? Virgil had himself told the story of Hylas in his Sixth Eclogue in such a way that for the moment the old myth lived again; but he has just professed repentance, so it seemed, and announced a practical theme — the farmer's care of flocks and herds. What has Ennius to do with this? The following lines explain.

The poet declares that he will return to his native Mantua, if his life be spared, bringing palms of victory and the Muses from their Grecian hill. He will first build a marble temple in the green field on the banks of the little Mincio, smooth-sliding river, fringed with vocal reeds —

> ubi flexibus errat
> Mincius et tenera praetexit harundine ripas.

The phrase takes us back to the Seventh Eclogue; it suggests the poet's love of his birthplace, and his early hopes. And now for still greater plans. The god in his new temple will be Caesar, and the poet, clad in triumphal purple, will set a hundred chariots whirling in the race along the stream. Little Mantua will become a second Olympia, with its shrine and its contests. Yes, the Nemean games and all the games of Greece will be transferred to this new site, where the poet, adorned with an olive crown, the emblem of peace, will assign the prizes. There shall be solemn processions to this temple, and the sacrifice of bullocks, and plays upon the stage, the curtain of which is embroidered with figures of Britons. The doors of the temple shall bear a battle-scene, carved of ivory and gold — the people of the Ganges yielding to Roman arms, the Nile surging with war, and towering columns of ships' beaks. The cities of Asia shall be there, beaten Niphates, the Parthian fighting as he flees, and a double trophy from the distant foes of east and west. There shall be statues, too, breathing images of Parian marble, of the god-descended kings of Troy, Assaracus and Father Tros, and of Apollo, founder of the city. Art will also show the fate of foes within the state; Envy shall cower before the Furies, the harsh stream of Cocytus, the writhing snakes of Ixion, the giant wheel, and the rock that never gains the summit. This for the future. Just now, Maecenas, I am wandering in woods and glades, obedient to your hard commands. You are the inspiration of my song. So, then, to horse! Cythaeron calls me, and the Spartan pack and horse-rearing Epidaurus, and their call is echoed by the groves. Anon I will sing of Caesar's glowing battles and herald his name to as long a glory as that which runs from the birth of Tithonus to his own times. (1–48.)

This seems a large order. Virgil likes to make rash promises, and to fulfil them. There is no renunciation of mythology in this challenge to Ennius. Virgil will take the beaten path after all, and rise to immortality by that very way. He will build his god a temple which will outshine the splendors of Greece. It is the sublimity of the theme, not the self-conceit of the poet, that prompts the ecstatic account of his undertaking and the confident prophecy of its success. In a word, the subject of Virgil's epic has come to him at last. He has found his hero in Octavian, and he will make his offering from his own little town. As Horace thought of his Apulian birthplace in the proudest moment of his career, so Virgil will build his Grecian temple on the banks of the Mincio. Of Virgil's many ventures, there is none more daring than this. He virtually proclaims that not only Ennius, but Homer himself, should look to his laurels.

It is of exceeding interest to compare this preliminary sketch of an epic with the finished performance of the *Aeneid*. In the main, it promises to be a narrative of contemporary achievement, the victories of Octavian over all the foes of Rome, those of the east, those of the west, and the rebels within. It will be, in a way, a Trojan poem; the supposed Trojan descent of the hero through the Julian line will make it appropriate to sketch the story back to the founding of Troy, and thus there will be place for eulogy of Apollo, the god who not only founded the city whence the Romans came, but saved the day at Actium. As in the *Aeneid*, there will be an Inferno, the purpose of which is to provide condign torture for those who have opposed the hero's will or sullenly disparaged him behind his back. No slighting of the myth in this part of the programme! All the traditional punishments of unspeakable sin will perform their ancient duty for the brood of unspeakable sinners.

Moreover, as Virgil turned the subject over in his mind, in the slow fashion in which his creative genius moved, the contemporary and historical elements in his epic design sank more and more into the background; the mythical and ideal became the ostensible subject of the poem. His real subject, the majesty of Rome and its mission of peace under a divinely appointed leader, had not changed, but it had acquired a profounder depth and a broader horizon. The change is well illustrated by the character of the Inferno in the *Aeneid*. This was at first intended as a place of torture for the enemies of Octavian; it eventually became, by a most daring and skilful application of Platonic metamorphosis to the demands of the plot, one of the two passages in the poem in which history pure and simple is described. The present outline has much to tell us of the art of the *Aeneid*, the poet's habit of work, and the character of his imagination. It may well have been put into final shape after the body of the poem was completed, perhaps not long after the news of Actium had come to Rome. But there are no allusions to the wars of Octavian definite enough to require a later date. With the *Aeneid* in its well-nigh finished form before him, Virgil could not, as has been suggested, have written the present passage shortly before his death.

On the west base of the beautiful statue put up by Virgil's countrymen at his birthplace, the verse

> primus Idumaeas referam tibi Mantua palmas

is inscribed; on the east, a verse from the Seventh Book of the *Aeneid*,

> et nunc servat honos sedem tuus;

the north bears Dante's lines,

> E quell' ombra gentil per cui si noma
> Pietola piu che villa Mantovana; [1]

and the south has the simple words,

> Pietole eresse il 21 Settembre 1884.

These inscriptions, tokens of gratitude, modesty, and pride, are, no less than the statue itself, a splendid monument to Virgil.

But we must to horse with the poet and follow the quarry through unbeaten woods, obeying those "hard commands" of Maecenas. Our object, as ever, is intensely practical. We first are to select good breeding animals, whether we are raising horses for the Olympian races or bullocks for the plough. Pick out the mother first. You can tell a good cow by her ugly head, abundant neck, and long dewlaps. Her flank is immoderately long. Everything about her is big, including her hoof. She has shaggy ears beneath her crumpled horns. Take no offence if she is dappled all over with white spots or if she resists the yoke. Her horn is vicious, her face like

---

[1] *Purgatorio*, XVIII, 83.

a bull's, her whole body is tall, and as she walks she sweeps her footprints with her tail:

> et gradiens ima verrit vestigia cauda.

There is something epic in this sweeping tail; our cow has an almost masculine dignity. But pretty she is not. Our poet is no aesthete; he wants the best breeder whatever she looks like.

The age for the rites of Lucina and lawful wedlock stops before the tenth and begins after the fourth year; offspring born out of time are good neither for breeding nor for work. So then, in the happy time of youth, bring on the males; be the first to initiate your herds into the ceremonies of Goddess Venus, and thus perpetuate your stock. The fairest day, poor mortals are aware, is always the first to flee; disease and drear old age come on; hard toil and pitiless death diminish the number. You will also find some cattle whom you would like to get rid of. Well, then, always replenish the stock. Forestall your losses and get you new offspring every year. These practical directions and energetic exhortations are occasionally seasoned, as appears in the metre as well as in the words, with touches of a grandiose style which, if the poet carried it a bit farther, would be mock-heroic. (49–71.)

You must take like pains in choosing your stallion, the hope of the race that you are to breed. The scion of a noble stock, a "generous charger," steps higher on the field, and plants a lighter limb. He is the first to dare a

venturous path, cross angry streams, and trust an unfamiliar bridge; nor does he start at idle sounds. His
neck is high; his head erect; short his belly and plump
his back, and his spirited breast luxuriates in muscles.
Finest in color are the bays and greys; worst are white
and yellow. Again, if he hear the call of battle from afar,
he cannot stay in place; he pricks up his ears, quivers in
all his limbs, and, snorting, rolls beneath his nostrils a
mass of fire. Dense is his mane; when tossed, it lies again
on his right shoulder. There is a double ridge of fat along
his loins. As he runs, he scoops the earth with clattering
hoof of solid horn:

> cavatque
> tellurem et solido graviter sonat ungula cornu.

This rapid verse is prophetic of the still more famous
galloping line in the *Aeneid*:

> quadrupedante putrem sonitu quatit ungula campum.[1]

This is a real horse, described by an expert as well as a
poet. We might have expected, after the preceding passage on the cow, that the good points of the bull would
be mentioned. But that is not Virgil's way; he exhibits
his customary "reticence," which does not tolerate explicitness when suggestion can tell the story; it is the
principle of the enthymeme applied to description.

So fine a creature as this horse is hard to get; there is
something of the mythical, the super-equine about him.
Yes, such was Cyllarus, whom Pollux tamed, as the

[1] VIII, 596. Cf. XI, 875:

Greek poets told, or the horses of Mars, or the great Achilles' span. And such was the form that Saturn took when his wife surprised him in his amour with Philyra, — one of the regrettable incidents of the Golden Age, — and he tossed his mane about his neck and scampered away, neighing till the echoes rang on lofty Pelion. (72–94.)

This is a considerable amount of the mythical after the denunciation of myth in the opening verses. But it is the way with Virgil, or any creative poet, to take the forbidden, the outgrown, the impossible, the lies of the ancient Greeks, and build his poetry of that. There is no mock-heroic in the present bit, nor is mythology invoked to dignify the rural theme. The horse is so splendid that we must search the fabulous to find his equal. There he has his peers; the story of the last of these is told with a dash and a rollicking humor that make good accompaniment for tossing manes and clattering hoofs.

The moment your stallion grows old or falls sick, turn him off; spare him not in the time of his disgrace. The old horse is too chill for love; in vain he undertakes unwelcome toil; and in battle he rages to no avail, like fire in a field of chaff. So know your animal's points — their spirits and their years, their traits and lineage, their defeats and their victories in the race. It is youth and vigor that count. Watch them when the chariots break from the barriers and course the plain, when youthful hope runs high and fears seize pulsing hearts. The

drivers let out the reins and ply the circling lash; the hot
wheel speeds amain; now low, now high, they seem to
rise in the light air and skim the breeze. No respite or
repose; a dusky cloud of sand is raised; the horses are
damp with foam and the breath of their pursuers — so
great is their love of praise and passion for victory.
Erichthonius was the inventor of the race of four-horse
chariots. The Lapithae first made bridles and practised manoeuvres, sitting on the horse's back, and
taught the steed with his armed rider to prance upon
the ground and gather up his proud paces.

Shall we call this a set-piece? The mention of the
chariot race has led to the description of it. The description is so vivid that for the moment we can think of
nothing else. It is not out of place to inquire who invented this glorious art and what were the steps in its
development. The brevity of the passage suggests,
rather than a set-piece, the sort of Homeric simile that
transports the reader to a different world, not relevant
in all its details to the subject in hand, but its own excuse for existence; when the falling shafts of Greeks and
Trojans are compared to flakes of snow, in a verse or two
we find ourselves in a snowstorm that covers the battlefield and all traces of human activity, bringing us nearer
to the heart of nature than many of the more self-
conscious endeavors of modern poets do.[1] Virgil does
not, as a rule, directly reproduce the irrelevant effect of

[1] *Iliad*, XII, 277–286.

the Homeric simile; he felt, apparently, that such a mode of imitation would be crude; he keeps his similes relevant and introduces shifts of the scene not by comparisons but by descriptions or reflections, which grow naturally out of the context. But, as ever, we easily glide back again. Youth and vigor, as the poet was saying, are the essential qualities. Ruthlessly demand these, though your charger has many tales to tell of pursuing the routed foe, and though he claim Epirus or Mycenae for his birthplace, and trace his lineage from Neptune. Out with these equine Nestors; in with the younger blood! (95–122.)

After selecting your breeder, feed him up. Give him fresh grass, good water, and abundant corn, lest he be unequal to his pleasant task and feeble offspring reproduce their starveling sires. But the mares must be kept thin; when they show the first symptoms of desire, refuse them pasturage and keep them from the streams. Sometimes they are given violent exercise and wearied in the sun, or worked at threshing, when the floor groans with its beaten grain and the light chaff tosses in the rising wind. This has a purpose, for if the mares are fed too generously the genital field is cluttered, the furrows are clogged, whereas the thirsty soil should seize the seeds of love and bury them deep within. (123–137.)

After conception takes place, your attention passes from the sires to the mares. As the appointed months pass on, they should not draw the yoke of heavy wagons, or jump across a road, or take too vigorous a pace across the field, or swim torrential streams. Let them wander in open glades along full rivers with moss-green banks, and seek the protection of shady caverns. There is a creature that swarms in the groves of Silarus and the green glades of Mount Alburnus; it is named *asilus* in the Roman tongue; 'tis changed in the Greek to *oestrus* — a fierce, harsh-throated beast, at whose coming the herds flee frightened through the woods, and bellow their fury to the upper sky, making the woodlands and the banks of Tanager's parched stream ring with their clamor. This is a dreadful commotion for a tiny gadfly to create! No wonder his prowess is described in epic terms, including a phrase — *asper, acerba sonans* — that Lucretius had applied to a dragon;[1] and no wonder that the poet turns to myth once more for the example of poor Io; the passage borders closely on mock-heroic. Such, then, is the creature from which you should shield your pregnant herd, especially at mid-day, when the gadfly is most lively, and take them out rather at the rising sun, or when stars appear at nightfall. One surprise in this passage is the sudden change in the subject from horses to cows. Virgil means both, but, with his reticent art, does not need to tell us so. (138–156.)

The new offspring now claim consideration. They are branded with the names of their stock or with signs that indicate which shall be breeders, which consecrated to

[1] V, 33: asper, acerba tuens.

the worship of the gods, and which shall plough the soil. All but the last-named can be turned out to graze, but the draft-animals you must now subject to a course of training, while they are easy of temper and docile of age. First put light hoops of osier about their necks, then, when their free souls are used to this amount of slavery, form pairs by joining these hoops and make the mates keep step; then let them drag a pair of wheels that leave the merest trace in the dust of the road. Afterwards harness them to a stout beechen axle that creaks beneath its load, with the brass-plated wagon-pole attached to a heavy yoke. Meanwhile you must feed the untamed herd not only with grass and willow-leaves and sedge from the swamp, but with the growing corn that you pluck by hand. Nor let your breeding cows, as in the manner of our ancestors, fill your pails of snowy milk, but keep for their sweet offspring all that their udders hold. (157-178.)

Your war-horse, or the racer whom you would have outrun the streams of Pisa and drag a car in the grove of Jupiter, must first have a sight of arms, and while in the stall stand the sound of trumpets, the rattle of the dragging wheel, and the sound of clanking reins. He must covet more and more his master's coaxing praise and the sound of patted neck. Thus much instruction must he get the moment he is weaned; next, put his mouth in a light muzzle, even when he is weak and trembling and ignorant of life. As the fourth year approaches, he may

begin his manoeuvres, step at attention, bend his legs
evenly in alternating curves, and present the appearance of exertion. Then let him challenge the breezes to
a race and, as though free from the rein, skim the open
field scarce touching hoof to the ground, like the north
wind when he descends from Hyperborean coasts, clear-
ing the Scythian showers and the dry clouds from his
path; then the tall corn and the floating fields of water
shiver in his milder blast; then the wood-tops catch the
sound, and the long waves dash upon the shore, while in
his flight he skims over the plain and sweeps across the
sea —

> ille volat simul arva volans simul aequora verrens.

Here is a simile, with powerful onomatopoetic effects,
that, Homeric enough in manner and in length, is nevertheless minutely relevant; we never cease to think of the
horse's flight, the ease of the course, and its gathering
intensity.

Such is the charger, who either at Olympia will sweat
and champ the bloody bit for the prize of victory, or else
with supple neck will draw the Belgian war-chariot.
When he is well trained, then, and not before, you can
stuff him with good mash. Ere this, much feeding will
rouse his proud spirit; he will not, when caught, allow
the lash or mind the bit. (179–208.)

The best way to get a strong stock, whether of horses
or of cattle, is to remove your animals from incentives to
love. Bulls are pastured in solitary fields with a moun-

tain or a broad stream in between, or else they are confined to comfortable stalls. For the sight of the female
preys upon their strength; her sweet enticements drive
out all thoughts of exercise or fodder, and prompt proud
rival lovers to fight it out in a duel of horns. There pastures in great Sila's fields a heifer fair to see, whose suitors engage in a mighty fight, exchanging thrusts and
plenteous wounds; black blood bathes their bodies; their
horns strain in full clash; their bellowings fill the woods
and the expanse of heaven. Nor will these warriors stall
together, but the vanquished retires afar to an unknown
coast, groaning from shame and the blows of his haughty
rival, grief for his lost love, and madness for revenge. All
this is in the look that he casts back on the stalls as he
moves away from his ancestral realms. So then he
trains, with all his might. He makes his unstrewn bed
on the hard rock; he diets on rough leaves and prickly
sedge; he tests his strength, and learns to throw his
temper into his horns, butting against a tree-trunk, lashing the wind with his blows, and making the sand fly in
prelude to the fight. Anon, when he has mustered his
might and repaired his powers, he orders "Forward,
March!" and charges headlong on his oblivious foe, even
as a wave that, foaming in mid-sea, curves onward from
afar and, rolling ashore, roars tremendous on the rocks
and like a mountain bursts, while the water at its depths
boils up in whirlpools and tosses the black sand on high.
(209–241.)

We have noticed touches of mock-heroic, or approaches to it, before, but here is a whole episode done in this style, admirable for its quiet humor and the dignity of the lines. There is no note of bombast or of the ridiculous. The description surges into an epic simile which like the wave itself washes away all flavor of parody and brings us to seriousness again. This short passage is one of the many bits in the *Georgics* each sufficient in itself to establish a reputation.

Every tribe of men and animals upon the earth, the fishes of the sea, the beasts of the field, the fowls of the air, all feel the hot driving of passion; all admit the sway of love. At such a time, the lioness, forgetting her cubs, wanders fiercely over the fields, and ugly bears spread havoc in the woods. Then raves the boar; then is the tiger at her worst; then is a bad time, ah me! for roaming the lonely plains of Libya. See you not how a horse's body quivers all over if but the familiar odor comes to him on the breeze? Then neither bridle nor lash nor rocks nor caves nor hills nor mountain-ruining floods can stop him. Yes, the great Sabellian boar rushes about, and whets his tusks; he paws the earth and rubs his ribs against a tree, and now on this side, now on that, toughens his shoulders for battle. This is mock-heroic description once more, with its humor helped out by the metre, especially in the placing of the monosyllabic hero impressively at the end of the line:

ipse ruit dentesque Sabellicus exacuit sus.

So Lucretius[1] had placed this word, and so Ovid[2] after
Virgil, but in a context of undoubted seriousness. Virgil
innovates, with daring, by fitting it to burlesque. This
noticed, we are prepared for another touch of humor in
the sudden introduction of the young man's passion just
at this point. It is the same unpitying love that lights
the fire in his bones. Aye, though the sea is tossed with
storms in the dead of a pitch-dark night, and the portal
of heaven thunders over him, and the waves burst roaring on the rocks, neither thought of his luckless parents
can deter him, nor the reflection that his rashness is
sheer cruelty; for it will bring both him and his beloved
to their deaths. Surely the young man, if Leander by a
typical example, shows as little sense in love as stallion
or Sabellian boar. And how about lynxes, continues the
poet, and the fierce tribe of wolves and dogs? What of
the mad battles waged by peaceful stags? These actions
all are blind, and yet nothing is blinder than the rage of
mares in love. Venus has specially inspired them, ever
since the time when the mares of Potniae, whom their
master Glaucus would not allow to breed, set teeth in
him and tore him limb from limb. Impelled by love,
mares cross the plains of Troy and the sounding stream
of Ascanius, climb mountains, and swim lakes. The
moment that the flame is caught by their greedy marrow, especially in the spring-time, when their bones take
heat again, they all face the west wind, standing on high

[1] V, 25.   [2] *Met.*, VIII, 359.

hills, snuff the light breezes, and, wonder of wonders, pregnant without wedlock by that wind, they flee over rocks and crags and levels of low valleys, not to the land of Eurus and the rising sun, nor towards Boreas, nor to the place whence black Auster saddens heaven with his chill rain, but straight to the fructifying west. The galloping mares have an accompaniment of galloping verses, especially the skilful line,

> saxa per et scopulos et depressas convalles,

where we seem to see first the bounding and clattering over high, rocky ground, and then an unimpeded letting out of legs along the level plain. That is alone the time when shepherds can gather the sticky juice that rightly called "mare's madness," oozes from the groin — baneful mess, that evil stepdames mingle with herbs and poisonous incantations. (242–283.)

A passage like the above, on the lusts of beasts, including the youth, on the mad flight of pregnant mares, and the gathering of the foul hippomanes, shows that the pure Virgil does not, like a pseudo-classicist, shy at unpleasant topics, but can turn most unpromising material into poetry. He had learned this art as early as the writing of the Sixth Eclogue, in which he makes pathos of the story of Pasiphaë. It is a token of his audacity — a greater audacity than our lewd moderns show, since they are merely writing out their minds.

But irreparable time is flying, the poet continues, while I dwell on this and that, through sheer devotion to

my theme. Enough for the larger herds. The task remaining is to drive our woolly and shaggy goats afield.
This means toil, my hearty farmer-folk; and it also
means reward. Nor am I unaware of the battle before
me as I essay to adorn a homely topic —

angustis hunc addere rebus honorem.

But the sweet love of Parnassus hurries me along the
desert heights. It is a joy to go where none before has
worn a path to Castalia. So then, worshipful Pales, now
is the time to call aloud in a lofty strain. (284–294.)

The lofty strain pertains to sheep and goats, and the
poet has just warned us that more mock-heroic is to
come. He takes his stand in a dignified position, and,
using the formulae of the law, issues a series of edicts,
like a praetor. The first is to give your sheep plentiful
fodder in comfortable stalls till summer returns with its
abundant leaves. Strew the hard ground with wisps of
straw and fern, lest the cold ice harm the gentle flock
and afflict them with mange or shameful gout. Passing to the goats, the poet requires that they have good
supply of leafy arbutus and fresh water, and that their
pens be faced away from the wind and towards the
sunny south when chilly Aquarius is sprinkling the close
of the year. Yes, your goats need just as much attention; their profit is no less, even though one can sell
at extravagant prices Milesian fleeces dyed in Tyrian
purple. For your energy will result in more numerous
offspring and a fine flow of milk; the more the milk-

pails have foamed at one draining of the udders, the more will the glad streams flow when next the teats are squeezed.

Further, your Cinyphian goats — for the farmer in this epic account must of course have the best of breeds — may be shorn of their bristly beards, which make excellent cloaks appreciated in camp and by the poor sailors out at sea. The beasts will find their fodder in the high glades of Arcady, in prickly brambles and briars that love the steeps. They will not forget home-coming time; they return with all their number, and scarce can get their udders over the threshold. And as they need but little human care, you will take the greater pains to protect them from ice and snowy winds, and joyfully bring them fodder, and not keep the hay-mow barred the winter through. This is not the moment for rustic exasperation; let the feeding of the goats be one of the pleasures of life; do it joyfully. Of course goats would make a mess in a hay-mow, but, for all that, don't keep it locked up all the time; let the poor goat in — once in a while. (295-321.)

So much for winter. When the glad summer, at the call of Zephyr, summons both flocks to woods and fields, let us with the morning star fare to the cool meadows, while the day is young and the grass shines, and the animals can find their beloved dew on the tender pasturage. Then when the thirsty hour of ten has come, and plaintive cicadas burst the thickets with song, I bid you take the flock to wells or ponds, or to give them a drink from water that runs in oaken troughs, and at mid-day to seek some shady valley, where a mighty oak of Jove spreads boughs of antique strength or a dark grove of ilex lies in its sacred shade. Then water them again, and feed till sundown, when the cool Vesper tempers the air, the dewy moon refreshes the glades, and the shores ring with the kingfisher and the thickets with the finch. Even without the aid of two echoes of the *Bucolics*,[1] this passage would transport the reader into the atmosphere of pastoral, where nature is fused with everlasting impulses and every oak under which the shepherd reposes is divine. (322–338.)

We pass to another pastoral scene, a description of the shepherds of Libya, that land of tents, where housetops are rare. Night and day through the long months the flock feeds and makes for the desert, with no lodging-place in prospect, out into the stretching plain. For the African herder carries all his belongings with him, — house and hearth and tools and Spartan dog and Cretan quiver, — just like the brave Roman soldier, who trudges on his way beneath his ungodly pack, and before the foe dreams it has pitched camp and formed before him in line of battle. There is a touch of humorous exaltation in this description. The Libyan really, as the ancient commentator observed, was armed with a lance,

---

[1] L. 326: et ros in tenera pecori gratissimus herba (cf. *Ecl.*, VIII, 15). L. 328: et cantu querulae rumpent arbusta cicadae (cf. *Ecl.*, II, 13 and also *Copa*, 27).

not with "Cretan" bow and arrows; and his dog was probably an Aethiopian mongrel rather than a Spartan hound. (341–348.)

Far different is the life of the Scythian shepherd on the bank of Lake Maeotis, where mad Danube whirls its tawny sands and Mount Rhodope stretches back under the very Pole. There they keep the herds tight in their pens; for no grass is in the fields or leaves on the trees, but mounds of snow and ice make nature level, buried full seven ells under its mass. Winter everywhere — winter and the blasts of Caurus, breathing cold. The sun never pierces the pale shadows of the mist, either when his chariot climbs the heights of heaven or when it drops into the glowing waters of the sea. Crusts of ice form suddenly on the running streams; the broad cart can turn its iron-bound wheels on the same way which before was cut by the sharp keel. Bronze vessels crack; clothes stiffen as you put them on; the liquid wine is cut with hatchets; pools turn into solid ice; and bristling icicles harden on unkempt beards. Nor is the snow less intense; the air is full of it; cattle die, enveloped in an icy shroud, and troops of deer grow torpid under the strange impediment that buries them all but their horns. Virgil may never have felt a northern winter, but his imagination is equal to describing it!

While the beasts of the forest are imprisoned in the snow, the hunters catch them, not with a pack of hounds, or toils, or the scare of crimson feather, but as the animals vainly push their breasts against the confronting hill of snow they butcher them at close quarters and with a joyful shout carry them home. Not much real sport in this hunting, any more than in the style of hunt that Lord Orrery, translator of the younger Pliny, indignantly called poaching. Once home to their dug-outs with the game, they make merry underground, pitching whole elm trees on the blazing hearth. They spend the night in revelry, and gleefully imitate a bowl of wine with yeast and sour sorbs; the beverage thus unenthusiastically described may perhaps have been beer. Such is the existence that men lead in the Hyperborean land under the north star, a race anarchical, buffeted by the arctic wind, and clad in bristling hides. (349–383.)

The reader may have expected before this that a set-piece would vary the georgic material thus far presented. His attention has been diverted by epic similes and descriptions, and by bits of mock-heroic; and it is now directed to a set-piece of an unusual sort. The matter is all germane, as it pertains to the life of shepherds. We first have an account, for which there is a practical justification, of how the shepherd should treat his flock in summer; the description grows naturally out of the preceding passage, which relates to the care of the flock in winter. But the duties of this summer day are given in such musical verses and with such pastoral charm that the setting of the picture is Arcadian rather

than Italian; or, better, the scene is the same Arcadian
Italy that delights the reader of the *Eclogues*, and to
which the quoted verses have called us back. This passage on an Italian pastoral day is the central picture of
a triptych, worthily consecrated to the altar of goddess
Pales. On either side, contrasting with it and with each
other, stand two other pictures, one a pastoral of the
parching south, the other a pastoral of the frozen north;
they remind one of the little scenes of summer and
winter that form an amoebaean pair in the Seventh Eclogue. Thus the whole coloring of this tripartite scene is
pastoral; and it thus, without ceasing to be relevant,
skilfully varies the atmosphere.

A word on the proper sorts of fodder. If the farmer
wants good wool, he must steer clear of brushwood, burs,
and briars. On the other hand, do not give your sheep
too luxurious pasturage, if you would grow the whitest
and the softest fleece. Choose only the whitest animals.
If your ram, white as his body is, have a black tongue,
away with him, for his offspring will have a spotted
fleece; look round in the broad field for another sire of
the flock. There is a charm in pure white wool. Pan, the
god of Arcady, if we may believe the fable, courted the
Moon with a present of snowy wool, and tricked her to
follow him into the dense woods, nor did she disdain his
call. This is one of the less-known amours of the Moon,
a curious and pathologic variant of the story of Endymion; Servius quotes the whole tale from Nicander, and

asks, "Who but a Greek could tell a thing like that?"[1]
Virgil dares to suggest, as in the Sixth Eclogue he dared
to describe, a myth in itself abnormal and revolting, but
in such a way as to leave the glamour and cast aside the
horror and the dross.

If you are more interested in milk than in wool, then
select a pasture thick with clover and lotus. There is not
much of the latter in Italy, but for clover one thinks of
the gay fields of *sula* in Sicily and of the extraordinary
goats of that happy island. And feed them yourself —
ipse manu! Bring salted grass to their pens. That will
give them an appetite for water, and thus fill their
udders, and likewise add a fine little salty flavor to the
milk. It is also a good plan to keep the new-born kids
from their mothers and put iron muzzles on their little
snouts. The milk that you get during the day is churned
at night; that which is milked at twilight is carried to
town in baskets at daybreak; or else the cheese is salted
and set by for use in winter. In verses of incomparable
brevity and "reticence," Virgil describes two milkings,
morning and evening, two kinds of cheese, one for immediate use and one for storing, and two destinations,
home and market. (384–403.)

Do not neglect your dogs. Feed your fleet Spartans
and bold Molossians on rich whey. With them to guard
you, you need never fear an attack on your pens by

[1] On l. 391: *huius opinionis auctor est Nicander: nec poterat esse nisi Graecus.*

nightly thief or prowling wolf or the never-to-be-con-
quered brigand of Spain. The last-named is an adver-
sary that the Italian farmer would apparently have no
special reason to apprehend, but, again, you never can
tell. The Spaniards, Servius[1] tells us, held the record for
robberies, and the Cantabrians kept the Romans busy
both when this poem was written and later. Your dog,
further, is indispensable for the hunt. He will track
the wild asses, or hares or roes; and he will bring the
boar to bay in his woodland slough, and with loud barking will drive the stag from the high hills into your nets.
Again this is not altogether an Italian hunt; for the wild
ass one must fare considerably far afield, to Africa or
Asia. (404–413.)

The care of animals, no less than that of plants, must
reckon with the pests. To drive out snakes, burn in the
pens fragrant cedar or the obnoxious galbanum. For
often a viper will hide there from the light, or a cobra,
fond of creeping up under the eaves and scattering its
poison on the herd. Take rocks and sticks, shepherd,
and as he rears his threatening head with hissing tongue,
down with him! Now in his flight, he plunges his timid
head deep in the earth. Cut him in two, and watch his
central coils relax, while his last fold drags in tardy
curves. Then there is that evil snake of the Calabrian
glades, with breast erect and scaly back and spotted

[1] See the comment (from Donatus) on l. 408: *de Hispanis ... quorum in
latrociniis fama praeponderat.*

belly. While streams are running clear and the fields are moist with the damp of spring and the rains of summer, he dwells by the pools and river-banks, saucily filling his black maw with fishes and with prattling frogs. But when the swamp dries up and the land cracks with the heat, he leaps out on the parched earth, and rolling his flaming eyes, fierce from thirst and scared by the heat, he rages over the fields. That is no time to pluck the fruit of gentle slumber under the open sky or to lie in the grass on a wooded ridge, when new-gleaming in his youthful strength, abandoning his eggs or his young brood at home, he glides along, towering to the sun and flashing his three-forked tongue. (414–439.)

Here, too, is an almost epic creature. The description begins, as epic descriptions often do, with an initial *est* in the verse and the hero at the end —

> est etiam ille malus Calabris in saltibus anguis.

There is a fine bit of humor — not found in the passage of Nicander that Virgil, in his way, used as raw material for a creation — in the picture of the talkative frogs insisting on having the last word as they slide into the belly of the snake. There is the sunshine of Italy in that line on a nap in the grass —

> ne mihi tum molles sub divo carpere somnos, —

that recalls Böcklin's painting of an Italian boy sleeping face upward under a cloudless sky. And there is movement, climax, and an awful dignity in the close of the description, that one will search for vainly in the verses of Nicander. The passage is a kind of companion-piece to that on the battle of the bulls.

We are now to consider the inevitable diseases that afflict the herds; we must know their causes and their symptoms. Servius remarks soberly [1] that Virgil in the following account deserts the "legitimate order" of treatment; for one would naturally speak first of the cause of a disease, then of its symptoms, and finally of its cure; we shall see the reason before long for our poet's transgression. He begins, at least, with causes. Your sheep will be subject to scab if they are drenched to the quick with a chill shower or chilled with wintry cold, or if patches of sweat are not washed away at shearing-time, or if a cut from a briar gives a chance for septic poisoning. That is why the master of the flock gives the beasts a good bath in sweet water and why the ram is ducked in a whirlpool and floated down the stream. Or they treat the shorn flesh with olive-lees, mixed with scum of silver and native sulphur, pitch of Mount Ida and oily wax, sea-leeks, rank hellebore, and black bitumen; surely such a prescription ought to work some effect! But the most present help in time of trouble is to put the knife to the ulcer. The wound festers and thrives if hidden, while the shepherd fails to lay on the healing hand and sits by, praying the gods to make it better. No Christian Science for the Virgilian farmer! He un-

[1] On l. 440.

derstands that Heaven helps those who help themselves.

Perhaps the malady may penetrate to the very bones
of the animals, and rave there with a burning fever. In
that case, it is well to open a throbbing vein of blood in
the foot, in the manner of the nomad Scythian, who in
his far northern plain drinks milk congealed with horse's
blood. It is not a pleasant beverage to contemplate —
fully as barbarous as beer — but the Scythian can at
least inform us that an animal's blood may be drawn
without destroying his life. (440–463.)

When you observe a sheep resort too often to the comfortable shade, or crop listlessly the tips of grass-blades,
or follow the last in line, or, as it pastures, lie down right
in the field, or take its lonely way home late at night,
then out with the knife; nip the disease in the bud, lest
contagion infect the entire herd. For not so thickly blow
the gusts in a wintry storm as pests descend upon the
flock. They seize not single beasts alone, but pounce on
whole camps of them — your hope, your herd, all their
race from its beginning:

spemque gregemque simul cunctamque ab origine gentem.

The impressive and swift-moving line does justice to the
suddenness and the completeness of the disease.

For an awful example, one has only to visit the Alpine
hill-forts of Noricum by the meadows of Timavus, and
mark, all these years after the calamity, the desert
realms of shepherds and the glade vacant far and wide;

the spot is not far distant from the scene of a more dreadful pest that fell on men, not beasts, in the late war, at Caporetto. A cloud of pestilence, says the poet, arose, catching infection from the air, and glowed with the heat of autumn. It doomed to death the tribes of cattle and the beasts of the woods; it poisoned the lakes and the pastures with disease. Nor was the mode of death direct, but when the fiery thirst drove through the veins and shrivelled the limbs a watery humor would begin to flow, and bit by bit absorb the crumbling and infected bones. Often at the very moment of the sacred rite, while the victim at the altar was being wreathed with the snowy fillet, he would drop dead, if the ministrant did not speed his task. If the animal were slain, then the altar did not blaze as the fibres were put on the fire, nor could the seer give answer to consultations, and the knives laid to the throat were scarce stained with the blood, which discolored but the surface of the sand in a meagre stream. (464-493.)

Virgil's purpose in deviating from a "normal" account is now clear; his description, climactic as ever, has led up, not to the remedy, but to a gruesome picture of the disease, in rivalry of the famous scene with which Lucretius ended his poem. On the way, we must not miss the minor challenge presented in the above passage. It recalls Lucretius's description of the ox slaughtered at the altar, a scene that he informs with both pathos and indignation; the murder of the dumb victim, no less

than the sacrifice of Iphigenia, is one of those crimes
committed in Religion's name —

tantum religio potuit suadere malorum.

Virgil's scene has its pathos and its horror, but the
horror comes not from outraged human justice, but
from wounded piety. There is no questioning of the
righteousness of the sacrifice; the awfulness of the death
is its occurrence at the most solemn moment of the
divine rite. Still, in all its horror, it is accepted; there is
no doubling of fists at the gods or sneers at their help-
lessness to save their very shrines. For all the calamity,
we are still with the poet in a world of simple faith and
rustic piety.

In the glad fields, young steers would drop in death,
or give up their sweet spirits in the full stalls. Dogs were
seized with madness, and sickening swine were racked
with coughing in their cluttered throats. The race-
horse stumbles at his tasks, forgetting to pasture and
forgetting his victories. He turns from streams, and
often paws the earth; his ears droop; he is covered with
a fitful sweat — aye, like the cold sweat of death; his
skin is parched and rough to the touch. These are the
earlier symptoms. As the disease hardens, his eyes
gleam; he fetches deep breaths and intermittent groans;
his groins are racked with hiccups; black gore flows from
his nostrils and his rough tongue fills his clotted jaw. It
helped to force open his mouth and pour in wine through
a horn; at least, that seemed the only remedy from

death. But soon it proved the animals' destruction; for they gleamed with a new fire and at the very moment of death's feebleness — O Heaven, save the righteous from such madness and visit it on our foes! — they tore asunder their very limbs and champed them with bared teeth. (494-514.)

The ox, too, smoking under the cruel plough, would fall, and vomit foamy blood, and heave his last groans. The sad ploughman unyokes the other steer, downcast at his brother's lot, and leaves the plough set in the unfinished work. No shades of deep groves, no waving meadows, can rouse his spirit, nor the brook flowing clear as amber over the rocks and down through the plain; but his flanks relax, his eyes droop in stupor, and, bending with his weight, his neck sinks slowly to the earth —

ad terramque fluit devexo pondere cervix.

What is the use of his toil and his good deeds? What boots it to have turned up the heavy earth with the plough? He never knew the harm of Massic potions or a round of feasts. His food was leaves and the simple grass; his bowls were fountains and the racing streams; and no anxiety disturbed his wholesome slumbers. Here again, in reminiscence of Lucretius's scene, is a chance for pathos, which Virgil takes, and a chance for defiance of an impious Heaven, which he declines. Instead, he adds a tribute to religion. Then it was, he declares, that when oxen failed for the rites of Juno they harnessed bisons to drag her sacred chariot. It may be that Virgil has here woven an anecdote from Herodotus into his Italian story, but that is of no moment. Wherever it came from, it is a symbol of reverence; the plague with all its dreadfulness endures but a day, while the worship of the gods lives on. (515-533.)

Left to till the fields with their own strength, men could but scratch them with the hoe, failing the good furrow of the plough, and dig in the seed with their nails; and with straining necks they would drag the creaking wagons over the high hills. But no wolf laid ambush against the folds, or prowled about the flocks at night; a care more serious kept him at home. The timid deer wandered among the dogs near the house. The boundless sea cast up all its creatures like shipwrecked bodies on the outer strand. Seals fled into the rivers — strange abodes for them; the viper looked vainly for shelter in his winding lairs; and a vain defence to the startled water-snake were his bristling scales. The very air was not safe for the birds; falling headlong, they would leave their spirits in the lofty clouds:

praecipites alta vitam sub nube relinquunt.

A change of fodder helped not; the remedies they sought worked harm; the masters of medicine left the field — Chiron the scion of Philyra, and Amythaon's own off-spring Melampus:

Phillyrides Chiron Amythaoniusque Melampus.

Lucretius ridiculed the impotency of medical science in the face of the overwhelming evil; it muttered in tacit timidity, as he puts it:

mussabat tacito medicina timore.[1]

Virgil cannot repeat the satire in quite the same way, but his is altogether a match. The stately epic names have the value of the appended letters of our professional degrees; a real plague is but guess-work even to the Professor of Pestilential Pathology. As human aid fails, Hell mixes in this chaos. Pallid Tisiphone, let loose from Stygian darkness, drives Disease and Fear before her into the light and lifts her greedy head higher and higher day by day. The bleating of the flocks and the bellowing of the herds come from the parched river-beds and the prostrate hills. The Fury piles her victims in heaps and loads the very stalls with putrefying corpses, till men learn to cover them with earth or stow them in pits. For their hides were of no use, nor could their flesh be disinfected with water or fire. None could shear the fleece that was rotted with disease and filth, or, if shearing, hand the putrid mass to the loom. Or if it were spun, and one donned the awful garment, burning pustules and dirty sweat covered his stinking limbs, and he tarried not long ere his body caught the plague of the accursed fire.

[1] VI, 1179.

II

The construction of this remarkable book is highly novel. It begins with an introduction of epic substance, in which, to our surprise, Virgil flings a new challenge; he promises to compete with Ennius and Homer himself in a new epic on a greater hero than theirs. The remainder of the book is not, like the first two books, diversified by set-pieces at regular intervals with long and formal passages of epic or reflective poetry at the end; it is all georgic. The topics are arranged in pairs — first horses and cattle, then sheep and goats. No word of description is wasted; by the help of his "reticent" method, Virgil can merge his subjects, speaking of one and leaving us to infer that he means both. In the middle of the book, the georgic flavor is varied with a new sort of set-piece, a pastoral triptych, which has the spirit of a different kind of poetry and the distinction of separate pictures. But the material, after all, is strictly georgic, much nearer to farm life, certainly, than the horrors of war or the triumphs of engineering or the birthday of the world which are sung in the set passages of the earlier books. All these have their justification; they are harmonized with the theme. Virgil's art in the present book takes precisely the opposite path. He starts with georgic material and moulds this in such a way that it gives the same effect of lift and relief that comes from the insertion of matter more obviously diverse; verily he knows how to have his cake and eat it

too. He further varies the prevailing tone with approaches to the Homeric simile and substitutes for it —
as though he were already whetting his steel for Ennius
and Homer. There are also the touches of mock-heroic,
with the poet's characteristic restraint and humor.
Humor is not often mentioned as one of Virgil's traits,
but it is profoundly a part of his nature. To most of us,
who have clots of chill blood about the heart, this humor
is not immediately obvious. But it comes by slow revelation, ever improving in flavor, like one of Virgil's
wines,

> That mild Lagean, which can gather strength
> To test the legs, one day, and tie the tongue.

Virgil's method of seeking diversity not apart from
his theme but in the midst of it is most brilliantly exhibited in the closing passage. The subject is strictly
georgic, and yet the episode is so striking that it has the
value of the formal endings of the earlier books. And it
contains another challenge to Lucretius, this time to the
poet's art. Nothing could exceed the grim and sombre
imagination with which Lucretius has made poetry of
Thucydides's account of the plague at Athens. It forms
a startling but terrifically appropriate close of the work
— the most awful indictment of the *dii falsi e bugiardi*
that one could well devise. The story as Lucretius gives
it is chaotic; there is something in it to justify the
ancient tale of his madness, as preserved by St. Jerome,
or at least to suggest that his spirit, like that of Pascal,

hovered sometimes on the borderland between genius and insanity. He ends his poem with a picture hardly to be surpassed in imaginative awfulness — funeral trains racing to be the first to bury their polluted dead, and battling with one another for the right of way. But again there is no leading up to the final scene. Horrors are piled up promiscuously, like the bodies of the dead in the temples. It were rash to improve on Lucretius's telling of the story; his way is a law unto itself. But Virgil takes similar material and treats it in his own fashion, with his mastery of delicate climax. We begin with the sense of the awfulness of the disaster, which somehow, though of long ago, still reigns in the abandoned fields. Its scope, which took in the very sky, next impresses us, and its mysterious strength, which could crumble the very bones. Then comes a pious shiver at the thought that not even the holy rites of religion stayed its progress. Science is useless; the powers of Hell are loose. The husbandman himself, if he attempt, too frugally, to utilize the bodies of his animals, falls a victim to the pest. There is a special sort of climax in the closing details, which Virgil noted in Lucretius,[1] and which with a fresh application of his "reticent" manner he reserves for his final stroke. There is horror in this account, the tragic thrill of pity and fear. No pathetic fallacy is allowed to intrude. Plants and trees shed no tears at the universal woe. Virgil, as we have seen, can

[1] VI, 1109-1207.

make of the pathetic fallacy poetry that has no touch of tawdry sentimentality; but this is not the place for it here; the poet intensifies the calamity by remaining true to nature; the grass grows joyously as before. In this epithet, *laetae herbae*, and in others, like *plena stabula*, *victor equus*, Virgil displays another of his preëminent virtues, contrast, which he here gains, in the manner that we have seen illustrated before, by the repetition in this dismal setting of a phrase or epithet taken from a previous passage of the opposite tone. But the strength of this daring attempt at rivalry is the careful application of climax, the economy of effort, wherewith Virgil makes amends for his less Titanic genius. We are invited to compare supreme power with supreme art.

CHAPTER IX

THE HUMAN BEES AND THE STORY OF ORPHEUS
A CHALLENGE TO HOMER

I

THE FOURTH BOOK

THE dark colorings of the story of the plague pass away as we turn to the Fourth Book. Here we are in clear sunlight again. It is the same contrast that Lucretius contrived between books, when he ends one with the picture of the world sinking to its grave and begins the next with the praise of Epicurus, the light of whose truths has put the shades of ignorance to flight —

E tenebris tantis tam clarum extollere lumen.

Milton shows the same art in the invocation to light at the beginning of the Third Book of *Paradise Lost*, after the dismal blackness of Hell in which the scene of the Second Book is laid.

The Fourth Book of the *Georgics* will tell of the heavenly gift of honey dripping from the skies, and of the bees who gather it. Read this chapter too, Maecenas; it will give you a wondrous spectacle of little things. My song is of great-souled leaders, and a whole nation's customs, energies, peoples, and wars. Great labor in a tiny field, but not tiny the glory of it, for one whom the evil fates do not impede and whom Apollo when invoked will heed. (1–7.)

This introduction, in contrast to those of the First and the Third Books, is as tiny as the subject. It is even briefer than that of the Second Book, and yet manages to pack into seven lines both the address to Maecenas and the invocation of the deity, whereas in the Second Book the former is postponed until the theme has been more elaborately stated. Here both the compass and the character of the theme are suggested most briefly and most completely. We are to hear how heaven makes the gift of honey to man and to learn the whole history of the bees. Further, it will be an epic description —

admiranda tibi levium spectacula rerum.

Bees may be small actors, but their doings will make the reader open his eyes. The god invoked is Apollo. Apollo was once a shepherd, though not of his own free choice, and as a shepherd he was invoked in the preceding book. As he never, to our knowledge, kept bees or patronized the bee-keeper, we shall have to read the present book to see why he is invited to preside over it.

First of all, the husbandman must pick out a fitting abode for his bees, well sheltered from the wind; for they find it a nuisance when home-coming with a heavy load, since it drives them away from the door. Do not have sheep or goats too near to trample their flowers, or a straying heifer to knock the dew off the grass. Mottled lizards should not congregate near the hives, or bee-

eaters, or Procne of the bloody breast. For these all are
foes; they will pounce on the little creatures in mid-flight
and carry them home, sweet morsels for their ruthless
nestlings. Have springs near by, and mossy pools, or a
thin stream slipping through the grass. A palm may be
their vestibule or a great wild-olive shade their house.
For then, when their kings lead out the swarm in their
own spring-time, and the young tribe, let loose from the
hive, begin their play, the neighboring bank may invite
them as the day turns hot, and the tree extend its leafy
hospitality to them. Whether you have pond or stream,
throw willows crosswise and hurl in mighty stones, that
they may have many a bridge on which to stand and
spread their wings to the summer sun, if perchance the
blast of Eurus sprinkle them where they rest, or duck
them headlong in Neptune's pools. Round about the
hive plant cassia and far-fragrant thyme and heavy-
scented savory, and let beds of violets drink the refreshing spring. (8–32.)

The poet is fulfilling his promise of exalting the theme.
He has turned it into a delicate mock-heroic. The tremendous stream of Neptune bridged by willows is two
or three fingers deep, and the *grandia saxa* that serve for
stepping-stones are called by Varro *lapilli*.[1] But this is
the world of the bees, not our world. We must adjust
the focus of our glass, and view the universe in Lillipu-
tian terms. As the vine looked up ambitiously to the

[1] *Res Rusticae*, III, 16.

tiptops of the elms that we can pat, so to the bee the
gentle breath of wind that knocks him into the stream-
let is the veritable blast of Eurus.

The hive, whether constructed of bark or plaited osier,
should have a narrow entrance; otherwise the entering
cold will congeal the honey and heat will melt it. The
bees understand this, and hence stop up the breathing
holes of their houses with wax, and plaster the rims with
pollen, or lay by for this use the glue they have gathered,
more sticky than bird-lime or Phrygian pitch. Fame has
it, too, and perhaps rightly, that they sometimes cherish
their hearth-gods in a dugout underground, or a hollow
in pumice-rock, or the cavity of a rotted tree. Despite
all their care, you can help make them comfortable by
smearing their creviced chambers with smooth mud, and
giving that a thin coating of leaves. And allow no yew-
trees near the hives, or let them smell burnt crabs —
from which the Italian farmer made a manure — or
dwell too near a rank and noisome marsh, or rocks that
make a ringing echo. Whatever modern naturalists may
say, there is no doubt that Virgil's bees were sensitive to
sounds and smells. They still are epic bees; the poet
speaks of their known habits with the cautious phrase,
si vera est fama, that is traditionally appropriate in the
announcement of some myth too majestic for human
credence. (33–50.)

Now for the way to get them into the hive that you
have built. When the golden sun has driven winter un-

derground and in the light of summer rolled back the covering of the skies, the bees at once fare to the woodland glades, reap their harvest in the gay flowers, and lightly skim the streams. Glad with some sweet mysterious joy, they hasten to make snug dwellings for their young, artfully fashion the new wax, and form the clinging honey. So when you see a swarm of them desert their cavity and swim the liquid summer toward the sky, or drive in a dark cloud before the wind, then mark you; they are on the hunt for a home by flowing water and protecting boughs. Scatter about the perfumes I prescribe, bruised balm and the plebeian honey-wort, and raise a din by striking the Great Mother's cymbals. They will settle of themselves on the scented restingplace, and of themselves will retreat into the inmost cells. Just one touch in this description suggests by the repetition of the phrase

nescio qua dulcedine laetae

that these bees, for all their epic acts and their instant reverence of the rites of Mother Cybele, are perhaps, after all, creatures of instinct and not reason, like the birds that unconsciously prophesy changes of atmosphere.[1] (51–66.)

If the bees go forth for battle, — for there is often discord between rival kings, — you can detect in advance the temper of the rabble and the quivering imminence of war; for laggards are stirred by the hoarse brazen

---

[1] L. 56. Cf. I, 412: nescio qua praeter solitum dulcedine laeti.

notes of Mars; yes, a sound is heard like the staccato tones of the trumpet. They gather in excitement, brandish the flashing targes of their wings, sharpen their stings with their beaks, get their war-legs on, and form in masses about the king, — yes, at the royal head-quarters, — and call loudly for the foe. And so, when they get a cloudless day of spring and open fields of air, they sally forth from the gates; they meet in conflict; there is a roar in the high air; they mingle in a mighty mass and fall headlong. Hail is not thicker, nor the rain of nuts that tumble from the shaken oak. The kings themselves, told by the lustrous insignia on their wings, flash in the thick of the fight, and bear valiant spirits in their tiny breasts —

> ingentes animos angusto in pectore versant.

Both armies fight stubbornly to the bitter end, when a crushing victory forces these or those to turn and run in flight. And yet this world-war is not eternal. As Blackmore translates the closing couplet,

> These outbreaks of the soul — this awful riot —
> Toss up a pinch of dust and all is quiet.[1] (67–87.)

The mock-heroic of the bees, the spirit of which has been obvious before, reaches its culmination in this delightful battle. It is one of the most skilful mock-heroics ever written, with its nice description, amused sympathy, and humorous adaptation of the habits of

---

[1] Ll. 86 f.: Hi motus animorum atque haec certamina tanta
pulveris exigui iactu compressa quiescunt.

bees to human conditions. One of the happiest touches is the comparison of the cloud of falling warriors to a storm of acorns under a shaken oak — a belittling comparison for the majesty of mankind, but not if we compromise our dignity and with the poet look on the world with the eyes of bees, to whom a cannonading of acorns would amount to a cataclysm. Into the zoölogical truth of the narrative we need not inquire. In Maeterlinck's phrase, it is one of those *erreurs charmantes* of which the ancient lore of bee-craft is full; the real equivalent may have been the killing of the males, which Maeterlinck describes with a delicious and Virgilian humor. But humanly speaking, Virgil's account is a *vérité charmante*. As often in the mock-heroic and in the beast-fable, there is an undercurrent of satire at our own expense. We see humanity in the patriotic commoners shouting for war, in the gallant armies each fighting to the last ditch for the right, and in the easy termination of our high moral emprises by the intervention of some natural force — a snowstorm, let us say, that puts the mightiest cannon out of commission. None of this moral is forced. It is crude, perhaps, even to call attention to it; yet it none the less flavors the story. It is a reading of human passions not less remarkable than that in the immortal Gulliver, and not less acute because indirectly set forth with gentleness of spirit. It is a delicate and unusual type of satire.

After the combat is over, take your armies back, and

inflict the death penalty on the defeated king; show no mercy; he will only be a nuisance. Let his better reign in his stead. And always pick your bees. There are two kinds: one is fair of feature, and resplendent with golden scales; the other is rough and unkempt, and indolently drags about a spacious paunch —

latamque trahit inglorius alvum.

Kill the brute! Like the monarchs are their subjects. One sort is foul and frowzy, like a traveller when he emerges from the deep dust of the road and spits the dirt out of his parched lips; the other gleams and glitters, its body evenly marked with flashing drops of gold. That is the better breed. From its work in due season you will strain sweet honey, and not so sweet as it is liquid, and potent to subdue the harshness of unmellowed wine. (88–102.)

When your swarms fly aimlessly in the sky and spurn their hives and leave them cold, you must divert their flighty spirits from the vain pastime of war. It is a simple matter; just clip the wings of their king. When he falters, not one of them will venture on the highway of battle or break camp. Get their minds off fighting by the lure of saffron-fragrant gardens, under the protection of the wooden sickle of that custodian of thieves and birds, the Hellespontiac Priapus. A scarecrow may not seem just the subject for epic, but here he is. A wooden sickle will not do much cutting, but it is majestic as a symbol. The humble god has a whole couplet to himself, in which his name is given a Homeric construction,[1] is accompanied by a stately epithet, and is revealed with imposing effect at the very end of the climax:

> et custos furum atque avium cum falce saligna
> Hellespontiaci servet tutela Priapi.

Considerable art and no little humor went into the building of these two lines.

The farmer should also bring thyme in his own hands and tine from the high hills and set them about the hives. Let him wear a callous on his hands with honest toil, and himself transplant the fruitful slips, and water them with a kindly shower. (103–115.)

The thought of gardens almost lures the poet beyond the bounds of his subject. Flower-beds are only an incident in the life of a busy farmer, but did time and space allow, account should be given of the care of gardens, how one grows the twice-bearing roses of Paestum, the watercress that loves its streams, the parsley on the bank, and the melon,[2] winding through the grass, and growing to a belly — the comfortable $\tau\epsilon\lambda os$ of its existence. The daffodil, too, shaking its late-flowering locks and taking — in antiquity — the winds of December with its beauty; the stalk of the twining acanthus; shimmering ivy; and the myrtles of the beach — such is the poet's garden, if not the farmer's, with its flowers and its vegetables. It takes his memory back to the days that

---

[1] *Tutela Priapi* is like ἱερὴ ἲs Τηλεμάχοιο.

[2] That *cucumis* means a watermelon and not a cucumber I have set forth in my book *In Quest of Virgil's Birthplace*, p. 21. See above, p. 58.

he spent by the turrets of Tarentum, where perhaps, as we saw,[1] Virgil wrote some of his eclogues, down by the tawny tilth that the black Galaesus waters. It was there that he knew that retired pirate from Corycus, who owned a few acres of abandoned soil, not arable or meet for grazing or suited for the vine. For all that, he made this scrubby brushland teem with vegetables, fringing them with lilies and vervain and poppies of the slender stalk. In his fancy, he rivalled the wealth of kings, and returning home in the late evening he would load his table with an unbought feast. He was first in spring to pluck the rose, first in autumn to gather pears; and when sad winter split the rocks with cold and bridled the courses of the streams with ice, he was already clipping the tresses of the nodding hyacinth, and chiding the late summer and the loitering breezes of Zephyr. Whether or not the ancient *hyacinthus* is our larkspur or gladiolus or iris, the old pirate managed, perhaps with the help of a cold-frame, to anticipate the seasons. That is why he was also the first bee-keeper of the place, raising a numerous swarm and straining the foaming honey from his hives. His bees fed on his groves of linden and pine. His fruit trees were covered with blossoms in the spring, and every blossom set in fruit. He could transplant whole rows of well-grown elms, and the hardened pear tree, sloes bearing their plums, and the plane tree with leafy branches, beneath which revellers were already

[1] See above, p. 75.

passing drinks. These are miracles in the art of transplanting, but miracles happen in Virgil's Golden Age, prompted by the intelligence and hard work of a pirate.[1]

We are sorry that this account of gardens is only a *praeteritio*. It is a new device for contriving a set-piece, like Cicero's regrets that he has not time to mention so-and-so, whom he sufficiently describes while expressing his regrets. While Virgil is presenting his apologies, the reader is diverted into a delightful and well-nigh magical scene, in which a garden contains all earthly possessions and the triumphs of the gardener exceed those of kings. But all this is structurally a part of the apology, and dependent, further, on the main issue. For what else was the outcome of the Corycian's gardening but that it won prizes for his bees? (116–148.)

Yes, it is all profitable and germane, but the poet, bound by the jealous limits of his space, must pass on, leaving the story of the garden for others to tell. Columella, in the reign of Claudius, took this remark as a personal suggestion; coming in his work on agriculture to the topic of gardens, he devoted his Tenth Book to it, and what is more, in honor of Virgil, put it into verse; there is honor in the idea, whatever we think of the execution, which is not half bad. Servius, somewhat unkindly, in view of Columella's feat, declares that Virgil is prophesying the work of Gargilius Martialis.

[1] Servius, on line 127, tells us that Pompey had settled some of the captured Cilician pirates in Calabria.

Our next topic is the nature of the bees, their remarkable qualities that Jove himself gave them in return for their kindly deeds to him when, attracted by the clashing of the cymbals of the Curetes, they fed the little king of heaven with honey in the Cretan cave. As their reward, bees were permitted to establish the only successful communism among mortals. They own their children in common, have common abodes, regulate their existence by mighty laws, and alone have a fixed and definite hearth and home. Looking ahead to the coming winter, they spend summer in toil, and set aside their acquisitions for the common store. They practise division of labor. Some watch over the provender; some have their assigned work afield; some stay within bounds and lay the tears of narcissus and sticky gum as the first structure of the hive, the dome, from which they suspend the clinging wax. Others take out the young hopefuls for exercise; others pack the pure honey and stuff the cells with liquid nectar. Some are set on guard at the gates, and keep a look-out for clouds and showers; or they relieve the incomers of their burdens, or, forming in line, drive off the drones, lazy incumbrances, from the hives. Hot glows the work; the fragrant honey breathes the smell of thyme. As when the Cyclops rush the work of turning ductile masses into thunderbolts, and some catch the air in bull's-hide bellows and puff it out again; some dip the hissing metal in the trough; some make old Aetna groan as they lay on at the anvil, and alternately raising their mighty arms in time ply the steel with gripping tongs — even so, if we may compare small things with great, the Cecropian bees, with their inborn passion for acquiring, tend to their several tasks. (149–178.)

If the reader should doubt the heroic character of what bees can do, this epic simile, in tone much like that which in the Third Book ends the story of the battle of the bulls, should convince him; for the present passage is set over into the story of the making of the hero's arms in the Eighth Book of the *Aeneid* with hardly the change of a word. Similarly, a phrase in the line preceding — *fervet opus* — appears again in the account of Dido's building of Carthage. These obvious signs of epic help to justify, if we need justification, the distinguished epithet of "Cecropian" applied to bees. Honey of Hymettus is traditionally sweet and is excellent today, but "Cecropian" more than describes its merits; the word connects the lineage of bees with the most illustrious community that history had known.

But to return to the allotment of labors, the aged are detailed to hold the town and fortify the hives and construct their artful dwellings. The younger come back late at night, their legs loaded with thyme; they feed where they will on arbutus and grey-green willows, cassia and glowing saffron, rich linden and rust-red hyacinth. They all rest from their toil together, and together work. In the morning, they rush out from the gates; no loitering. Again, when the evening star bids them to have done at last with pasturing afield, they make for home, and then they take refreshment. They raise a din, and buzz round the enclosure and the thresholds of their hives — it is their brief hour for gossip. After they have settled in their chambers, silence falls and deepens into night; their tired bodies sink into their own repose; sleep is their own, for they have won it:

> post ubi iam thalamis se composuere siletur
> in noctem fessosque sopor suus occupat artus.

The sleepy sibilants in these untranslatable verses describe, better than words, the drowsy bees as they buzz into slumber, the sound gradually dying down, with one small buzz at the end.

In their excursions, they do not venture far from home when a shower is impending or a breeze stirs in the sky, but they make safe trips for water near the shelter of their city walls, and often carry little stones, like the ballast of boats that toss in the swirling tide, and thus they keep their balance in the aëry clouds. This, I fear, is another of the *erreurs charmantes*, unless the bees of Mantua were more resourceful than those of more sluggish regions and times. (178–196.)

Small wonder that the gifted creatures like the bees should come into the world in no ordinary way. They do not indulge in sexual intercourse or waste their strength in love, or suffer the pangs of childbirth, but the mother-bees find their young amid the flowers and sweet herbs, and take them home in their mouths. The mothers alone furnish the king and the brood of young Romans, and support their palace and their waxen realms. This delightful legend, which perhaps was invented for the edification of the youngest bees, is responsible for a charming bit, no longer possible, of the liturgy of the Catholic Church. For in ancient times, much to St. Jerome's indignation, at the ceremony of the Blessing of the Wax on Holy Saturday, Virgil's story of the creation of the bees was read in a lesson, their virgin birth making it an especially appropriate selection.[1]

Bees do not live for long; their life is too intense. Often as they wander amid the hard rocks they bruise their wings and willingly lay down their lives beneath their load. But though their term on earth is slight, — it does not reach beyond the seventh year, — the race lasts forever; a family preserves its fortunate estate for many years, and counts back from grandsire to grandsire. (197–209.)

Their king is a despot absolute. Egypt or mighty Lydia or the Parthian tribes or Median Hydaspes have not his peer. While the king lives, they are all of one mind; if they lose him, they abandon their allegiance, tear down their piles of honey and demolish their latticed combs. He is the mainstay of their toil; he is their general admiration. They stand about him in a dense

---

[1] See H. M. Bannister, *Journal of Theological Studies*, XI (1909), 43 ff. Some of the scenes on the *Exultet* Rolls are Virgilian in character. See E. Bertaux, *L'Art dans l'Italie Méridionale*, I (1904), 216, 221, plates X, XI.

roaring mass and press him tightly and carry him on their shoulders; for him they bare their bodies in the fight, and court a glorious death in action. (210–218.)

This is a curious case of myth-making. When Virgil puts fresh meaning into the story of Hylas or of Pasiphaë, he is aware that he resuscitates them from fable. But though he imparts the same life to the tiny hero of the present story, he happened not to know that the King Bee has no existence whatsoever.

With these tokens in view, some maintain that the bees are endowed with a portion of the divine spirit and a draft of heaven itself; that God goeth through all the lands and the tracts of the sea and the deep places of the sky; that flocks and herds and men, and every tribe of beasts, derive their birth and slender thread of life from him, since to him all things return and are resolved again into his essence; hence there is no room for death, but rather they fly living to the starry hosts and mount the heights of heaven. (219–227.)

The philosophy at which the poet hints is pantheism, reconcilable with an atomic materialism, which the phrase *resoluta referri* might imply, in the matter of personal immortality. There is no chance for this in either system; the whole is immortal but not the parts, combined in temporary union. They fly living to the immortal stars, in a universe alive, but are absorbed again into its being. The passage is no proof that the poet accepted the immortality of the soul.

Further, as we have just seen, the language harbors two warring philosophies. They agree in barring out personal immortality; they differ in the nature of the universal force that they assume. The system of Epicurus, to which Virgil had devoted much study, starts with a primal rain of atoms, leaving fortuitous concourse and the physical forces thereby engendered to account for the universe as it manifests itself to us. The rival system accepts a deity, whose presence, immanent everywhere, explains the display of intelligence in creatures like the bee. In the First Book of the poem, Virgil held to a purely naturalistic view: the feathered prophets of weather are not really intelligent, but merely respond, like barometers, to atmospheric changes; nor does he, in the present passage, suggest a recantation. But the spiritual theory is most akin to his temperament. Virgil was born to religion, and to religion he returned. The Fourth Eclogue is built up entirely on the idea of a divine spirit that moves in all things, —

terrasque tractusque maris caelumque profundum, —

a verse that he instinctively repeats in the present passage; and deity is further manifested in a new-born Messiah, the heir of Jove. Hence, though the poet declares no creed, he reveals his state of mind; his desires are impelled in two directions. He subscribes at once to *Felix qui potuit*, but he at once adds *Fortunatus et ille*. There is no confusion of thought here, as some have found, but rather the clear recognition of opposed appeals, between which the poet does not decide.

When the time comes to approach the bees' holy of holies and broach their treasured honey, first cleanse your face and rinse your mouth and hold before you a torch of penetrating smoke; for unpleasant odors irritate them, while the fumes of smoke will stun or drive them away. Twice a year is the harvest gathered, once when the Pleiad Taygete turns her glorious face to earth and spurns the ocean at her feet—her rising is in May—and again when she sadly descends from heaven to the wintry waves — her setting is in November. If you manage to stir up the bees in this process, remember that their anger knows no bounds. If offended, they inspire their bites with poison; fastening on a vein, they leave their unseen stings there, and put their whole souls into the stab. In case you fear harsh winter and, pitying their crushed souls and broken fortunes, decide to spare their stores, there at least is no objection to fumigating the cells with thyme and cutting them back. For the comb may be eaten by the unseen newt or by beds of light-hating beetles, or by the drone, who sits scot-free at another's feast. Or a nasty hornet starts an unfair fight, or moths, that evil tribe; or the spider, Minerva's detestation, hangs her yielding web athwart the doors. But be not too considerate. The more you exhaust your bees' possessions, the more resolutely will they all turn to and repair the ruins of their fallen race, filling the cells and weaving their granaries with flowers. (228–250.)

Life has inflicted on the bees the troubles to which
humanity is heir; they languish with melancholy ail-
ments, which you can tell by no uncertain signs. The
sick at once change color; their faces are squalid and
haggard. The bodies of those bereft of the light of day
they carry from their houses in a sad funeral train, and
perform the last rites; they hang with feet linked together from the lintel, or all stay within closed doors,
sluggish from hunger and listless from the stiffening
cold. Then a deeper hum is heard, and long-drawn
whisperings, even as chill Auster when it murmurs
in the woods, or the strident sea when it tosses its
refluent waves, or the consuming fire when it seethes
in a closed furnace. At such a time, burn the strong-
smelling galbanum and insert honey in pipes of reed,
rousing the bees' tired spirits and spurring them to their
wonted food. It will also help to mix the flavors of
pounded gall-nuts and dry rose-leaves, or must, thick-
ened over a hot fire, or raisin-clusters of the psithian
vine, Cecropian thyme and heavy-perfumed centaury.
There is a flower in the meadows, — aster, the farmers
call it, — a plant not hard to find, for a whole forest of it
grows from a single sod; it is golden at its centre, but the
petals that surround it in profusion are dark violet, with
crimson shimmering through. Often it adorns the altars
of the gods in twined festoons; its taste is bitter to the
lips; shepherds gather it in the close-cropped vales and
by the winding stream of Mella. Steep its roots in

scented wine, and set it for the bees' food in basketfuls before the doors. (251–280.)

If all your stock should suddenly give out, and if you have no resource for getting you a new one, it is time to recount the discovery of the Arcadian keeper, and how bees may be generated by the festering blood of a slaughtered bullock. I will set forth the whole story somewhat fully, says the poet, going back to its very beginning. For where the fortunate race of Alexander's town Canopus dwell by the inundating Nile, and travel their own fields in gayly painted skiffs, and have the quivered Persians for near neighbors, and where the river spreads into diverse mouths and fertilizes verdant Egypt with black sand, descending from the far lands of the swarthy Indians — all this region rests its hope of safety on the art that now will be described.

First they choose a small place, confined to suit the special need. This they enclose with a small tiled roof and cramped walls, making four windows, letting in the light obliquely from the four quarters of the compass. Then they look for a calf whose horns are of the second year. They stop its nostrils and its mouth for all its struggling, and beat it to death, mashing its flesh within the unbroken hide. Thus they leave it in the cabin, laying boughs beneath its ribs, with fresh thyme and cassia. The deed is done when the zephyr first stirs the sea, before the meadows are bright with new colors and the twittering swallow hangs her nest beneath the eaves. Meanwhile the warm liquid seethes in the soft-ened bones and creatures may be seen in wondrous wise, first destitute of feet, but soon equipped with buzzing wings. They flock together and more and more essay the unsubstantial air, until they burst forth in a cloud, like rain downpouring from the summer clouds, or like the arrows sped from the twanging bow when the nimble Parthians start off a battle. (281–314.)

What god was it, Muses, that devised this art for us? Whence did this strange experience enter the goings of man? It was the shepherd Aristaeus, who, as the legend has it, fled from the vale of Tempe after the loss of his bees through some mysterious illness and sadly standing at the sacred spring of the river Peneus thus made com-plaint to the ocean nymph who bore him:

"Mother Cyrene, that dwellest at the bottom of the sea, why the vain boast of my divine parentage — if verily Apollo be my father — when fate thus scorns me? Where is thy love? What boots my hope of heaven? Even my crowning glory, triumph in the art of fruits and flocks, I must resign — and thou my mother! Come, then, uproot my thrifty woods with thine own hands, set fire to my stalk, burn my harvests, and ply the ruthless axe in my vineyards, if thou art so indifferent to my praise!" (315–332.)

This passage marks a turning-point in this book and an epoch in Virgil's poetry. It is the full fresh wind of epic that catches his sails and speeds him exultingly over the waters which he had only skirted before. It is the great surprise of the *Georgics*. And other surprises are in store.

The farmer-lad, whose extravagant reproaches, like those of Damon in Virgil's pastoral, are set forth with quiet humor, soon gains an answer from his goddess mother. She is sitting amid a bevy of water-nymphs in a chamber of the river's bed far below. They are spinning Milesian wool, the best variety on earth, but its color of crystal shows that it is good texture for creatures of the deep. The nymphs have, naturally, Grecian names, and what is more, they are Homeric —

Drymoque Xanthoque Ligeaque Phyllodoceque.

This is a daring challenge. Of a sudden we are transported into the fairy-world of the *Odyssey*. In its delicate charm and its delicate naughtiness, the scene is French. Clymene is telling the rest what Ovid called

the smartest scandal Heaven ever heard—

the tale of the loves of Mars and Venus caught in Vulcan's meshes. Anticipating Ovid again, she is rehearsing all the amours of the gods from Chaos down. Meanwhile the nymphs, like merry French housewives, ply their glassy needles without stint — no toil without gossip, no gossip without toil.

But the wailing of Aristaeus interrupts them. Arethusa rises to the surface and informs her sister Cyrene of his woe. He is bidden to join them, and down he comes

by a magical parting of the waters and looks wonder-
ingly at the vast caverns and the sounding groves and
the rushing of mighty waters. Is this merely the bed of
the river Peneus? Rather we have been mysteriously
transported to the floor of old Ocean, where are the
springs of the mighty rivers of earth — Phasis and
Lycus, Enipeus and Father Tiber, the little Anio along
with the giant Hypanis, Caicus of Mysia and Virgil's
king of streams, Eridanus —

> With visage of a bull and golden horns,
> Maddest of rivers to rush through teeming tilth
> Down to the wine-dark sea.

At last the youth reaches the grotto of the nymphs
with its hanging pumice, and Cyrene, knowing that his
woes are not beyond consoling, orders a banquet, after
proper washing of the hands and drying them on
smoothest napkins — both acts ordinarily impossible at
the bottom of the sea. The tables are loaded, the gob-
lets are filled, and the altars glow with fires of Araby —
smoking, that is, with incense. First a toast to old
Ocean, and a prayer to him, the father of the world —
their world, certainly — and to their sister nymphs, the
guardians of woods and streams. Vesta's hearth is
thrice sprinkled with nectar, and thrice the flames leap
and lick the roof. These must be magical, hyaline
flames — no, they are real, for the poet himself is a
magician and has made the impossible real. (333–383.)

The omen from Vesta is good. Cyrene can tell her son

the cure for his misfortune. He must visit Proteus, the infallible seer of the sea, taking him when he brings up his herd of seals from the waters to have his siesta in a secret spot. That is the time to put the fetters on him and hold fast! For he will turn into all shapes conceivable, — a bear, a tiger, a scaly snake, a lion, — or he will crackle into flames or slip into tenuous water. Hold him fast till he resumes his own form, and then he will tell you all. (384–414.)

Then Cyrene breathed from her body an ambrosial perfume that encompassed her son and gave his comely limbs a magical strength. Together they came to the hillside cave on the beach — known as a refuge for shipwrecked sailors — where Proteus was wont to take his naps, after barring the entrance with a huge rock. The nymph and her son hid in obscure corners. It was the hour of that tropic heat that scorches the dwellers of India. The blazing sun, halfway through his journey, was withering the grass and

> Parching the thirsty throats of hollow streams
> He turned their waters into steaming mud.

With a verse of sizzling sibilants —

> iam rapidus torreus sitientis Sirius Indos —

Virgil has pictured the hottest noon-hour on record. Proteus, thinking it high time for his siesta, mastered his seals, who came up from the brine shaking themselves like dogs after a bath. Careful shepherd of his flock, Proteus proceeds to tell his tale, when Aristaeus

with a shout has the manacles on him. The old man resorts to his metamorphosis, but at last admits defeat
and, glaring at the lad, champs his teeth and mutters his
grim oracle. (415–452.)

"It is no slight crime for which the wrath of heaven
seeks atonement. The punishment comes from Orpheus,
justly enraged at the loss of his Eurydice. For while she
was fleeing in hot haste from your amorous pursuit
along the stream, she saw not before her feet the huge
water-snake that guarded the stream in the grass."

That is the crime, and Proteus needs no further words
to make it plain. But he is a bard as well as a seer, and is
now aroused to song. He sings of the grief of Eurydice's
sister dryads, whose lamentations made the mountain-
tops ring. Aye, the mountain fortresses of Rhodope, the
high nest of the Pangaean mountain, the wilds of Thrace
and Scythia, Hebrus the great river, and Attic Orithyia,
all mourned for her. Her spouse consoled his broken
spirit with the music of his harp, singing of thee, dear
wife, thee on the solitary shore, thee when came the day
and thee when it departed. Aye, he made his way to the
gates of Hell, entered the gloom, and approached the
shades and their awful king with heart that no human
prayers can soften. His music stirred the shadowy
ghosts from the infernal depths, like thousands of birds
that hiding in the leaves of a tree are routed by evening
or a chill storm from the hills — matrons and men,
great-hearted heroes, boys and maidens unwed, youths

put on the pyre before their parents' eyes, all now imprisoned by muddy Cocytus and the dismal swamp and the nine circles of the Styx. (453–480.)

These lines are familiar to readers of the *Aeneid*. Virgil, after his wont, does not hesitate to repeat his best passages for a new purpose. The setting in the Sixth Book of the *Aeneid* is more sombre; here, though sombreness is not lacking, the aim is to suggest the countless numbers of the dead who gathered to hear Orpheus's song. Yes, it penetrated to the inmost abodes of Death, to Tantarus; the Furies with their serpent-locks were listening; Cerberus was agape, with all three mouths; and the wheel of Ixion stirred not in the wind.

Then had Orpheus triumphed by the power of song, and was leading the way for Eurydice to the upper air, when he forgot the terms imposed by Proserpine and, crazed with love, committed the transgression — pardonable, if Hell knew how to pardon — and looked back at her. Then was all his labor wasted, with the breaking of the tyrant's pact, and thrice sounded the crack of doom in the pools of Avernus.

> Ah, Orpheus, who has ruined me, and thee?
> What madness this? For back the cruel fates
> Call me, and sleep beclouds my swimming eyes.
> And now, farewell. Encompassed by the night
> I am borne on, and stretching out to thee
> My feeble hands, alas no longer thine —

She spoke, and vanished before his eyes, like smoke. He grasped the shadows vainly, and the ferryman of

Hell allowed him not to cross the stream again. Seven months he mourned by an aëry cliff near Strymon's river, pouring forth under the chill stars songs that calm tigers and draw the oaks to hear. Such does the nightingale sing, mourning her young whom the harsh ploughman has snatched from the nest. Such, we may add, sings the romantic lover in Propertius's elegies, fleeing like Orpheus from the haunts of men to the wilds of nature —

> Hyperborean fields of ice and snowy Don,
> And plains ne'er widowed of Rhipaean frost.

Unlike the Propertian lover, Orpheus had no thought of love, except for that which death could not sunder. That was enough for the women of Thrace. Orpheus had protracted his lament into a denunciation of womankind. Maddened by Bacchanalian rites, they tore him limb from limb and cast his head into the Hebrus. "Eurydice!" the lips still cried; "Eurydice!" as breath and life departed; and "Eurydice!" echoed the riverbanks, as the head floated on

> Down the swift Hebrus to the Lesbian shore. (481–527.)

This triple echo made its impression on Dante. At a moment of high pathos, when at the summit of Purgatory he takes leave of his master and good guide, he honors him with a threefold calling on his name:

> Ma Virgilio n'avea lasciati scemi
> Di sè, Virgilio dolcissimo patre,
> Virgilio a cui per mia salute die' mi.

Master of Virgil's reticent art, Dante states without words, to those who know the *Georgics*, that his grief at parting from Virgil was no less than that of Orpheus when Eurydice faded back into the shadows.

While Cyrene and her son are listening spellbound, old Proteus, choosing his moment, leaps with a splash into the sea. He has said too much and not enough. He has explained the need of atonement imposed on Aristaeus, for his involuntary sin that led to the death of Eurydice. The seer has charmed his hearers with the full tale of Orpheus and his tragic end, but he has not told Aristaeus how to replace his bees with another swarm. But the lad's mother knows. He must make sacrifice to the nymphs, Eurydice's playmates, and then, taking four bulls of form surpassing fair and as many heifers, whose necks have felt no yoke, offer them up at four altars of the goddesses and abandon the bodies in the leafy grove. At the dawn of the ninth day, after consecrating Lethaean poppies to the shade of Orpheus and sacrificing a black sheep, he must visit the grove again and by the slaughter of a heifer pay homage to Eurydice.

These directions are obeyed to the letter, and are repeated by the poet to the letter that there may be no flaw in the liturgy or its effect. Milton observes this propriety, not improbably in reminiscence of Virgil, in describing the penance paid by our primal parents after the transgression in Eden.[1]

---

[1] *Paradise Lost*, X, 1086 ff.

And then the miracle.

> They saw a sudden wonder, strange to tell,
> About the cattle's liquifying flesh —
> In all the belly and the broken ribs
> A humming swarm of bees; in giant clouds
> They trailed and on the tree-tops gathered dense,
> Or swung in clusters from the drooping boughs.

The poet's song of the farm is ended. He adds a little epilogue:

> These strains I sang about the care of fields
> And flocks, the while great Caesar thundered war
> By deep Euphrates and on willing lands
> Imposed the victor's laws and aimed his course
> Skyward. 'T was then that sweet Parthenope
> Nourished me, Virgil, basking indolent
> In lettered ease, who sang the shepherd's songs,
> Bold in my youth, and, Tityrus, sang thee
> Under the shelter of a spreading beech.

II

Virgil's *Georgics*, we have seen, is an intensely practical work. Ask Fairfax Harrison, who among other things is a practical farmer, and who, though he doubts that Virgil had much experience with the actual work of the farm, can "thank God that one of the greatest poems in any language contains as much as it does of a sound tradition of the practical side of his art." [1] Ask Donald Grant Mitchell, who, in those profitable "Wet Days at Edgewood," finds it "inconceivable that a man of his [Virgil's] intellectual address should have given so much

[1] *Roman Farm Management*, p. 14.

of literary toil to a work that was not in every essential fully up to the best practice of the day." [1] Ask M. Billiard, not a philologian but an agriculturalist, who in a recent work [2] on ancient agriculture as illustrated in Virgil's *Georgics* declares that this "chantre divin de la terre" is sprung from the same earth that he exalts and that his art is as closely conjoined to the matter of the poem as the skin of a fruit to its substance.[2] If I may add the testimony of a practical gardener on a very small scale, I myself astonished my better-informed wife, when first we started our own little garden, with bits of agricultural lore which came straight — though I did not tell her at the time — from Virgil's *Georgics*.

As, with Mr. Mitchell, we "slip along the dulcet lines" — for nothing can stop us if we once begin — we find nothing that does not bear on the poet's subject. He sings of rakes and harrows with an epic ease; he sings of the breeding of horses and the care of goats; he exults in the joy of hard labor in the dirty soil; he gets good and dirty; he does what, as we have seen, the dainty-handed Pope could never do — he flings manure about. And yet he does many other things. He sings of Caesar's death and the crime of civil war; he praises, and rebukes, the outlook of the man of science upon the world; Libya and Scythia are part of his scenery, and so are the dolorous realms of the shades whither Orpheus descends in

[1] P. 48.
[2] Raymond Billiard, *L'Agriculture dans l'Antiquité d'après les Géorgiques de Virgile* (Paris, 1928), p. 10.

his vain quest of Eurydice. Not all of this is helpful for the horny-handed tiller of an Italian farm. We have been tricked, as usual, with incongruities; the master magician has raised impossible growths from common soil. Some of us, like Mr. Conington, will protest against such practice. Politics, philosophy, and eschatology are not fit subjects for a georgic poem; it isn't done! The rest of us, if we are wise, will reply that it *is* done. We should not have believed it before; but here it is, before our eyes. The spirit of God has moved upon the waters.

It is beyond me to resume the diverse acts of magic in the *Georgics* whereby that which never should have been touched at all is made an indispensable part of the poet's design. One irregular extension of his proper boundaries we have noticed, though it is not observed, I venture to say, by ninety-nine out of a hundred, or a hundred out of a hundred, modern readers. It is Servius who pointed it out, with reference to the beginning of the Third Book. He remarks, as we saw,[1] that a prooemium was particularly in place at the beginning of this book, since it was virtually a new poem — pastoral rather than georgic. The modern reader imagines that the "georgic part" is not finished till the last line of Book Four. "Georgic" does mean, literally, "that which applies to the tillage of the soil," and in the last two books of the poem we pass from the soil to the animals of the farm

[1] See above, p. 268.

and to the most human of its insects, the bees. Thanks to Servius, we appreciate better than before the pastoral character of the invocation in the Third Book and certain delightful reminiscences in the later books that carry us back to the simple charm of the *Eclogues*. Such is the reappearance of the beloved Mincio —

Smooth-flowing Mincio crowned with vocal reeds —

in an elaboration of the very verse that had described the river in the *Eclogues*. Such also is that triple painting that describes the life of shepherds in three widely different regions. But these scenes,[1] of course, however alien, are cunningly adjusted to the larger design.

III

An even greater boldness is exhibited in the composi tion of the Fourth Book. Its matter is not more georgic, if we must use technical terms, than is that of the Third Book; it is "melissurgic," since it treats, from first to last, of the care of bees. In tone, from first to last, it is epic, the part between the brief introduction and the brief epilogue falling into two little epics, or epyllia. The former, the tale of the bees, is delicately mock-heroic in tone. Virgil's sense of humor is aroused mainly by the contrast between gigantic performances and tiny performers —

ingentis animos angusto in pectore versant.

[1] See above, pp. 291 f.

He expresses such humor, naturally, in mock-heroic. As a lad he wrote the poem on a gnat, and at various places in the first three books of the *Georgics* he paints in little touches of mock-heroic — in the Third Book he just manages to refrain from turning didactic narrative into a mock-epic of the goat. After these premonitions we are quite prepared for the story of the bees. And even there, mock-heroic is flavor and not substance; the poet is true to the purpose of his work.

With the story of Aristaeus, we pass to real epic. The latter part of the book may be lifted out of its context and printed as an epyllion, reminding us of the Sixty-fourth Poem of Catullus, in which, as here, one story is enclosed within another. How different it is from the youthful epyllia, *Culex* and *Ciris*! In its spirit, it challenges not Catullus but Homer. The gauntlet is thrown down at the line that I have called the turning-point of the book.[1] Virgil comes to his own at last and is ready for the fray. It is the *Odyssey* at which he aims. It is sometimes remarked — Servius said it first [2] — that the first half of the *Aeneid* is an *Odyssey* of travel and adventure, while the last half is an *Iliad* of war. This looks like a neat observation, but it is pertinent merely to the outline of Virgil's epic and the external events in the narrative. Otherwise there is little of the *Odyssey* there. Here we have it — the romance of adventure and the charm of fairyland set forth in music as different from that of

[1] L. 315.   [2] On *Aen.*, VII, 1.

Homer as the Roman temperament is different from the Greek.

One may defy the higher critic to point out any detail in the Fourth Book that is not germane. One might reason that Cyrene could have told the whole story to her boy, but the narrative gains in richness and impressiveness by the introduction of Proteus — and in veracity, as well, for Proteus is a seer. He pronounces authoritatively on the sin and Cyrene can tend to the rest. Similarly, she merely explains the ritual of the atonement and does not hint at the marvellous reward, the miracle of the creation of the bees that comes to the reverent youth as a glorious surprise and to the reader of the book as the swiftest of climax-capping *dénouements*. Again one is astounded at the magic with which heterogeneous elements are fused into a harmonious whole. As we contemplate the finished design it seems impossible to imagine that anything else had ever entered the poet's fancy, much less that the original ending of the poem had contained matter of quite a different sort.

It is Servius, again, who informs us — not as minutely as we should like — of a daring change that the poet had made in the composition of Book Four. It had ended, so Servius declares, with a panegyric of Virgil's beloved brother-poet Gallus, but Virgil had substituted for that the story of Orpheus and Eurydice after Gallus had incurred Augustus's displeasure and met his death.[1]

[1] On *Georg.*, IV, 1: sane sciendum, ut supra diximus, ultimam partem huius libri esse mutatam: nam laudes Galli habuit locus ille, qui nunc

Gallus had been the poet's most intimate friend, so far as we can judge — heart of his heart. But as governor of Egypt he had evidently been faithless to his trust. A side of his character was revealed that Virgil had little suspected before. Broken was the adoration of so many years, and the praise of Gallus was blotted out from the end of the poem.

Just how much of the original was occupied with the praise of Gallus has been variously estimated. Much of the story of Aristaeus would have been there, for the poet needed it to account for his explanation of the method of producing a new stock of bees. In fact, he tells us that he is going to give us this story.[1] There is an exuberance in the description of the Nile and its seven mouths quite different from the scorn that Juvenal levelled at Canopus.[2] The dwellers at Canopus are fortunate, declares our poet [3] — fortunate, we may guess, because they had Gallus for a ruler. We can do no better than follow Servius, who says explicitly that the panegyric of Gallus was replaced by the story of Orpheus.[4] Possibly the

Orphei continet fabulam, quae inserta est, postquam irato Augusto Gallus occisus est.

[1] Ll. 281–285.
[2] *Sat.*, XV, especially l. 46.   [3] L. 287.
[4] See the comment on *Georg.*, IV, 1, just quoted. It must be admitted that Servius in another comment on *Ecl.*, X, 1, declares that the panegyric of Gallus replaced the story of Aristaeus as well (fuit autem amicus Vergilii adeo, ut quartus georgicorum a medio usque ad finem eius laudes teneret: quas postea iubente Augusto in Aristaei fabulam commutavit). Confronted by the necessity of choosing between these two conflicting accounts, we may prefer that which the commentator wrote with the text of the *Georgics* before him.

panegyric was not quite so long, though no such conclusion may be deduced from the extent of the present
form. Exclusive of the epilogue, which pertains to the
whole poem, the length of Book IV is approximately
that of any of the first three books.[1]

It is unprofitable to speculate as to when the new episode was written. Certainly it was added after 26 B.C.,
the date of Gallus's suicide, but we are going outside of
our evidence in thinking with some scholars that the re-
vision was not accomplished until the very year when
Virgil died.[2] According to ancient testimony, the poet
spent three years on the *Bucolics*, seven on the *Georgics*,
and eleven on the *Aeneid*; the last two poems would on
this basis be assigned to the years 37–30 and 29–19 re-
spectively. This is a helpful statement, but it must not
be too rigorously applied. We must not divide Virgil's
activities into water-tight compartments and suppose
that so epic a passage as the story of Orpheus could not
have been written until the *Aeneid* was almost or nearly
completed. Some of the *Aeneid* had of course been
written by 26 B.C. In fact, some may well have been
written while the poet was at work on the first edition
of the *Georgics*. Such speculations are of little pith. We
may rest with our feeling that, whenever it was done,
the art of the Fourth Book in its present form is perfect.

[1] It contains 558 lines. The contents of the first three books are respec-
tively 514, 542, and 566 lines.
[2] See the note of H. E. Butler, *The Sixth Book of the Aeneid* (Oxford,
1920), on ll. 305–312.

It is the hand of a magician that tore his finale to pieces and made it as good as new or better.

IV

The *Georgics* presents us with Virgil's philosophy of life expressed in his characteristic art. It is Hesiod's philosophy of Justice, Industry, Contentment, and Religion adjusted to the needs of the hour and reflected through country life. The life of science makes the first appeal to cultivated young Romans of the day; Lucretius cannot be passed over in silence. But Virgil, as the *Ciris* showed, had not been a dogmatic Epicurean, and he never was to be. He did not shrink from a scientific reading of the universe, and in fact delicately illustrates it in this poem. At the same time, he feels instinctively that after one has explained each crevice of the universe, in Lucretius's triumphant way, something lies unexplained after all. The triumph is its own defeat; the countryman with his faith in Pan and Silvanus and the sister nymphs is truer to the heart of reality. Virgil is no dogmatist in religion any more than in science, but his temperament with its mystic yearnings is written here, and is written more clearly still in the Platonic vision of the Sixth Book of the *Aeneid*.

We saw, also, that the longing for universal peace, the need of the hour, inspires the epic passage at the end of the First Book of the poem. This is the background of his thought, as the desire to free mankind from superstition is the ethical force in Lucretius's philosophy. It is no idle fancy, no merely negative programme, this dream of peace. In the epilogue of the poem, the hero reappears. Caesar Octavian not only has won his victories, but will proceed to dictate law to nations that are anxious for his sway. It is a programme of reconstruction and the hint of a prophecy that the poet will later return to this theme. For the moment it is that same pastoral Virgil, taking his ease in Naples, who once in the hardihood of youth sang of Tityrus, piping in the shade of a spreading beech.

The scenery in the *Georgics* is more definite than that in the *Bucolics*. It is more obviously national. The poet sings a song of Ascra through Roman towns and glorifies the soil, the vines, the lakes, the hills, of Italy. There are glimpses of little Mantua, his birthplace, again. But Virgil can never be wholly realistic. Actualities are given a larger and imaginary setting. Spanish brigands and wild asses appear on the scene, and the farmer's bees are raised to epic dignity by the epithet Cecropian. Moreover, the echoes of the *Bucolics* recall the pastoral Arcadia of these poems, and though the *Georgics* in general are anything but Arcadian, the country scenes at the end of the Second Book, while still Italian, are made to recall that earliest Italy when Saturn ruled in the Golden Age.

Tennyson's picture of the wistful Virgil brooding over "the doubtful doom of human kind" is true to only one aspect of his nature, or rather, even, only to certain of his moods. There is little of this mood in the *Georgics*. It is a poem of joy, joy in life and in work and in simplicity. Plunge lustily into work, and the simplest relaxations become the most extravagant of pleasures. Sweet is pleasure after toil.

The music of the verse heightens the reader's joy. In a most delicate appreciation of the poem published in an out-of-the-way place by an *anima candida* who knew and loved Virgil well,[1] the work is likened to a symphony with four movements and various themes plainly set forth and harmoniously interwoven.

The art of the poem is a constant joy. The diverse feats of the magician were not lightly tossed off. Many hours of the golden day were spent in their perfection. Our poet is a builder.

> He knew
> Himself to sing and *build* the lofty rhyme.

Magician though he is, he does not wave temples into being from the air. Stone upon stone, column by column, tile by tile, till the temple is done. Its architecture, though Roman, reflects the noble simplicity of the age of Pericles. The high levels have been regained after the complexities and sentimentalities of Hellenistic art. The poet's story of Orpheus and Eurydice may be written around the beautiful relief in the Naples Mu-

[1] Charles Pomeroy Parker, "Virgil and the Country Pastor," *The Churchman*, April 18, 1914, reprinted in *The Classical Weekly*, VIII (1914), 74–77 (with Virgil's name spelled as Parker did not spell it).

seum; the spirit of Virgil's art is that of the unknown sculptor of the fifth century.

Virgil wrote the *Georgics* at Naples, and great is our joy if we can read or reread the poem in the place where it was written. Virgil was basking in the studies of ignoble ease as he wrote. So says he, though in reality he was as busy as any of his bees, making his honey through all the golden day. It is that blessed *otium* of the ancients, that rest of the body though not the mind, that brings the quintessence of leisure. *Felices nimium* who, *Georgics* in hand, can stretch out under the shelter of a spreading palm in the garden of Naples, or on her heights, or on the beach at Sorrento, wherever imagination may place the altar of the poet's vow to Venus, and, slipping along the dulcet lines, look out from time to time over the blue waters toward opal Capri and the glistening stretches beyond.

CHAPTER X

VIRGIL AND THE DRAMA

THE modern reader wonders often at the almost entire lack of a drama in the Augustan Age, and regrets especially the loss of Ovid's *Medea* and the *Thyestes* of Varius, the only plays of the period, apparently, which impressed later critics as significant. Horace, in a passage which suggests an anti-Philistine diatribe of Matthew Arnold, bewails the depraved taste of the popular audience, which resorted to the theatre to glut the eye, not feed the understanding.[1] It may be, indeed, that the plays of Ovid and Varius gained no general hearing at all, but were closet dramas, presented to a circle of friends at the *recitatio*. Yet admitting that the stage, as such, played no part in the development of contemporary poetry, the poets themselves, deeply versed in the different types of Greek literature, could not fail to draw inspiration from the Greek drama, whatever their opinion of the early dramatic art of their own countrymen. Horace's *Art of Poetry* is concerned mainly with the drama. Several of his odes are essentially dramatic in plan, and his Cleopatra, though treated in the compass of a single lyric, deserves a place with the heroines of tragedy. In his *Satires*, Horace turns to a form of

[1] *Epist.*, II, 1, 177–213.

poetry which possibly was dramatic in origin, as the ancient critics believed, and at least suggested an affinity with the Greek old comedy in the boisterous gibes and racy wit of Horace's master Lucilius. Horace's relation to him is much like that of Menander to

Eupolis atque Cratinus Aristophanesque poetae.

He mildens and refines; he makes the villain not less but more uncomfortable by illuminating his folly instead of cudgelling his guilt. He summons against his victims, not the Furies, but those comic imps who in our generation owe chief allegiance to George Meredith. Surely the comic spirit comes to its own in the *Satires* of Horace; and supreme tragedy we find in Virgil.

There are some, but not many, indications in Virgil's early poems of dramatic genius. His main impulse from the first was to epic. Like Milton, he cherished from his youth a great plan, destined to ultimate fulfilment after various attempts and changes of purpose. There was the epic on the Alban Kings of Rome, on which the youthful Maro toiled

Ere warning Phoebus touched his trembling ears;

there was the inappropriate Inferno of the *Culex* with its dull galaxy of Greek and Roman heroes, — at which Phoebus must have tweaked the trembling ears right vigorously. These and other failures discouraged Virgil for the time, — *offensus materia*, as his ancient biographer remarks, — but they led to the triumphs of his

Bucolics. In the *Bucolics*, as we have seen, we find a literary creation; pastoral they are in essence, *molles atque faceti*, and favored of the Muses who love the countryside, as Horace said of them, but breathing, too, a new spirit, the unmistakable touch of epic feeling, forever present in the undercurrent of Virgil's thought. Some touches of the dramatic are noticeable in Virgil's eclogues. Eclogues contain dramatic elements in the dialogue and in the amoebaean debate, and in the time of the Renaissance they developed into actual drama. The rustics of Theocritus are often intensely individual and might appear without a change in a mime. In Virgil there is enough dramatization to tempt a recent writer to wish that Virgil had undertaken *fabulae togatae*, plays on a Roman theme.[1] Further, the tragic problem had early engaged the poet's mind, as passages in the *Culex*, the *Ciris*, and the *Bucolics* suggest.[2] In the *Georgics*, there is tragic as well as epic feeling in the story of Orpheus and Eurydice, and while he was occupied with the *Aeneid*, Virgil was meditating profoundly on the problem of Greek tragedy.

I

Few readers can have failed to remark that the Fourth Aeneid is essentially a tragedy, and in the Renaissance playwrights of various nationalities sought, with indifferent success, to reset the story into actual dramatic

[1] See J. Hubaux, *Le Réalisme dans les Bucoliques de Virgile* (see above, p. 79), p. 95, and above, pp. 127 f.
[2] See above, pp. 38, 48, 125.

form. Such tragedies bear Dido's name as title and present her fate as the chief, if not the sole, dramatic motive. To most of these writers Aeneas is a shadowy figure, and, by implication, a villain, the more detestable for his *pietas*. Jodelle has more than the ordinary sympathy for Aeneas, yet the chorus condemns the hero in the end. To Marlowe, he is almost a comic villain. Such criticism was, of course, nothing new, and it did not cease with the Renaissance. Imogen's dreadful indictment that

> True honest men being heard, like false Aeneas,
> Were in his time thought false

echoes the sentiment more mildly expressed in a mediaeval lament of the repentant Aeneas,

> Non semper utile
> est diis credere —
> nam instigaverunt
> me te relinquere,[1]

and is typical, too, of much that has been written on the Fourth Aeneid in recent years. Mr. T. R. Glover remarks, in his *Studies in Virgil*:[2]

And yet in Dido's anguish it is written that the gods think more of seven hills beside a river than of human woe or of right and wrong. Here, then, our tragedy fails and is untrue. On the side of Dido it is true, vividly and transparently true.

---

[1] *Carmina Burana* (herausg. von J. A. Schmeller, Breslau, 1894), pp. 58 f.

[2] London, 1904, p. 190. In the second edition, called *Virgil* (New York, 1912), p. 206, the passage reads: "And yet Dido's anguish seems to suggest that the gods think more of seven hills beside a river than of human woe or of right and wrong. What are we to say?" What Mr. Glover proceeds to say could not be better put. There has been a notable change of sentiment — in the right direction, I believe — on the part of this eminent Virgilian.

Certainly the tragedy fails if the hero is a scoundrel in disguise,—if Aeneas is but another Theseus. The lament of an Ariadne, as in Catullus's beautiful poem, has room for intense pathos, but not for tragedy. The solution here is simple; the villain is punished, and the heroine is consoled. But punishment and consolation are unthinkable remedies for the *dénouement* of the Fourth Aeneid. The reason is that the deep emotions and high ideals of Aeneas are, no less than Dido's passion and suffering, a part of Virgil's tragedy.

One cannot understand the plot of the Fourth Aeneid apart from the books preceding. They are important not only for the main idea of the poem, but for the drama of the Fourth Book. In the First, the chief actors in this drama are presented. Dido, queenly and competent, yet ever the woman, immediately fascinates. Aeneas needs deeper study, but his character, once Virgil's meaning is grasped, is quite as clearly conceived. It is given in his address to his men at a moment of utter despair when, after the shipwreck, part of them have landed on a foreign shore.

Comrades, — aye, comrades, for no strangers are we ere this to hardship — O ye who have suffered harder woes, for these, too, heaven will ordain an end. Men, you have drawn near to Scylla's fury and her deeply echoing cliffs; you have risked, too, the Cyclops' stones. Call back your hearts and banish mournful fear. Haply, some day, this too will be pleasure to remember. Through diverse haps, through many a peril by the way, we push our course to Latium, where the Fates show us a resting-place secure; there, they decree, the realms of Troy shall rise again. Bear up, and keep yourselves for better days.

So spake his voice; sick with mighty cares, he wore hope on his face, and crushed the deep woe in his heart.

These are the words of a brave man of action who has encountered perils and knows sorrow, but who does not wear his feelings on his sleeve; his vision is set on the distant goal, which somehow he shall reach. Deep woe at heart, but mastery of emotion, supreme reserve and resolution — these are the fundamental traits of Aeneas's character. Virgil has taken a suggestion from the speech of Teucer in the splendid ode of Horace — if indeed that is the earlier poem — and both Dante and, following in his steps, Tennyson have, in the words which their hero Ulysses addresses to his disconsolate men, caught again the spirit of Virgil's lines and shown their understanding of his Aeneas. Virgil knew of a historical counterpart in the character of Julius Caesar, and he portrays his hero with the same masterly reserve with which the character of Julius Caesar is presented in Shakespeare.

Toward the end of the book, the plot of the drama is stated. When Aeneas and his attendant stand forth refulgent from the cloud, the effect upon Dido is immediate:

> obstupuit primo aspectu Sidonia Dido.

The artifice of Venus seems almost unnecessary; after it and before, the dramatic problem is revealed as Dido's passion and its relation to the hero's ideals. Following

an accepted device of the dramatist, Virgil does not proceed at once to the solution of the problem, but, now
that the reader's interest is aroused, interposes other
matter to lengthen the suspense. And yet Virgil's
Second Book, though deferring the dramatic problem, is
relevant to it. The purpose of the new narrative is to develop the character of the hero, as outlined in the First
Book. After the horror of the last night of Troy, where
Aeneas, despite the divine command of Hector, fought
desperately on till all was lost, after the weary voyages
and purposeless settlements dutifully undertaken in
obedience to an undefined and forever retreating ideal,
we read with new understanding the words of Aeneas's
speech, and see again in the hero a man of brave deeds
who encounters tragic calamity and — what is sometimes harder to bear — sickening deferment and the
jests of brute chance. For all this, the hero can crush the
deep woe of his heart, and hopefully push on to his goal.

But the moment of temptation is at hand, for Aeneas
and Dido both. A very natural temptation it is for
Aeneas, coming at the moment of extreme despair and
after so many attempts to raise the walls of a new Troy.
Might not the rising Carthage fulfil at once the oracle
and his dream? And for Dido the temptation is both
natural and fated. Before Aeneas half feels its presence,
she has yielded to her sister's entreaties, to the god's influence, and to her own heart. Sin, the poet believes, is
complete at the moment of decision; while Aeneas, like

the shepherd who hits a doe with a random shaft, is still "unaware," [1] she by mentally consenting has "given hope to her wavering heart, and loosed her chastity." This is the same *pudor* to which she has sworn sacred allegiance in the speech given not many lines before. To Dido, too, belongs the guilt of the act, when on the day of the hunt the lovers meet, and Juno and the elements sanction the union as best they may.

No more cares Dido for appearance or report; no more does she brood a secret love. She calls it wedlock, and cloaks with this name her sin.

Fame, that horrid monster of the feathered eyes, reports that Aeneas and Dido are wasting the long winter in riot, "heedless of their realms and bound by low desire." Thus whispers gossip, coloring basely the truth, but true to one part of it, for the poet himself speaks, a few lines later, of "lovers forgetful of their higher glory." Up to this point Virgil has betrayed by no word the feelings of Aeneas, but now we see that he, too, has yielded to passion and a change of purpose. He proceeds with what he may have thought his mission; he "founds towers and makes houses new," but wears meanwhile a cloak of Tyrian purple, the work of Dido's hands.

When the stern message comes from Jove,

Aeneas at the sight is dumb, his sense gone . . . he longs to flee away and leave that lovely land, overwhelmed at such a warning, such mandate from the gods.

[1] *Nescius* (IV, 72).

His first thought is, How shall he now approach the queen? What plea will win forgiveness and approval?[1] Aeneas orders his men to make ready in secret for sailing at a moment's notice.

He, meanwhile, since his good Dido knows it not, nor dreams such love could be dissevered, would ponder the best chance of approach, what the time for gentle speaking, what mode of action most auspicious.

Two possible inferences may be drawn from this passage. Perhaps this is a callous hero, or else a lay figure, a mere emblem of Roman destiny. But perhaps we may read in these lines what we have learned before of Aeneas. He is a man of deepest feeling, his passion has been intense, but in the face of such a revelation he masters himself in an instant. He sees his infidelity and in an instant resolves. Best to have done once for all with what was sin for them both. It cannot be a separation like that of Antony from Cleopatra, which

> so abides and flies,
> That thou, residing here, go'st yet with me,
> And I, hence fleeting, here remain with thee.

Nor can Dido stand, as Lorenzo thought of her,

> with a willow in her hand
> Upon the wild sea banks, and waft her love
> To come again to Carthage.

The parting must be brief and forever.

[1] This is the meaning of *ambire*, l. 283. The word is used of the politician who "solicits"; it is also used, as here, of the worshipper who implores. Some editors turn Virgil's tragedy into farce by translating literally, "get around."

Certain recent critics have claimed that we have no right to find pathos in the story of Dido; this, it is said, is an intrusion of modern romanticism which ancient feeling would not have tolerated.

Nor, though Virgil in his powerful picture of Dido's grief and despair . . . arouses our sympathy for the forsaken heroine, need we suppose that such was his intention, or such the effect upon Roman readers. For them and him Dido symbolized Carthage, as Aeneas symbolized Rome: and her fate, to Roman eyes, was only right, an echo of the old cry *Delenda est Carthago*.[1]

But ancient readers found pathos enough in similar narratives of Catullus and Ovid, and when Ovid assures us that the Fourth Aeneid was the most popular part of the poem[2] we are sure that, whatever the truth of this statement, the readers whom he has in mind did not go to the story of Dido for political allegory. Nor did the youthful Augustine shed tears for memories of the Punic Wars,[3] nor is this why Macrobius includes a lengthy treatment of this book under the rubric of *pathos*.[4] If the speech of Dido in which, *omnia tuta timens*, she reproaches Aeneas for his intended cruelty is not pathos, and intended pathos, then we had better look further for a definition of this term. She begins by reproaching him for his base resolve to steal away from her, heedless of their love, his pledges, and the cruel

---

[1] Papillon and Haigh, *P. Vergili Maronis Opera* (Oxford, 1892), II, 181. See below, p. 411.

[2] *Tristia*, II, 535.   [3] *Confessiones*, I, 21.

[4] *Saturnalia*, IV, 2, 2 *et al.*

death in store for her: by this she means that natural death by which the slighted lover dies — but the reader knows the terrible meaning of this tragic irony. But if Aeneas must go, why should he brave a wintry sea? Such action she calls cruel — cruel to her and to himself. Does he flee *her*? She implores him by her tears and his pledges, by their "wedlock just begun," to pity her and save her from the surrounding foes, who will pour in at his departure. For his sake she had consented to shame. "To whom dost thou leave me to die, my guest? Since this name alone is all that is left from that of husband." With a supreme appeal to the most sacred of human feelings, she laments that there will be no child to console her, no little Aeneas to bear his features and his name. "Then should I not seem utterly captive and forlorn." The Dido of Ovid's Seventh Heroid invokes a curse on her betrayer, in that he may have left her with child, doubling his legacy of cruelty and shame. This bit of Ovid's subtle characterization presents a prouder Dido, a scornful heroine; Virgil portrays for the moment a weak and loving woman.

Thus she spoke. He, at Jove's behest, bent firm his glance and, struggling, crushed the anguish in his heart.[1]

Obnixus curam sub corde premebat —

these words show that we have inferred aright the meaning of Aeneas's resolve when the warning comes. The very phrasing recalls that passage in the First Book in

[1] Ll. 331 f.

which his character was first presented — *premit altum corde dolorem;* we see again the man who deeply feels, but is strong to control. Conington renders *curam* by "great love,"[1] but Virgil has not yet spoken so plainly; with supreme skill he heightens his final impression by gradual explicitness and growing intensity.

Aeneas replies, as he says, briefly. Conington well observes that his speech is actually longer than that of Dido: "But the words come slowly and with effort, and bear no comparison to what the lover would have said had he given way to his emotions." He begins by acknowledging the justice of her appeal to his protection.

I never will deny, O queen, that thou has deserved of me a thousandfold more than thy words can ever utter, nor shall I be loth to bethink me of Elissa, so long as my memory lasts and breath inspires this frame.

Surely these are heartless words, if they express all that Aeneas feels — an almost condescending esteem instead of the passion on which the two had fed — but they are tragic words for him as well as for her, if they crush deep anguish of spirit. He answers in a word her charge of base desertion; he had not meant to steal away, but, as the reader has seen, prepared for instant departure after his last words with her. "Nor did I hold the bridegroom's torch before me, or enter into such a covenant." These are the most cruel words of all, because the plain truth. But cruelty is the only kindness if

---

[1] Of course *cura* may have an amatory meaning, but in the sense of "darling" — *mea maxima cura*, as Venus says to Cupid (*Aen.*, I, 678).

the separation must be at once and irrevocable — and it is demanded by the Fates. Aeneas has obeyed the will of heaven before against his own desire — else he never would have started on his weary quest; he would have built again the walls of his native Troy. But Italy, Italy — the words come ringing in like a motif in Wagner — is the predestined goal. "This is my love, and this my native land." And has she not a mission, too, a city to build? They both had been faithless to their ideals; may he not cherish an ideal as well as she? In visions of the night his father Anchises comes to reproach him; the sight of his boy Ascanius, whom he is robbing of his destiny, is a constant reproach. Now appears the messenger of the gods with a final command. So "cease to torture thee and me with thy complaints" — tears and sympathy are the cruel course now. "To Italy, not of my will, I follow on." These last words resume in brief compass the elements of the tragedy that confronts Aeneas: *Italiam* — his mission; *non sponte* — his love; *sequor* — his resolution.

Those who object to what they deem the impassiveness of Virgil's hero should note that Dido in her retort makes precisely the same charge. Rock-born he is, the nursling of tigers.

Had he a sigh for my weeping? Turned he his eyes to me? Did he yield and shed tears? Did he pity her that loved him?

Virgil, we see, was not blind to this opportunity. He might have evoked compassion from Aeneas at this moment — if he had chosen. And when Dido, kindling to the sense of her lover's ingratitude, scoffs, with just a touch of blasphemy, at his divine mission, when proudly she bids him go and exults at the doom that she, as minister of the Furies, will visit on him, when faint from such excess of feeling she is borne off by her attendants, Aeneas in anxiety for her [1] can hold back passion no longer.

But loyal Aeneas, though he would fain soften her grief with words of consolation and assuage her cares, deeply grieving, his whole heart upheaved with his great love, fulfils for all that the mandates of the gods and again repairs to his fleet.

Multa gemens magnoque animum labefactus amore — [2]

amor — passion: that is the word that Virgil has not spoken till now.

After Dido's final appeal — the messages sent by Anna — Virgil gathers up in one simile the impressions made thus far in an ascending scale. We have learned of the hero's amazement and his fixed resolve at the moment of the revelation — *obmutuit*. We have seen that his outer calmness disguised deep anguish — *curam sub corde premebat*. He has made virtual confession to Dido that love is the fee exacted by obedience — *Italiam non*

---

[1] Ll. 390 f.:

> multa metu cunctantem et multa parantem
> dicere.

Some editors again stage this scene for comedy, seeing in *metu* "the dread of arousing her *wrath* still further."

[2] L. 395. Ribbeck remarks that Parrhasins omitted this line *fortasse recte*, citing ll. 438 ff., 448 ff., and V, 5 — a curious array of proof.

sponte sequor. Finally the anguish that racks the heart is openly called love — *magnoque animum labefactus amore*. Allusive description and the gradual approach — these are methods characteristic of that peculiarly Virgilian quality, reticence, which is another name for artistic reserve.[1] It is perhaps the most fascinating and distinctive trait of Virgil's personality, one which his reader greets on page after page; it reveals in the written word the same impulse that prompted the shy poet to take refuge in the nearest doorway when passers-by pointed him out in the streets of Rome.[2]

After the last of Dido's messages, we are told:

He, for all that, is touched by no laments, nor is he pliant to hear her supplication. The Fates oppose: God shut the hero's steadfast ears. And even as an oak, mighty with years of strength, now here now there is tossed by the blasts of Alpine Boreas who struggles to uproot it — loud it creaks, and as its trunk is shaken, deep-piled leaves clutter the earth: the tree clings to the rocks, and as far as it stretches its crown into the higher air, as deep its roots toward Tartarus are stretching — even so the hero on this side and on that bears the blows of entreaty and knows anguish in his great heart. His will abides unshaken; and tears are showered in vain.

I believe with St. Augustine[3] and Servius[4] against many editors, from Heyne down, that these are the

---

[1] See above, p. 91.   [2] See above, p. 6.
[3] *De Civitate Dei*, IX, 4.
[4] On l. 444. The comment on l. 449 (from Donatus?) shows that the ancients were aware of the other explanation and that some indeed thought that there was an outpour of weeping on the part of all concerned: *quidam tamen "lacrimas inanes" vel Aeneae, vel Didonis, vel Annae, vel omnium accipiunt*. We may take Dido's tears for granted, but may wonder whether Anna could weep.

tears of Aeneas. They are the outward and visible sign of the inward and spiritual anguish just described —

> magno persentit pectore curas.

In this simile, the falling tears match the falling leaves, symbol of the storm that does not touch the substance; the comparison is exact in all its parts. There is a battle on, as St. Augustine, a master of psychology, set forth, between Aeneas's emotions and his will. But his will, the inner self of him, stands firm.

One more passage in Book Four gives indications of the hero's feelings — a passage susceptible of gross misinterpretation. After those liquid lines on the calm of night, brought in painful contrast with the anguish of the queen, it is said of Aeneas[1] that "he, in his high ship, determined, now, on going, was plucking the flower of sleep, all being now in readiness." *Carpebat somnos* — enjoying sleep to the full. Is this a sign of heartlessness? Rather, after the anguish of his own struggle and the pain of his sympathy with Dido's grief, he gains that peace which succeeds a bitter fight, and yields to his exhaustion when all has been done that he can do — *iam certus eundi, rebus iam rite paratis.*[2]

It would be easy to cite throughout the narrative of

---

[1] Ll. 554 f.

[2] Lucan has a similar situation at the beginning of his Third Book (ll. 4–9). Pompey, sailing away from his foes at Brundisium, *solus ab Hesperia non flexit lumina terra* until the last speck of land has passed from view — *dum dubios cernit vanescere montes.* Not till then *soporifero cesserunt languida somno membra ducis.* So, too, the sleep of Ariadne and of Andromeda as described by Propertius, I, 3, 1 ff. In fact, we are dealing here with a traditional theme in both literature and art.

the Fourth Book, and especially toward the end, the various bits of incident or description by which Virgil suggests that the external setting, the scenic adornment of the story, is that of the tragic stage. These would mean little, however, if the inner plot were not of the essence of tragedy, as it is. It brings us face to face with the ancient motive of the Greek drama, the conflict between human will and an overruling fate; tragedy lies in the bitter conclusion that the actors, though pursuing right paths, or at least natural paths, run into disaster despite themselves. They cannot be villains, else tragedy would not purge the emotions with the thrill of pity and fear, but merely awaken indignation and suggest an obvious remedy — the flaying of the villain. Not that the actors need be spotless. We demand not a triumphant, logical insight into every move in the ethics of the narrative, but pity and fear at the calamities of creatures like ourselves, involved in the play of forces passing their control. Both Aeneas and Dido are faithless to an absolute moral standard and their own ideals, but their infidelity is so natural — almost irresistible — that we are ready to condone.

> Si fuit errandum, causas habet error honestas.

Thus Dido pleads for herself in Ovid's *Heroid*,[1] and Virgil, too, acquits her in his closing words —

> nec fato merita nec morte peribat,
> sed misera ante diem subitoque accensa furore.

[1] VII, 109.

Dante acquits her by placing her near the entrance to the Inferno, not in the seventh circle of the lower hell. Aeneas's yielding to so reasonable a temptation at the moment of utter dejection is pardonable too; many a reader will allow that who cannot pardon his return to duty, who does not see that his struggle with his heart-shaking emotions and his mastery of them are as tragic for him as for Dido. His passion and hers, natural and condoned, clash with the purpose of a righteous and ir-resistible fate. This makes the tragedy. No other end-ing could be conceived save that which Virgil gives. Aeneas must sail away. George Meredith, with a strik-ingly similar plot in his *Lord Ormont*, ends in revolt and a curious consequence — banality: his Aeneas stays in Carthage. But Virgil is writing tragedy.

II

We must not forget that the gods take part in the drama of the *Aeneid*. A measure of Dido's guilt reverts to Venus — not all, for Dido, it would seem, had been ready of her own accord. But Virgil's gods are not merely human passions writ large, adding nothing to the plot but epic mechanism and the contrast of shifted scenes; they are larger human actors, more powerful, but submissive, like men, to the Fates. Standing in rank midway between, they descend to the human plane, help or retard, and withdraw. Their action has interest in itself and their characters have personality. Thus

Venus in the First Book seems charmingly unintelligent in encouraging her son to run so great a peril; she thinks, apparently, of Dido merely as an enemy who may destroy the shipwrecked Trojans if she is not enamored of Aeneas in time. The goddess does not consider that the hero's infatuation delays the Fates and his ultimate triumph. Juno has more sober sense: she will entangle him in the very trap that Venus has set. Pretending indignation at such artifice, she proposes to her fair rival that the passion which Venus has aroused be further strengthened by wedlock.[1]

> Now thou hast what thou soughtest with all thy heart. Dido is afire with love and has sucked passion to the marrow of her bones. Let us, therefore, you and I, rule with equal auspices this race conjoined. Let her be slave to a Phrygian lord, and entrust her Tyrians as dowry to thine hand.

Venus, perceiving the trick, answers with a smile:

> Who so mad as to spurn an offer like this, or prefer instead to take up arms against thyself — if only good fortune may attend the plan that thou proposest? But I drift doubtful of the Fates — whether Jove will that there should be one city for the Tyrians and the voyagers from Troy, or approve the union of their tribes and bonds of federation. Thou art his spouse, thou hast the right to test his temper with entreaty. Lead on: and I will follow.

Juno, oblivious to the delicious irony and coquetry of Venus's assent, undertakes to arrange things by herself. She sets the stage for the fatal hunt and the storm, for the meeting in the cave, for the liturgy which she will

[1] Ll. 93 ff.

improvise to sustain the act. She presents the plan explicitly to Venus. And Venus "opposed not her request, but nodded, and smiled at the invention of such a snare." Venus smiles first at the cleverness of Juno's plans — for it is a downright good trick — but also because she perceives that it will all come back on Juno in the end. In short, Venus is far more sagacious than the reader suspected at the start.

This incident shows well enough the purpose of divine machinery in Virgil's drama. Gods complicate the plot, appearing as superhuman actors. They help or hinder mortals without being mere personifications of their qualities. They hasten or retard the Fates, without being mere symbols of ultimate purpose. Their coming shifts the scene to the radiancy of Olympus and gives the relief of contrast. In the scene before us, and elsewhere in the *Aeneid*, as in Homer, they afford comic relief for the setting of tragedy. Comedy for the gods; tragedy is reserved for mortal men — *miseri mortales* — whom Virgil's gods can sometimes pity too. In a word, Virgil's world has place for both the human and the divine.[1]

III

The Fifth Aeneid, that counterpoise of graceful comedy to the tragedy of the Fourth, gives us further insight into the character of the hero. After this book, in which he appears at the games as a dutiful son and

[1] See below, p. 403.

princely entertainer, and after the following book, we are ready for the summary of his qualities that Dante gives in his *Convivio* [1] — *Lealtà, Cortesia, Amore, Fortezza, Temperanza*. The meeting of Aeneas with Dido in the Mournful Fields of the underworld [2] shows us directly again what the Fourth Book has developed in a careful climax of explication — that deep feeling underlay the severity which it was kindness to assume.

When the Trojan hero saw her dimly through the shadows, even as one who at the month's beginning sees or thinks he sees the rising moon, he poured forth tears [3] and with sweet love addressed her:

"Hapless Dido, had then true message come to me that thou wert dead, and with the sword hadst taken desperate measure? Was it, alas, to the grave I brought thee? By the stars I swear, by gods above and whatsoever faith is beneath the earth, against my will, O queen, I left thy court. By the mandates of the gods that impel me now to go through these shades, through places grisly with decay, through profound night, they forced me to their will; nor could I think I brought thee grief like this at my departure. Stay thy steps and withdraw not from my look. Whom dost thou flee? The last word fate allows me with thee is even this."

Thus did Aeneas, as she stood with fire-glaring eyes, seek to calm her spirit and summoned tears. She with eyes fixed on the ground bent away, unmoved in aspect at the words essayed, as though she stood a hard flint-rock or a Marpesian cliff. At length she flung herself away, and fled defiant into the shadow-bearing grove, where her consort of old days, Sychaeus, answered her grief with his and mated her love. But none the less Aeneas, overwhelmed at her unjust fate, followed her from afar with tears and pitied her as she went.

[1] IV, 26.　　　　[2] VI, 450 ff.

[3] These tears, at least, are those of Aeneas (l. 455). A bit later (l. 476) they burst forth afresh.

Relations have been exactly reversed. Aeneas, now that the divine will has been fulfilled and Dido's act is past recall, may give utterance to what he feels and felt: it is Dido's turn to be relentless.

In another way, further, the Sixth Book, apart from its own deep meaning, is related directly to the tragedy of the Fourth. We have found tragedy there in the clash of human wills, well directed in the main, with an overruling Fate. Pathos is not excluded thereby. On the contrary, the more human the actors, the more poignantly does their disaster move pity and fear. If Aeneas is Fate itself masquerading as an epic hero, "the passive recipient," as Sellar finds,[1] "both of the devotion and of the reproaches of Dido," if Dido is simply *delenda Carthago* in person, Virgil should have written plain history in prose. A touch of the allegorical, and, in Dido's case, direct allusion to the Punic Wars, are apparent,[2] but the main interest in the Fourth Book is in human beings and their battle with Fate. Now this Fate, as the reader feels at the time, is a power essentially for the good. It is not a malignant arbiter, as in the novels of Thomas Hardy; it is not what Hardy misconceives Aeschylean fate to be. Aeneas is fulfilling divine destiny, and that destiny is the *fatum Romanum*.

But the nature of this principle needs elaboration. The reader might ponder the story of the Fourth Aeneid

---

[1] *The Roman Poets of the Augustan Age:* "Virgil" (Oxford, 3d ed., 1897), p. 398.

[2] See below, pp. 411 f.

alone and find, as Sellar finds,[1] merely "the doctrine of predestination in its hardest form." Roman Fate conceived in the abstract has, indeed, even less personality than Calvin's deity — an idol of wood or stone. In the Sixth Book the vision is summoned into the clear light; all history sweeps before the hero; a sublime apocalypse connects the remote past with the triumph of imperial Rome. Something more than "seven hills by a river" is cause of Dido's suffering; it is a principle of justice and civilization — the Roman temperament actively and beneficently at work in human history. This is not, I believe, a conception "much inferior both in intellectual subtlety and in ethical value to that of the Fate of Greek tragedy in conflict with human will." [2] It is a different conception and a noble one: it is more, not less, a spring for true tragedy. The Fate of the Greek drama has no moral development. In Aeschylus it is the accumulation of guilt which involves the partly innocent; hence the battle, and pity and fear for those who are doomed to defeat. But the triumph of Zeus and Apollo is the triumph of personal theism and the twilight of the Fates; the closing scene of the *Eumenides* would be conceived by Dante as *Commedia*. In Sophocles, most clearly in his *Oedipus*, righteous humanity is brought to ruin through conflict with divine law. One cannot repress the query, hovering on the poet's lips, it would seem, whether this law can be just. The query grows

[1] *Op. cit.*, p. 344.   [2] *Ibid.*

more urgent still for Euripides: it is no righteous divinity that sends Hippolytus to his doom. A new motive is thus introduced into the dramatic problem — human revolt at these helpless conflicts. If too much is made of this element, indignation drives out pity and fear, and thus the very principle of tragedy.

Now in Virgil here and there are touches of protest against the *iniquus casus* in which several of the actors are involved; many of them occur in Book Two, where the indignation of the narrator is dramatically appropriate. These are the sum total of Virgil's inheritance from Euripides, so far as tragic plot is concerned. He is akin to Euripides in his pathos and his far-reaching humanitarian sympathies, but his spirit — supposing for the moment that I know just what the spirit of Euripides was — belonged to a different order. If a whirl of faith and doubting mingled in his mind, as they did in the mind of Euripides, if Virgil never fought out the battle between philosophy and poetry, if he was majestic in his sadness

At the doubtful doom of human kind,

he at least cast no scorn at the gods, in the fashion of Euripides at times or in that of Lucan always. His tragedy would have suffered had it presented merely an indictment of divinity; for verses made by indignation are good for satire, or for sermons, but not for tragedy. Virgil abides by Aristotle and purges his readers with pity and with fear.

In both his art and his theology, Virgil is bound by far closer ties to Sophocles.[1] What indeed is the "ideal truth of Sophocles — the ideal of final purification and reconcilement of a noble human nature with the divine nature"[2] but the theology that Anchises teaches his son in the fields of Elysium? Personality, too, is at the heart of the Roman ideal. It is not true that the Fates act "irrespective of right and wrong, regardless of personal happiness or suffering,"[3] and that thus the *Aeneid* fails of the highest rank as a work of art because it "does not touch the heart or enlighten the conscience." The Fates consider right and wrong, for both Aeneas and Dido, though acting constantly, and, to sympathetic humanity, pardonably, have crossed the moral law; retribution follows as inexorably as it would in Aeschylean tragedy. There is plenty of moral edification in the story of Aeneas, as Dante and all the Middle Ages were only too well aware.

[1] For an excellent statement of the kinship of Virgil and Euripides, see Mr. Glover's *Virgil*, pp. 53–55. But this, I feel, is only half the story. The readers should also ponder a profound article by A. P. McMahon ("Seven Questions on Aristotelian Definitions of Tragedy and Comedy," in *Harvard Studies in Classical Philology*, XL [1929], 97–198), who shows by a searching historical survey that the Aristotelian definition of tragedy that controlled literary criticism well-nigh to the nineteenth century was not the famous doctrine of κάθαρσις of the *Poetics*, but the more general statement, made probably in the work *On Poets*, and that the notion of a conflict of human wills with one another or with destiny is a purely modern idea. Modern it is, but truer to the essence of Greek tragedy, or any tragedy, than is either of Aristotle's descriptions, helpful though they are. These give the indispensable outlines, but the modern notion is an undeniable part of the complete definition.

[2] Sellar, *op. cit.*, p. 344.

[3] *Ibid.*, p. 354.

What Virgil has done is to infuse into the idea of Fate an ethical content that it did not display in previous drama. He identifies it with all that is best and most sacred in the Roman ideal and the fulfilment of this ideal in past and present history. The *fatum Romanum* is no malign tyrant, but a power for good, a power that makes for righteousness; it is no barren abstraction, but the poet's vision of beauty, as well as of grandeur, an ideal colored with the charm of that Italy whose praises he had sung before; he makes his point delicately, by a phrase or two from his rhapsody on Italy in the Second Book of the *Georgics*. Its clash with human wills is as tragic as before, but the reason is at hand in human error and sin, however natural. The final solution, therefore, brings us still farther away from Euripides: it is essentially the solution of Aeschylus, through the rational vindication of the moral law. This is the Fate, then, revealed in the Sixth Book of Virgil's poem, which is therefore an indispensable guide to the tragedy of the Fourth.

IV

It would be strange if Virgil had given dramatic structure to the first half of his poem and devoted the remainder to epic of a simple type; it would be difficult to achieve harmony with such a scheme. Even as it is, according to George Woodberry,[1] "the dramatic power in the episode of Dido threatens to overbear the moral

[1] In an appreciative essay on Virgil in his *Great Writers* (1907), p. 135.

unity of the structure." Possibly the reason why certain critics — Mr. Woodberry is not among them — find the latter books an anticlimax is that they are unaware of the essentially dramatic plot and its connection with that of the first half of the poem. Voltaire, in *Candide*,[1] indulges in lavish vituperation of all but the Second, the Fourth, and the Sixth Aeneid, and Mr. Saintsbury,[2] perhaps subconsciously influenced by this very passage, speaks of the Seventh Book as

the point when, to modern readers, the interest of the *Aeneid* is all but over, and the romantic wanderings of Aeneas, the passion of the Fourth Book, the majesty and magnificence of the Sixth, are exchanged for the kite-and-crow battles of Trojans and Rutulians, the doll-like figure of Lavinia, and the unjust fate of the hero Turnus at the hands of a divinely helped invader.

Mr. Saintsbury is a facile maker of phrases; his criticisms are always good reading. But pertinence is also a virtue of the critic, and hardly one of the above characterizations is to the point. How human we are after all! Mr. Saintsbury's indignation at the "divinely helped invader" is not far removed from that of the rustic at the villain in the play, with whom Macaulay also is at one, in his cry of "Poltroon!" when Aeneas sails on from Carthage. Righteous wrath at injustice is the beginning of literary appreciation in such situations as these,

[1] Chap. XXV. To be sure, the speaker is Pococuranté, who is obviously a target for the author's satire. Voltaire is perhaps having a fling at the great authors for the fun of it.

[2] *A History of Criticism and Literary Taste in Europe* (Edinburgh and London, 1900–04), I, p. 339.

but the rustics should first be sure that they have caught the right villain, and even then not descend upon the poet with their flails.

Virgil himself did not feel that his work was over at the Seventh Book. Toward the beginning he declares

maius opus moveo.

His first problem in the ensuing Iliad of war is to create an antagonist worthy of Aeneas. It is no easy task to match the splendid strength and reserve of the hero's character. Yet Virgil is so successful that the sympathies of not a few readers besides Mr. Saintsbury are enlisted for Turnus. Like Dido, Turnus has a vigorous and immediately engaging personality. He is young and goodly to see, brave and aristocratic — "potent in grandsires and greatgrandsires," [1] and, above all, patriotic and Italian. By careful suggestion, by deliberate contrast with other characters, like that of the plausible but weak-spirited Drances, Virgil prepares us for his final array of qualities at the end of the poem.[2]

In one breast, reverence and madness, mingled with grief, fury-driven love and conscious valor.

No reader gainsays when Turnus cries out that he descends to the shades a "sacred soul." [3] It is the fate of Turnus that makes up the tragedy of the latter books: the drama is worked out step by step. The Seventh Book presents the issue, the combat for Lavinia, to

[1] VII, 56: avis atavisque potens.
[2] XII, 666 ff.   [3] XII, 648.

which Turnus is impelled not only by the Fury but by his own resolve. The Eighth interposes dramatic delay in the embassy of Aeneas to Evander; the Ninth records the hero's ἀριστεία, his deeds of valor within the Trojan camp. In the Tenth, the slaying of the lad Pallas marks the acme of the ascending series, for Aeneas's vow of revenge, sworn sacredly to Evander, means Turnus's death. The Eleventh Book fixes once for all the character of Turnus as the splendid champion of a lost cause. At a moment of utter discouragement, when the Latin envoys return from their fruitless mission to Diomede, when the king, as ever, wavers, and Drances has presented cogent arguments for peace, Turnus breaks through all opposition and carries the day for war. The disasters in the ensuing fight, especially the death of Camilla, prophesy the tragic outcome, and the agreement of the armies to stake all upon a single combat draws the toils still more closely about Turnus. From this point the action proceeds rapidly to the catastrophe.

One quality of Turnus repels the reader from the start, his *violentia*, ὕβρις, which, in keeping with the tragic conception, calls down divine vengeance, ἄτη, on the transgressor. For this, Allecto is not wholly responsible, any more than Venus is for Dido's passion, for Turnus has a crude and savage strain in his nature, which is contrasted at various points with the courtesy and chivalry of Aeneas. But from the moment when the Furies descend upon their victim,[1] Turnus has our sympathies. There is no further mention of *violentia*; his actions are no longer under his own control. He arms himself madly, — like Macbeth in a similar situation, — though the night is coming on. In the first combat his very manhood ebbs away: he moves as in a dream, raises a rock and can scarcely throw it. His qualities desert him, even his bravery: he is hardly more than a shade when he is put to death. His death is inevitable; it is a stern duty laid upon Aeneas by his pledge to Evander. At the last, when his chivalry prompts him to spare, the sight of the belt of Pallas on his foe calls forth the final stroke. But this act is not the punishment of a villain; it is the victory of the good over the good, as in the slaying of Hector, a deed fated but lamentable. The soul of Turnus "flies reproachful to the shades." It utters the reproach of humanity laid low by a fate that it does not altogether deserve; so Dido had fled "defiant" (*inimica*) from Aeneas in the Mournful Fields. The Fate is, however, inevitable and a power for the final good; it is the same Fate which controls the drama of the Fourth Book, and whose nature is revealed in the Sixth.

But apart from this personal tragedy which furnishes the external plot of the latter books, a larger drama is on, the play of ideal forces, which bear the ultimate meaning of the poem. The struggle is not merely between the chieftains of heroic quality; it is between the

[1] XII, 101.

native strength of Italy and all the influences of foreign civilization that developed a rude community into imperial Rome. This element adds new significance to the drama of Turnus and intensifies the tragedy of his fate. The Seventh and the Eighth Books present the actors in this larger drama. The first of them has a distinctly Italian coloring. The mustering of the native forces has a deeper tone of patriotism than the Homeric catalogue of the ships, the epic model for Virgil's description. This book, more than any other of the *Aeneid*, has the simple pastoral charm of the *Eclogues* and the *Georgics*, and in its patriotic sentiment recalls the latter poem. The Eighth is a Roman book.[1] The embassy of Aeneas to Evander skilfully transports the reader to a new scene, where the rude huts on the Palatine suggest by contrast the splendor of imperial Rome. The legend on the heaven-wrought shield has the same purpose as the vision of heroes in the Inferno of Book Six, presenting the sweep of Roman history down to the triumph of Augustus himself. Turnus and the Latins and Rutulians, therefore, represent native Italy; Aeneas and the Trojans, the influence of civilizing forces from without. I need hardly add that Virgil does not set forth this allegory baldly or mechanically; his heroes are persons, not types. But the larger ideas shimmer through the narrative, and are suggested clearly enough, in Virgil's way. Both of

---

[1] A fuller exposition of the meaning of Books VII and VIII will be found below, pp. 422 ff.

these ideal forces are bone and marrow of the Rome that had developed in the poet's time; the combatants, engaged in inevitable struggle with one another, are fighting for the same goal.

> Di quel umile Italia fia salute
> Per sui morì la vergine Cammilla
> Eurialo e Turno e Niso di ferute —

Dante saw that the latter books of the *Aeneid* had other battles than those of "crows and kites."

In Book Nine, the general coloring is that of sorrow and defeat for the Trojan side during the absence of its leader. In Book Ten, hope brightens for them as Aeneas returns and renews the fight. In the Eleventh Book, the sadness of the Ninth is deeply reinforced: it is sorrow and defeat for the Italians now, as well. The last book effects the reconciliation of the warring principles, and reveals Virgil's final estimate of the Roman temperament and Roman achievement. It supplements the famous lines of Book Six:[1]

Others shall chisel more delicately the breathing bronze, so I believe, and draw features from marble; plead causes better; mark with the rod the courses of the sky and name the rising stars. Remember thou, O Roman, to subject the nations to thy sway. These shall be thine arts, to crown peace with law and order, to spare the humble and beat down the proud.

The splendid poetry of these lines is proof in itself that the Romans were capable of other *artes* besides that of war. The passage emphasizes what is most appropriate

[1] Ll. 847 ff.

for the immediate setting, and it gives, I believe, only part of Virgil's meaning. For the rest, we must look to the latter books of the poem.

Sacra deosque dabo, says Aeneas,[1] *socer arma Latinus habeto*. Military strength is a national characteristic, but it is to be enriched by other elements introduced from without. By "religion" I understand not merely the ancient ceremonies that Augustus was so anxious to revive, but spiritual enlightenment in general. "They are to bring to Italy," says Mr. Glover,[2] "all that is signified to a Trojan by Troy, all that Evander found wanting in the old life of the country—*mos* and *cultus*." May we imagine further that Virgil is thinking here of the part played by Greece in Rome's development? In any case his meaning here is larger than that of the prophecy of Anchises. More important still is the ultimate effect that foreign influence is to have on national character. It is not to lead to servile imitation, the abandonment of native traits; Juno insists upon that:

> Sit Romana potens Itala virtute propago.
> Occidit occideritque sinas cum nomine Troia.[3]

Jupiter smiles assent:
> commixti corpore tantum
> subsident Teucri.[4]

[1] XII, 192.
[2] *Op. cit.*, p. 115 (2d ed.), p. 123. The two chapters (V and VI) "Italy" and "Rome" are splendid.
[3] XII, 827 f.
[4] Ll. 835 f.

Virgil differs from Horace, it would seem, in his reading of the intellectual history of Rome. To suit Virgil's meaning, the Sabine poet's famous verse

Graecia capta ferum victorem cepit

must be transformed — I will not attempt a verse — into something like

Italia capta humanum victorem cepit.

The decree of Jupiter announces the *dénouement* of the larger plot of the latter book — that is, the main idea of Virgil's epic. Here, surely, the gods are not mere epic adornment; the divine actors convey a message that could hardly be given by anybody else. By disposing first of the ideal problem, Virgil can keep the present tragedy, the fate of Turnus, for the end of the poem — certainly a triumph in dramatic arrangement. Here is one important detail in which Virgil diverges from his epic model, the *Iliad* of Homer; for even if those are right who regard the last two books of the *Iliad* as later additions, the poet of the Twenty-second Book does not end with the moment of Hector's death.

An analysis of the *Aeneid* in the light of the foregoing discussion reveals an epic poem presenting a unified narrative and yet constructed of two tragedies, the tragedy of Dido and the tragedy of Turnus. These tragedies are linked together by the Sixth Book, which is indispensable for the plot of either, as it sets forth the nature of the fate that controls both. The larger ideas in which personal action is set are disclosed with completeness only in the later books — *maius opus moveo*.

A bare summary of the events in the narrative of the *Aeneid* — a storm at sea, funeral games, a hero's story of his adventures, a hero's descent to the lower world — suggests the influence of Homer at every turn. Despite these details, despite the echoing of beautiful phrases and imagery — which is not "imitation," but a part of the ancient poet's sacred function — the discerning reader is astonished to find that there is nothing Homeric in the total effect of the poem or its total plan. One great difference is the strong national sentiment of the *Aeneid*, whereas the *Iliad* and *Odyssey* both are essentially personal narratives. Another difference, more striking still, is the element I have discussed in this chapter. For the poem is not solely epic; in structure it is a fusion of epic and of Attic tragedy, which Virgil enriches by creating a new conception of fate. The poem is indeed *alta tragedia*, as was said by one who, though limited by mediaeval conceptions, "knew it all in all." Whatever the plays of Varius and Ovid may have been, Virgil's *Aeneid* alone is proof that the Augustan Age still cherished the drama.

CHAPTER XI

TRAGEDY FROM ROMANCE

THE amazing tangle of historical and mythical traditions, poetical models, and his own fancies that Virgil, after long process of his fusing thought, worked into a harmonious epic of Rome has been vaguely suggested in the first chapter of this book. The more one studies the *Aeneid* and its background, the more one is astounded at the multitudes of problems that faced the poet at every turn — amorphous fragments of chaos, awaiting the creator's touch, impossible acts of magic, driving him, momentarily, to despair.

One of the hazardous essays to which I referred was his combination of epic and tragedy in a new form — or, no, the absorption of tragedy into epic in such a way as to preserve its own character without disrupting that into which it was absorbed. In the preceding chapter, I have endeavored to set forth the character of the two tragedies that are absorbed into the *Aeneid* and their relations to the plot of that epic.[1] We have been contemplating the finished product. I would now ask the

---

[1] The same theme is worked out admirably in different ways by H. H. Yeames, "The Tragedy of Dido," *Classical Journal*, VIII (1912–13), 139 ff., 193 ff., and by M. B. Ogle, "Vergil's Conception of Dido's Character," *Ibid.*, XX (1924–25) 261 ff. On the topic of the present chapter, see R. M. Henry, "Medea and Dido," *Classical Review*, XLIV (1930), 97–108.

reader to consider, all too inadequately, the art of the magician who evoked these tragedies, and particularly the tragedy of Aeneas and Dido, out of the chaos that he had accumulated in the deep well of his mind. The venture is perhaps foolhardy and impious, but let us see if we can put ourselves in his place at the time when incredible feats confronted him and thus better appreciate the incredible success with which he performed them.

I

We noted the change, the revolution, that took place in Virgil's mind when his early plan, sketched in the *Georgics*, for a contemporary and historical epic gave way to a larger idea, bolder and vastly more poetic. He changed his point of outlook from the Rome of his day to prehistoric Italy and sang not of the triumphs of Augustus but of the coming of Aeneas and the building of Rome's ancient walls. It was a view of the present age, as I remarked, from the remote past *sub specie aeternitatis*. This meant some adjustment of his original design

The hero of the new epic, so the poet thought, — or so we will imagine him thinking, — is bound to be a success. For is he not Augustus in disguise? The disguise will be transparent and all Rome will applaud. Of course Aeneas will need to be made over a bit. Some of the historians have made him out pro-Hellenic during the siege of Troy. Only he and Antenor were allowed to leave the doomed city and settle in Italy where they would. Our hero must be of finer metal than that. Instead of being let off, he must fight to the end and be forced to retreat only when Heaven has decreed his going. For the bearer of Roman destiny, of the will of the gods, must be pious; he founds the faith of the fathers, which our Augustus, the prince of peace, so nobly sustains. Peace is the mission of Aeneas — peace after the inevitable war. For war is decreed for the Trojans when they land on the shores of Latium. Their victory will mean not the crushing of the inhabitants of the land but the union of two splendid forces — culture, enlightenment, a higher religion, from without, the native strength and sweetness of Italy from within. For they are Italians, those primitive ancestors of ours. For Italy they die. Worthy the conquerors, worthy the defenders. It will be a task to construct for these defenders exploits fit for epic. Their primitive strains must be heard in the full music of eternal Rome. "Barbarous Turnus," Tibullus called him.[1] But that surely is not the final word — Turnus must be worthy of Aeneas's steel.

And the hero's voyage! There must be a nice selection from among the legends that have recounted that. He cannot die at several places along the way; he cannot die till the journey is done. He cannot have love affairs at various stopping-places. He is no Don Juan; an *Aeneis immoralizata* such as Byron wrote, or such as Ovid, had he only thought of it first, could have written more deli-

[1] II, 5, 48.

cately than Byron, naturally could have no part in
Virgil's plan. Perhaps some writer of our day, intent on
a best seller, may yet write *The True History of Aeneas's
Voyage*. One episode of love, Virgil finds, there well
may be, for love-stories are sanctioned by epic tradition.
They are sanctioned at the start by Homer. Yes, Homer
must give the main outlines and many of the details of
the new epic; let there be an *Odyssey* of travel succeeded
by an *Iliad* of war. Let Homer now, as Hesiod in the
poem just achieved, be sung through the towns of Rome
— aye, through the provinces of Rome, through all the
Roman world. Let the whole poem breathe Homer
by the most painstaking imitation — the imitation that
challenges attention and that frustrates the critic who
would condemn the thefts. There are no thefts; it is
easier to steal the club of Hercules than a verse of
Homer's. Not petty larceny, but robbery in the grand
style — that is the programme. It will baffle the ac-
cuser, who never can say just what the theft is and how
it is made. He can never point it out; it will elude him;
for the poem from first to last shall be the epic of Rome.

So the voyage, once more. It is the voyage of another
Odysseus, as like and as different as can be. Odysseus is
a resourceful explorer of many lands and many minds,
and many are his adventures; Aeneas is the bearer of
Roman destiny. And again, as Dryden later remarked,[1]
the one hero went home and the other sought a home.

[1] *Dedication of the Aeneis* (Cambridge Edition, G. R. Noyes, Boston,
1908), p. 505.

The *Odyssey* is brim full of romance; Ovid saw that, and made it live again, after his own fashion, in a tremendous epic on a novel plan. But the voyage of Aeneas has no place for adventure. It is the quest of a Galahad balked by deferment, in the form that the poet's imagination finally conceived, by a series of false hopes, and brave struggles, and final triumph. Through it all, the character of the hero is constantly enriched. He is not merely a prototype of Augustus. He must be a human being and appeal to any human heart, if the poem is to survive.

For allegory, as Virgil soon found, or rather already knew, is a tawdry device if crudely applied. Had he not mastered the rare and illusive sort of allegory that we have seen in the *Eclogues*? His epic, his masterpiece, the great work that had appealed to his boyish ambition and was to express at last his mellowed imagination, could have no room for symbolism of the baser sort. What Virgil would have thought of a recent discovery that all, or almost all, of the persons of his poem have Augustan counterparts — that Achates stands for Agrippa, and Mnestheus for Maecenas, in virtue of their initial letters — may readily be guessed. There would have been laughter unquenchable, I doubt not, especially if Horace were there to hear.

No, that way madness lies. Even Augustus must not be too much in evidence. He is directly mentioned in the prophecy in the First Book, which with a stroke of happy art takes the place of a dedication; and the greater prophecy of Anchises in the Elysian fields leads up to him. His deeds are emblazoned on the hero's shield, and he shimmers through the narrative at times, as in the Eighth Book, when the victory and the rites of Hercules, another mortal raised to divinity, are described. But Aeneas is not Hercules, and he has ceased to become Augustus; he is a hero in his own right. Stroke by stroke the poet sets his character before us.

I have endeavored in the preceding chapter to do justice to the character of Aeneas for the benefit of those who would regard that character as abstract piety in its least attractive form. I cannot refrain from adding one little episode in the closing book which shows that the hero had intensely human moments. After his miraculous healing, he thinks it now an easy matter at last to come to close quarters with Turnus. But most mysteriously, most provokingly, the latter's chariot is steered out of his way. There is some witchcraft abroad, but he cannot make out how or where. At that moment Messapus hurls a javelin at him and strikes his helmet. That is the last straw. It is often some definite little accident that makes a state of general nervousness explode. Aeneas, to use a human phrase, gets mad — *tum vero adsurgunt irae* — and lays out right and left.[1] This incident is but one among many that illustrate the poet's pains to make Aeneas a man of flesh and blood.

[1] XII, 494.

II

For the creation of the hero of the *Aeneid* Virgil could thank first of all his own genius. But the final act of creation, the magic act, was preceded by an attentive study of whatever in the poetry of the past bore on his theme. The part of that theme that required the most profound attention was the love of Aeneas and Dido. It is probable — though not all scholars agree on this point — that the visit of the hero to Carthage was already a part of the legend as Virgil found it. It is not the kind of embellishment of the legend that a poet like Virgil would be apt to devise. The poet's business was to repeat the myth and interpret it, rather than to change it. "It is reprehensible," says Servius in one of his comments, "for a poet to invent something that is entirely remote from truth." [1] The pretty story about the baby Camilla, who, tied to a spear-head, was thrown by her father across a stream, was called by Probus an ἀπίθανον πλάσμα, "an incredible fiction." [2]

The myth-maker, therefore, proceeded with caution. When Virgil at the beginning of his poem makes what appears to the modern reader the innocuous and apparently unimpeachable assertion that Juno "is said" to have preferred Carthage to any spot on earth, Samos not excepted, —

[1] On *Aen.*, III, 46: vituperabile enim est poetam aliquid fingere quod penitus a veritate discedat.

[2] See Servius on *Aen.*, XI, 554 ff.

quam Iuno fertur terris magis omnibus unam
posthabita coluisse Samo, —

the word *fertur*, "is said," may seem to the modern
reader otiose; if it means anything, it would apparently
imply that the poet was a bit doubtful of the truth of
the story. Nothing of the kind. Servius informs us,
what we little suspected, that the use of *fertur* is a stroke
of art on the part of the poet, who took pains not to resort outright to poetic licence in a matter of myth, but
pretended to follow the established belief and only incidentally resorted to the poet's devices.[1] *Fertur* is an
appeal to establish tradition.

This remark of Servius I find most illuminating. It
may often prove an unexpected clue to what is invention
and what tradition in a poet's work. Our English classic
poets doubtless understood the point; for they read their
ancients and the ancient commentaries upon them.
Pope, in retelling one of Chaucer's Fables,[2] employs the
phrase "'Tis sung" in a passage of unsavory quality
with a sly touch of mock-heroic that might not be appreciated by those unfamiliar with Servius's remark:

> What next ensued beseems me not to say;
> 'Tis sung, he labored till the dawning day. . . .

Ah me! How many fine flavors there are in our English
poetry that never can be tasted save by palates acquainted with the viands and vintages of the ancients!

[1] On *Aen.*, I, 15: FERTVR, dicitur. et ingenti arte Vergilius, ne in rebus
fabulosis aperte utatur poetarum licentia, quasi opinionem sequitur et per
transitum poetico utitur more.

[2] "January and May," l. 383.

But I have told only half the story. On another passage in the First Book, Servius, whom no real reader of Virgil can neglect, makes another profound observation. When the hero declares that Venus, his mother, guided him on his way — *matre dea monstrante viam* — Servius explains that Virgil incidentally, *en passant (per transitum)*, is alluding to history, which by the law of poetic art he may not set forth outright.[1] The particular history in this case was what we should call the delightful myth of the guiding star, Venus's own star, that made the hero's path plain till he came to the Laurentine shore. Servius refers to Varro as authority, and it were rash to deny an authority like his; the myth had become *historia* when Virgil took it up. I rather think, however, that Virgil rejected the story of the star not because it was plain history but because, for all its beauty, it interfered with his idea, a brilliant idea, that the hero's journey should not be made too plain; it is not like that of the Children of Israel, or that of the Magi. The principle involved in Servius's remark is in any case admirable. He says in conclusion that Lucan did not observe it and therefore wrote history rather than poetry.

I have quoted the helpful Servius at such length since his comments enable us better to picture the state of the poet's mind as he proceeded to mould tradition to the new demands of his story and the actors in it. He would find for the story of Dido a certain warrant in tradition

---

[1] On *Aen.*, I, 382: hoc loco per transitum tangit historiam, quam per legem artis poeticae aperte non potest ponere.

from the *Odyssey* down. Whether he invented it or found it, he turned inevitably to the many romantic tales that presented a similar situation. Of the *Odyssey* I have briefly spoken. It is constantly suggested, but its matter is rarely abstracted. Odysseus and Aeneas, as I have indicated, have little in common; the one is typically Greek and the other is typically Roman. Calypso and Circe are charming, as fair women generally are, but their charm is taken for granted. Virgil borrows little from Homer here; Dido's charm is the work of his own hands. Calypso and Circe are also enchantresses, and have bequeathed a touch of their power to Dido. Virgil pays but scant homage to the tradition here, even though it includes Medea too. Some witchcraft there is in the dim background, and Dido professes acquaintance with the art. But she stoops to it reluctantly, and before long the reader knows that it was but grim pretence; the magic pyre containing her lover's weapons and their bridal bed was meant only to receive her dying body. What fashionings and unfashionings of the tradition must have taken place in the poet's mind before he knew how much of it would serve his end! He paints in just a stroke or two from these old stories of witchcraft. Connoisseurs will recognize the appropriate colorings. More would spoil the picture; for Dido needs no alliance with the powers of darkness — her radiant self is all the magic that she needs.

Of this art of "painting in" Virgil is a master. He exhibits it in certain passages in which certain sober scholars, ancient and modern, have found him culpable. I am thinking of the comparison of Dido and her courtiers to Diana and her bevy of nymphs, a comparison for which Virgil has been rebuked by Probus and many after him. I would start with the comment of Servius, as usual, who points out that comparisons sometimes aim at a general effect, not an agreement in all particulars.[1] We may go a bit further, I think, and recognize, as the cultivated reader in the poet's day would recognize, that Virgil by his borrowed simile is calling our attention to Homer's inimitable description of Nausicaa where the same simile is used. The general situations are the same; a princess is giving shelter to a shipwrecked hero. Virgil's smooth hexameters are not devoted to equating dancing nymphs with respectable noblemen of Carthage. He is painting in a dash of Nausicaa in his portrait of Dido, a touch of her charm to match the *lumen iuventae purpureum* that Venus had poured about the hero. Milton understands this art of "painting in," whether he learned it from Virgil or not, and illustrates it finely in the lines that tell of Eve as she departs from Adam and the Angel.

> With goddess-like demeanor forth she went,
> Not unattended; for on her as Queen
> A pomp of winning Graces waited still,

[1] On *Aen.*, I, 497: STIPANTE CATERVA, ad hoc tantum sequens pertinet comparatio, quam vituperant multi, nescientes exempla vel parabolas vel comparationes adsumptas non semper usquequaque congruere, sed interdum omni parte, interdum aliqua convenire.

And from about her shot darts of desire
Into all eyes, to wish her still in sight.[1]

"Not unattended" — οὐκ οἴη; just two words irresistibly set before us Helen of Troy on her way to the tower by the Scaean gate. What an audacious Puritan, to associate Mother Eve with Helen of Troy! Sometimes I wonder whether the inner heart of Milton was Puritanic at all.

III

It is far from my purpose, and my ability, to review all the extant poetry that Virgil read, or may have read, before the images of Aeneas and Dido came clearly to his mind. One poem was of surpassing importance to him as a model of both what to do and what not to do. It is the *Argonautica* of Apollonius of Rhodes. Says Servius in his opening comment on the Fourth Aeneid:

Apollonius Argonautica scripsit et in tertio inducit amantem Medeam: inde totus hic liber translatus est.

This is a surprising statement. The hunter of sources gets out both texts and finds to his chagrin that the Fourth Book of the *Aeneid* is anything but a direct translation of the Third Book of the *Argonautica*. Servius must have meant something else. Let us try to find out what he did mean. I will first sketch briefly some of the characteristics of the poem with remarks about Virgil strewn in, and then speak of its relation to Virgil's developing plan for the story of Aeneas and Dido.

[1] *Paradise Lost*, VIII, 59.

The *Argonautica* of Apollonius of Rhodes, a younger contemporary of Theocritus, is a well-constructed poem, which tells a story of romance and adventure. The first two books describe the journey to Colchis. The beginning lacks art. The poet does not plunge *in medias res* in the fashion prescribed by Horace and illustrated by Virgil. He suggests rather the unfortunate bard mentioned by Horace [1] who, impelled to sing the tale of Troy divine, started in with the egg from which Helen was hatched. Apollonius similarly begins with the sandal that Jason lost in the mud, a fact noted by Pelias, who was destined to be slain by a man wearing one sandal and who promptly dispatched Jason on the impossible emprise of recovering the Golden Fleece. Then comes a most tiresome catalogue of the heroes who took part in the expedition; it takes two hundred verses to tell their tale. Valerius Flaccus, who under the Flavians retold the story of the Argonauts, saw his predecessor's mistake and sensibly reduced this catalogue. So did Virgil in his summoning of the Italian clans. He may not have put the final touches on that passage, but whatever its roughness it lacks not charm or climax, with the unforgettable picture of the virgin Camilla at the end.

The account of the fitting and the launching of the Argo comes as a relief, and when the voyage is once begun the reader's interest does not flag. The stop at Lemnos adds variety. Hypsipyle suggests at least one

[1] *Ars Poetica*, 147.

of Dido's traits, as we shall shortly see. The story of
Hylas is beautifully told, and the rage of Hercules at his
loss is admirable. The whole episode is fitted to the
poet's needs, since if Hercules had kept on with his comrades Medea would have been forced into a secondary
rôle.

In the Second Book, the boxing-match of Pollux and
Amycus is a fine and bloody affair. Apollonius can reproduce the delightful savagery of Homer. Poor Virgil,
who tries as conscientiously to be fierce as the younger
Pliny tries, in doggerel verse, to be naughty, does not
succeed. The prophecy of Phineus is effective. He fore-
shadows awful events, and only a part of their solution.
Virgil, probably in a late stage in the composition of his
poem, applies this device in the prophecies that attend
the hero's voyage.

Apollonius, like Virgil, is a religious poet. Above the
narrative hovers the will of Zeus, as it does in Homer.
The phrase at the beginning of the *Iliad*,

$$\Delta\iota\grave{o}s\ \delta'\ \grave{\epsilon}\tau\epsilon\lambda\epsilon\acute{\iota}\epsilon\tau o\ \beta o\upsilon\lambda\acute{\eta},$$

which has echoed down the centuries, — I once heard it
again in a sermon of Canon Farrar's, — is caught up by
Apollonius:

$$\tau\grave{a}\ \delta\grave{\epsilon}\ \pi\acute{a}\nu\tau a\ \Delta\iota\grave{o}s\ \beta o\upsilon\lambda\hat{\eta}\sigma\iota\ \tau\acute{\epsilon}\tau\upsilon\kappa\tau o.[1]$$

However, with so many special interventions of divinities by the way, a general Fate or Providence is not
needed; for Virgil, it is inherent in his design.

[1] II, 154.

In the Third Book, Erato, Muse of Love, is invoked. Virgil does not forget this when he repeats this invocation at the beginning of his Seventh Book and announces a larger subject — *maius opus moveo*. A struggle on Italian soil no less heroic than the fight for the Golden Fleece is at hand, and the hand of a princess is the prize. With the winning of the fleece, Jason has gained his goal. Of course, the heroes have to get back to Greece, and there are hair-raising adventures on the way, but on the whole the poem ends in anticlimax.

In general, this voyage challenges comparison with that in the *Odyssey*, and the moment the challenge is made the weakness of the *Argonautica* is shown. It presents, like the *Odyssey*, a great adventure thrilling with dangers; the adventure, in fact, is greater. The quest is hard and the goal is won, that is all. There ought to be something else, some guiding idea above the adventure, and there is none. Virgil has profited by both his models. He avoids the weakness of the one, and he assimilates in his own way, with a guiding idea quite different, the strength of the other.

Moreover, in the *Argonautica* the difficulties are too easily solved. A god is always at hand, or a woman — the woman. The blasphemous Idas, who, Hercules always excepted, is the only human being among the warriors, voices the reader's feelings when he protests against salvation at the hands of a woman. The adventures become tiresome because they are always helped out by magic. Mediaeval romance — one form of epic — gained much by throwing mythology away, not because mythology seemed dangerous in mediaeval eyes, — for there is a long tradition of literary paganism in the Middle Ages considerably before Chaucer's day, — but because mythological devices for the solution of an epic plot had no contemporary value. The *Chanson de Roland* is vastly more human than the *Argonautica*. The only human characters in the latter poem are, as I have said, Hercules, who might have smashed these divine arrangements, and Idas, who chafed against them.

The poem is also less human than Homer's, whose gods of course interfere with the action, but in a human way. Virgil's originality, too, becomes the more impressive when we are aware of the weight of tradition represented by a poem that he had studied so deeply as the *Argonautica*, from which he broke loose. Those who talk of the Alexandrian Age as one of a new individuality, or personality, — awful words, — would do well to compare the persons in the poetry of Apollonius with those of Homer, and to reflect on the use that Virgil made of them both.

Before passing to the episode with which we are specially concerned, I cannot refrain, now that I have said so much ill of Apollonius, from calling attention to one of his merits, namely, the astounding wealth of similes in the *Argonautica*. They are perpetually fresh and original — the shining wake of the ship like a white path in a green plain, the heart of Medea creeping like a dream after her hero as he went his way.[1] Such similes were not taken from Homer, and the like of them is not in Virgil. The majority of Virgil's similes are Homer's; he adopts and refines, but he does not invent. When the reader, to his surprise, comes to new matter for comparison in Virgil, — the sunlight quivering on the water in a caldron, the early morning hour when the poor widow arises to light the fire and ply her task,[2] — he will find both these pictures in Apollonius.[3]

But the hero and the heroine — here is where Apollonius is weak and where Virgil, profiting by his precursor's failure, is strong. Jason seems a far remove from a hero. He is lacrimose, and is rebuked by Idas for his tears. He suffers from a New England conscience. He is always at a loss as to what to do; ἀμηχανέων is a standing epithet. The passing of the Symplegades, the moving rocks that might crunch the vessel in their jaws, is a thrilling incident. But where is Jason as a leader of men? It is Tiphys who guides the ship and Euphemus who cheers the oarsmen. Tiphys consoles Jason when it is over, but Jason is downhearted still. He is a man of sorrows, reproaching his conscience for involving each and every one of them in such woes. Only when they shout encouragement to him does he take heart — and makes a rather good recovery.

[1] I, 546; III, 446.   [2] *Aen.*, VIII, 22, 407.
[3] III, 291, 756; IV, 1062.

Jason is tender-hearted and courteous. The very reason for his success is that once upon a time he had carried an old woman — Hera in disguise — over a stream. Hera did not forget, — elderly women always appreciate gallantries, — and without her help the fleece would not have been won. When Medea appears on the scene, there is tragic irony, if it is not comic irony, in Jason's sigh that they have come to a pretty pass if their hope depends on women. This is precisely the situation, as Idas understands. Jason's men know that he is no leader. They offer in turn to go for the fleece in case he does not feel equal to the effort. Nobody would say that to Aeneas.

Nor is Jason overwhelming as a lover. His speech to Medea has not one particle of love. Cupid had not directed his shaft in his direction. His reference to Theseus, the prince of deceivers, is peculiarly *mal à propos*. Medea does not desire an Ariadne's crown; she desires Jason. She does not dislike his speech; she would swallow anything to have him. At last we see that he is in love. Apollonius has portrayed the development of his passion with a sense of climax that Virgil noted and deepened immeasurably as he set forth step by step the mastered emotion in his hero's heart, the emotion struggling for expression, the emotion, at last called love, that shakes his very being.

The moment when Jason fell in love is not plainly marked in the *Argonautica*, but we can see the time when

he was in love and the time when he was not. The heart
of Aeneas is a deep and silent heart. We know its secret
at the end, but when did it begin? Dido, despite her vow
to be sacred to her husband's memory, despite the new
life and character which loyalty to that vow and the triumphant success of her career had apparently ensured
forever, Dido, whose generous heart was moved to compassion—near neighbor to affection as that is to love—
gave her inmost self to her hero the moment that he
stepped from the cloud, godlike in form, with the ruddy
light of youth playing about his locks and shining in his
joyous eyes. After the hero's words of gratitude and
homage the poet says of Dido:

obstipuit primo aspectu.

Of Aeneas nothing is said. But wrapped in the cloud he
saw Dido as she came to the temple — *pulcherrima
Dido*, a queen among her people. He heard her speech
to his men, and marked her gracious courtesy, her open-
hearted hospitality, her tribute to his fame, her desire to
see him. What could the hero's feelings be, with such a
rescue from disaster? We are not told. We see him at
the last

multa gemens magnoque animum labefactus amore.[1]

At what moment before that time may we infer from the
words of the poem that he was not in love with her?
There is no such moment, as there surely was in the ex-

---

[1] See above, p. 361.

perience of Jason. Am I for arguing that Aeneas fell in
love with Dido at first sight, or that a love for her ripened from gratitude, or that, though fascinated with her
at the start, he had never meant to take the affair so
seriously as she, poor woman, took it?   Perish the
thought. I could argue eloquently as to what his emotions on beholding her ought to have been, and I know
what they were at the end. We need not go beyond what
we read. Virgil, says Dryden, has the art of saying much
in little, and often in silence. And sometimes his silences
contain a multitude of possibilities all the more impressive if left unguessed.

These silences of Virgil's — they are the supreme sign
of his reticence and the height of his art. Perhaps we
might call them his songs without words. There is a
silence of Aeneas when the warning from Mercury
comes. There is a silence of Dido when the hero meets
her in the Mournful Fields. There is a silence of the poet
as he weaves his tragedy about them both. Much pondering of the theme, much practice in the art of magic,
preceded those eloquent silences.

Jason is no hero in love—neither is he in battle. In the
poem of Valerius Flaccus, an intelligent if not an inspired composer of verse, Jason takes part in the war
that was in progress between King Aeëtes and his
brother Perses, who also coveted the Golden Fleece.
The poet thus has a chance to develop the bravery of his
hero, who earns the fleece by his prowess and then is

cheated of it by the wiles of Aeëtes. He has a right, at
such a pass, to resort to Medea's art. The Jason of
Apollonius has no such excuse. He merely is presented
by Medea with a box of magic salve. He goes out to perform the midnight rites "like a stealthy thief," [1] wearing the robe that Hypsipyle gave him. One thinks in
contrast of the robe wrought by Dido for Aeneas, —

ipsa suis quondam manibus,[2] —

which he laid on the bier of young Pallas as the highest
honor he could pay. It was one of two robes, *geminas
vestis*, that she had made for him — he is not giving
both. If all the charm of all the Muses flowers in many
a lonely word of our poet, he also can pack a tragedy
into a word, as he does in *quondam* here. But what a
magic change! The cloak of Aeneas is a symbol of the
distress through which he had lived. The cloak of Jason
is a badge of the romantic in its worst form, the sentimental; it comes from his last sweetheart. Jason has
neither the virility nor the cynicism to make a Don
Juan. He is fond of women, however, and his present
passion will not last for long.

Such is our hero as he approaches the dragon "in
fear," πεφοβημένος [3] — but Medea's potions, luckily, are
mightier than his fear. One manly speech is contrived
for him, in which, as they leave Colchis, he declares
to his men that he will defend Medea to the end. His

    [1] III, 1197.   [2] *Aen.*, XI, 74.   [3] IV, 149.

only heroic deed, however, is the dastardly killing of Apsyrtus in cold blood. The climax of unmanliness is reached in the marriage scene. Of course he was postponing the ceremony until his return, but to have it depend on the ultimatum of Alcinous relieves it of the last vestige of romance. If Medea is still virgin, so Alcinous decrees, she must be sent back to her home, but otherwise the Argonauts may help her. Hence the immediate decision that she must not remain virgin. *Mariage forcé*, of a truth.

Medea has our respect, or at least our sympathy, throughout. Her conduct is entirely determined by the shaft of Cupid. She is a pawn for Hera, who has arranged the affair with Aphrodite. The debate within her breast, therefore, between shame and passion, αἰδώς and ἵμερος,[1] is somewhat gratuitous. She is a character for "Euripides the rationalist." Human action in the *Argonautica* as a result of human resolve is a superfluity; in the *Aeneid* the superfluities are the gods. Cupid did not need to assume the shape of Ascanius or to be fondled in Dido's arms; Dido was already aflame. But let me quickly retract that phrase about superfluities, into which that false divinity Epigram, in her most pernicious form, Antithesis, has tempted me. It is true, rather, that Virgil's world is half human and half divine. *Forte quadam divinitus*, "jewels upon which I chanced divinely" — Virgil is at one with Livy and Tennyson and

[1] III, 653.

with all who read the world for both its aspects.[1] Meantime, a little magic has been applied to Apollonius of Rhodes.

Not that there is any lack of human feeling or of penetrating psychological analysis in the *Argonautica*. After Medea has received the fatal shaft, she has won our utter pity. She supplicates her hero when he should have supplicated her. She feels continually that she has done wrong; on board the boat, she stretches out her hands to the shore. The cause of her calamity is well set forth by Arete, consort of Alcinous. One act, the gift of the magic charms to Jason, led inevitably to all the rest — and that act was really Cupid's. It is a chain of fate, with the murder of Apsyrtus as the last link. The heroine's character has shown little development. She has the power, an inherited power, of working magic spells, but not until the slaying of Apsyrtus is there a suggestion of Medea the awful witch, whom tradition had celebrated for centuries. Apollonius has softened her outlines, discarding everything that did not fit his picture of a tender, passionate, resourceful woman deeply in love. The poet is at one with the tendencies of the period, which was as adept as the Middle Ages in making over the stern nobility of the past into an easy modernness and romance —

> Nec nocet auctori mollem qui fecit Achillem
> Infregisse suis fortia facta modis.[2]

[1] See above, p. 366.   [2] Ovid, *Tristia*, II, 411.

One sees nevertheless in Medea a touch of those traits that would, after the mishap in store for her, turn her into the slayer of her children. There is premonition in her threat to invoke a curse on Jason if he abandons her. His reply is partly prompted by fear.[1]

Enough has been said of the portraiture of Jason and Medea in the *Argonautica* to show that there is matter for tragedy there, only that Apollonius has not cared to follow in the wake of Euripides and other dramatists who had used it for such an end. Possibly an epic of so small a compass as four books could not contain a tragedy too, or possibly Apollonius was not — he surely was not — possessed of the audacity of a Virgil, who commingled the categories without compunction.

There is no doubt that Virgil had devoted as much attention to the *Argonautica* as to the *Iliad* and the *Odyssey* themselves. A host of minor echoes might be assembled to prove this point. I will add but one instance to those that we have noticed by the way. One of the traits of Apollonius is a weakness for αἴτια, the mythological origins of persons, places, or events. The narrative is strewn with references to the establishment of religious rites or the founding of towns that resulted from the Argonauts' voyage. A certain impressiveness is gained; the voyage is dated thereby far back in those times when certain age-long institutions had their beginning. But there are too many of them. The poet is

[1] IV, 380 ff., especially 394.

suddenly revealed as one of the learned Alexandrians famous for special research in little-known myths; the tale of hairbreadth 'scapes in the imminent deadly breach is strewn with doctor's dissertations. They crowd at the end of the poem. Even the delightfully human touch at its very close, the banter of the maids with the men, is brought in to show the origin of a rite. The cloven hoof of the philologian also appears when the sowing of the dragon's teeth is described. They are the very teeth, we are told, of the dragon whom Cadmus had slain at Thebes; apparently he had not sown them all. Thus are two similar stories harmonized as the maker of a *summa mythologica* would harmonize them.   Ovid blithely tells them both in their proper places, leaving his readers to make of the coincidence what they will.

Now Virgil recognizes the presence of αἴτια as one of the necessary flavors of the kind of epic that he was writing, and obeys as ever the demands of tradition. He, too, is a *doctus poeta*; he had spent untold days in the amassing of his material and in the adjustment of it to epic procedure. But Virgil's learning never protrudes. He had allowed it to mellow and to mingle with poetic fancies. His poem has room for a few αἴτια, enough to create that impressiveness of which I have spoken, and to deepen Roman sentiment. He has also, as I have intimated, made over the gods of Apollonius by restoring them to their Homeric estate and by fitting them to the demands of tragedy. Above all, he has made over the persons in a story of romance to suit the same demand.

We return, for a moment, to that surprising statement in Servius in a better mood for comprehension:

Apollonius Argonautica scripsit et in tertio inducit amantem Medeam: inde totus hic liber translatus est.

Whatever Servius thought he was saying, the value of his words is precisely this: Virgil's starting-point was the *Argonautica* of Apollonius of Rhodes. From that poem — *inde* — he took over the outline of the story of love that he tells in the Fourth Aeneid. But before telling it, he had translated it — translated it into that upper region where tragedy is at home.

IV

What, then, at this juncture, turned Virgil to Greek tragedy?[1] He doubtless had studied other poems besides the *Argonautica*. He doubtless knew of the story of Demophoon and Phyllis, of Paris and Oenone, of Theseus and Ariadne; the latter he had read — read many times — in the Sixty-fourth Poem of Catullus. He transformed the Birth-Song of Achilles there chanted by the Fates into a new prophecy of a Golden Age, set not, romantically, in the dim and blessed past, but in the present, or the immediate future, of Italy, in which a Prince of Peace has just been born. That, as we saw, is one of the achievements of the Fourth Eclogue. Equally

---

[1] What use he made of Roman tragedy we may only guess.

impressive is the metamorphosis of the tale of Theseus and Ariadne into that of Aeneas and Dido. Virgil wants us to see what he has done. Throughout his story he weaves in phrases or even lines from Catullus's poem, inviting us to compare, and to contrast.[1]

The trouble with the heroes of the poems thus far mentioned is that they contribute little to Virgil's demands. They are all, except Odysseus, villains. They woo, win, and abandon. Odysseus is wooed, is won, and escapes. He receives our congratulations. The other heroes arouse our indignation, and their victims have our pitying sympathy. Pathos may be there intensely, as in the poem of Catullus, but there is no tragic problem to call for our solution or despair. All will be solved if we can catch the villain and treat him as he deserves. Somehow it would do no good to capture Aeneas. We should not know just how to chastise him. The hero cannot play the part of a common deceiver. He could not found Rome after that. Aeneas must be kept on the level of high epic. And Dido, too, must be made of sterner stuff than the swooning sentimentality of an Ariadne.

Tragedy, then, is the solution, and to tragedy the mind of the poet turns, possibly, first of all, to the many plays about Medea. In that of Euripides, the only one we know, he found no better model in Jason as there por-

[1] See "Catullus and the Augustans," *Harvard Studies in Classical Philology*, XVII (1906), 25-27.

trayed. He is even less satisfactory than the Jason of
Apollonius. The time of the play gives a later point in
the story. Jason is now an arch-hypocrite, a self-
righteous Pharisee, who would throw off his own base-
ness on somebody else. One might call him a caricature
of Aeneas, or an equivalent of what certain indignant
readers would take Aeneas to be. If that was so, no
wonder the poet wished to burn his masterpiece!

Nor is there much help in other plays of Euripides or
his fellow-dramatists. Love had only gradually been
taken up by the tragedians as a theme worthy of their
art. There are the love episodes in Homer; the face
of Helen had launched a thousand ships against Troy.
Doubtless from the very dawn of history the clue for the
unraveller of causes should be "Cherchez la femme!"
But at least, so far as we know, an elaborate, psychological treatment of love waited for Euripides, and it was to
Euripides that Virgil, in his present perplexity, chiefly
turned.

Once more, he found no fitting models for his hero. In
the plays in which love plays a prominent part, egoism
is no less prominent. This is the cardinal sin, in which
ὕβρις is involved, that Euripides lashes with a subtle
ridicule that George Meredith would have applauded —
possibly did applaud. Jason is an egoist; so is Hippolytus; so is the father of Admetus, for whose sake Alcestis
consented to die; so is, just a wee bit, I am afraid, Alcestis herself. There may be some suggestions for Dido's

fate in the death of Alcestis or that of Ajax in the play
of Sophocles. The speeches of Jason and Medea are
models in outline and dramatic tone for those of Aeneas
and Dido — but ah, how different their substance, their
inner feeling, is!

The play that, next to the *Medea*, perhaps most attracted Virgil in this quest was the *Hippolytus*. The hero
is pious — overmuch so; he is even something of a prig,
a superman, περισσὸς ἀνήρ; he thanks Heaven that he is
not such as Aphrodite is. And yet he is sweet and pure,
wholesome in his love of nature and the hunt. He is lovable — others besides Phaedra find him so. He keeps his
vow to the end and is noble in his death. Phaedra is detestable, of course — but is she wholly detestable? Her
passion, though fierce, is pure and, after all, nothing in-
cestuous. Moreover, it is fated, partly by heredity, completely by the will of Aphrodite. Phaedra struggles but
cannot overcome. She makes atonement by her death
and descends to it an *anima candida*. Ah, there is a
tragic complication at last! What are we, puppets in the
hands of the gods? May we throw off our evil on them,
and, if so, do they merit our worship? Euripides, religious, almost mediaeval at times, leaves the question of
Hippolytus and Phaedra in a blur.[1] Virgil, who had
pondered this tragic problem early in life, as we have
seen,[2] now took it up afresh. He retained the Euripidean
gods, relieving their malignity with a touch of Homeric

[1] See above, p. 369.   [2] See above , p. 349.

humor. But the gods themselves, as well as men, act in the presence of a power that makes for righteousness, and the ultimate happiness of the world — the *fatum Romanum*.

One way to exalt the hero is to depreciate the heroine. If Aeneas must abandon her, she must deserve to be abandoned. Perhaps that is the easiest way out. Carthage was the traditional foe of Rome and no faith should be kept with Punic heretics. If Naevius, who fought in the First Punic War and wrote an epic on the Second, told, as seems likely, the story of Aeneas and Dido by way of preface, his lines were doubtless spiced with patriotism and indignation. Perhaps he inserted a little hymn of hate, vastly popular with his contemporaries. For Virgil's Dido prophesies the coming of her avenger who shall sweep through the land of the Trojan colonists with fire and with sword. Or, to come down to Virgil's time, there was a fateful Egyptian queen who played havoc with one great Roman and thoroughly disgraced another. Let Dido be a symbol of the Punic Wars and embody something of Cleopatra's poisonous charm, and all right-minded Romans will applaud when Aeneas casts off from Carthage. The Emperor himself will read with both pleasure and profit, noting what the Ruler of Rome is not and what he should not be.

To the lure of such allegory, a temptation of the Evil One, our poet gave no heed.[1] A great work of art al-

[1] See above, p. 356.

ways inspires moral lessons and incites to particular ap-
plications. Certain modern students are much concerned with both. I greatly doubt, however, that at the
end of their reading of the Fourth Book of the *Aeneid*
young Romans shouted "*Delenda est Carthago!*," which
Augustus was just trying to build up, or that old Romans caught up the strain with "*Pereat Cleopatra!*"
Lucan has his chance to reflect Virgil when he comes to
Cleopatra in his epic. From the spirit of the *Aeneid* few
later poets could escape — the story of the Argonauts
meant something new to Valerius Flaccus because of
Virgil's hero, and Ovid's story of Phyllis, thanks to Virgil, almost rises to the tragic plane. If current interpretation had identified Cleopatra with Dido, we should
expect some trace of that idea in Lucan; but to Lucan,
Cleopatra is a simple beast.[1]

No, that is not the way — to make a vampire of Dido.
Heroine and hero both must be noble, despite the lapse,
a pitiable but undeniable lapse, that brought them to
disaster. In a word, when romance is exalted to tragedy,
they must remain human, become more intensely human, though involved in the interplay of powers *über
unsere Kraft*. Allegory is unnecessary and base if real
human beings can be created. Part of the growth of
Aeneas in the poet's mind I have endeavored to suggest.
Touches of Dido are apparent in the heroines whom her
creator had contemplated — the passion of Phaedra,

---

[1] She is *incesta soror* (VIII, 693). Her character is displayed in Book X.

the suffering of Medea, the queenly competence of Hypsipyle, the steadfastness of Alcestis, all this and something more. Her creator watched her day by day, as Pygmalion watched his statue until the magic moment came when

ad lumina lumen
attollens pariter cum caelo vidit amantem.[1]

Poor Aeneas! He, the easier creation, had now, by this irony of magic, become the harder. The intention of the poet is clear; the question, very variously answered, is whether he succeeded and whether he thought that he had succeeded. For one, I am ready to take Aeneas on faith, remembering his silences, like the silence of Hamlet in his love of Ophelia; for he at the end of the play, like Aeneas in the Mournful Fields, becomes eloquent enough.

In some such way as this, Virgil had transmuted romance into tragedy. I would not be numbered among the foes of romance or think our poet incapable of it. Nothing is too romantic for Virgil — nothing too romantic to transmute into the right mood for tragedy or epic. Perhaps we are juggling with words. John Addington Symonds calls the story of Dido "the only classic masterpiece of pure romantic pathos."[2] I associate with romance the sentiments of wonder, adventure, love, a wistful longing for a Golden Age in the dim past, or for

[1] Ovid, *Met.*, X, 293.
[2] *The Renaissance in Italy*, Vol. II, "The Revival of Learning" (2d ed., 1882), p. 23.

one in the dim future. None of these feelings is alien to
Virgil, but they do not master him. His vision of life
sweeps over past and future, but is concentrated on the
present. His mind is its own place. His sympathy for
the fate of his characters has no room for rebellion
against the governing issues of life. In his larger out-
looks he returns, after much loving study of the Alexandrians, to the noble severity of the dramatists of the
fifth century and to the radiant calm of Homer.

Such is our magician when his epic is done and tragedy
has been interwoven in its tissue harmoniously. Both he
and his critics might wish for some improvement here
and there. But one act of magic at least is perfect, destined to resist the ravages of time. It is perhaps the
hardest magic of all. Homer had achieved it, but Ovid,
though master of all the secrets of the art of love, and
master of Pygmalion, did not even attempt it. It is the
creation of a real woman, eternally appealing in her sufferings, eternally compelling in her charm.

CHAPTER XII

PRIMITIVE SIMPLICITY FROM
IMPERIAL ROME

VIRGIL's revolutionary plan for his epic of Rome involved, as we have seen, an abandonment of the triumphs of Augustus and a retreat into the primitive past. This backward movement in time was accompanied, necessarily, by a backward movement in space. The scenery of the new epic could not, any more than the persons or events, be that of Augustan Rome. And yet, shimmering through the mythical narrative, Augustan places no less than Augustan persons and events must be discerned. More magic, an extraordinarily subtle magic, must be invoked. Temples and palaces familiar to Roman eyes must be suddenly swept away. The latest triumphs of engineering must dissolve from the scene, and a realm of mystic awe and pristine simplicity take their place.

I

There is no reason, really, from what *historia* could tell the poet, why Aeneas should have gone to Rome at all. We learn from Livy, for instance, that he landed on the shores of the Laurentine community, the northwestern part of Latium, and there, after either a battle or a conference of the two leaders, made a treaty with Latinus, king of the inhabitants of the land, and received the hand of the king's daughter Lavinia in marriage. Thereafter, Turnus, king of the Rutuli, who had been betrothed to Lavinia before the advent of Aeneas, smarted for revenge and attacked both Trojans and Aborigines. He lost the first battle, but Latinus was slain. Turnus then appealed to Mezentius, ruler of the mighty Etruscans. Aeneas gained the affection of the Aborigines by giving them equal rights with the Trojans and led a united army against the foe. The Latins — so now the new people is called — won the day, but for Aeneas it was the last of his earthly works. He lies buried, whatever it is right and proper to call him, says Livy cautiously, by the banks of the river Numicus; and is invoked as the local Jupiter. The popular belief was that he was translated to the skies.

Where is Rome, in this version of *historia*? Aeneas never reached the seven hills on the Tiber. Why then did Virgil make over the accepted account? I am afraid that here, as in the story of the last night of Troy, he has offended against the law laid down by Servius, and thrown tradition to the winds. The schoolboy, winning his way along the dulcet lines, is not aware what audacities the poet has committed. Virgil starts with the form of the legend that recorded an alliance made immediately with Latinus, but for the poet's purpose this alliance cannot stand; it runs counter to the will of Juno, who, through the Fury, rouses Turnus to revenge. The fight will now be between the Trojans and the joint forces of the Latins and the Rutulians; Latinus, who sees the sight but weakly cannot follow it, has yielded to his consort Amata, to whom young Turnus, handsome, noble, and bold, seemed a most acceptable son-in-law. The combat between Aeneas and Turnus must be kept till the end of the poem, and it must match in interest and in sublimity the combat of Achilles and Hector in the *Iliad*.

How can the Trojans, noble warriors, but a handful, win the fight? The gods could help, but the gods are on both sides, as in the battles of Homer. It must be a human fight — or rather, as was indicated in the preceding chapter and as is admirably portrayed by my friend Conway in various of his essays, Virgil, with his customary view of our little world, will have events both human and divine commingling on his battlefield. In brief, the Trojans need allies, and the allies must come from some other part of Italy. They will be the Etruscans, Virgil's own ancestors, with a delegation from little Mantua among them. For Virgil, we may note parenthetically — and I am depending on a fine little essay of my friend Professor Nardi tucked away in a recent issue of a daily paper [1] — Virgil was most probably an Etruscan; no Celtic blood flowed in his veins, and no evidences of the Celtic spirit, whatever that may be, need

[1] *Il Popolo d'Italia* of Milan, April 2, 1930.

be gathered by discerning critics from his poetry. But what chance would the invader have by appealing directly to the Etruscan king? That Mezentius was on the side of the Rutulians seemed too deep-rooted a part of the tradition for the poet to deny. He therefore becomes a refugee, a hero bold and bad, in revolt against Heaven itself and no worthy representative of his race. A part of them he had dragged along with him, but the people themselves remain true — true to the ideal that the poet set for them. The hero, however, turns not to them but to Evander, a traveller from Arcadia, who had made a little settlement on the very spot where Rome was later to be. To Evander, joined to Aeneas by ties of ancestry, the appeal must be made. Hence the voyage up the Tiber to the spot where stood the seven hills.

The meaning of the voyage and of the visit to Evander, thus motivated by the demands of the obvious narrative, is something deeper still. The plot of the *Aeneid*, like that of most epics after Virgil wrote, is of a twofold character. Something of the sort may be made out in the *Iliad*, and Virgil doubtless saw its presence there. But in the *Aeneid* it is written into the very texture of the poem and is the clue to its ultimate greatness. Mr. Saintsbury, as we have seen,[1] in one of the jaunty utterances that make his *History of Criticism* lively reading, remarks that when we come to the Seventh Book of the *Aeneid* the interest of the poem is all but over. Virgil

[1] See above, p. 373.

himself seems not to agree with Mr. Saintsbury. After lines of an unparalleled music at the opening of the Seventh Book, he invokes the Muse again and declares that a greater order of events and a greater work are now to be created:

> maior rerum mihi nascitur ordo,
> maius opus moveo.

This greater work, this larger plan, necessitated a certain amount of allegory in the *Aeneid*. If we seek to identify the persons of the poem with those in Homer's epic or with characters in Roman history, we shall come to grief. Aeneas, with the model of Homer ever before us, is another Achilles, chief of the invaders, and Turnus is another Hector, mainstay of the defence. But in their characters this relation is reversed; the gentle Aeneas is another Hector, the violent Turnus another Achilles. If contemporary parallels are sought, Aeneas is Augustus, and Turnus, therefore, Antony. But if Hercules, as has been recently maintained, is Augustus, then Cacus is Antony. Readers of the poem in the Augustan Age may have endeavored to detect such resemblances, just as readers of a successful novel today are sometimes prone to identify its characters with persons of the author's acquaintance. I know of one such novel which was given one set of identifications in a certain city in the East and another in a certain city of the Middle West. If Virgil meant to flash such resemblances before us, in the next instant those resemblances are gone. His art of allegory, as ever, is something transitory and elusive. We may not pin it down. The characters in his poem are not lay figures for allegorical drapings, but living persons, just as real to us today as the actual historical characters, the major and minor figures of the Augustan Age whom they vaguely may foreshadow.

There is, however, in the poem a general and pervasive sort of allegory, which constitutes one aspect of what I should call its larger plot. Its lesser plot, concerned with the actors in the story, is the problem of how the hero, with the help of his new allies, is to defeat his valiant foe, win his promised bride, and found a new Troy in Latium. The larger plot is concerned with the ideal aspects of the Roman temperament. As I have already tried to make clear,[1] it tells of a battle between the native qualities of Italy and the civilizing influences that came to it from abroad, and particularly from Greece. Aeneas is a symbol of these influences; Turnus and the natives are the qualities on which these influences work. The city founded is a *civitas Dei*, the Roman ideal in its richness and strength, with a mission of peace for all the world. This larger plot is nowhere stated in the poem as crudely as I have stated it here. It is subtly infused throughout the narrative, giving it tone and strength.

The different books of the *Aeneid* are unities in their action and in the general coloring that pervades them.

[1] See above, pp. 376–380.

This fact did not escape the notice of Servius, who designates at least the first six each with a single word, declaring them to be pictures of life.[1]   The First he calls *omina*, the Second *pathos*, the Third *errores*, the Fourth *ethos*, the Fifth *festivitas*, the Sixth *scientia*. These words I would partly translate and partly replace with the following, which have a more modern, perhaps a too modern ring, and are intended to suggest the tone, or coloring, or mood of the different books.

The First is the Quest, or the Vision. The Second is Disaster. The Third is Deferment. The Fourth is Tragedy. The Fifth is Gayety, Servius's word. The Sixth is Majesty, or Sublimity, befitting Philosophy, which Servius rightly finds the essence of this book.

But let us boldly extend this series, in the fashion already set forth, to the latter half of the poem. The Seventh Book I have called Italy, and the Eighth is Rome; we shall examine them more carefully below. The Ninth is Sorrow and Defeat, the reverses that meet the Trojans when their leader is gone. The Tenth is Hope and the Battle, the courage that they recover when he returns. The Eleventh is again Sorrow and Defeat, the general sorrow that now broods over the protracted fight, and the defeat that now threatens the

[1] On *Aen.*, III, 718: epilogos dedit sex istis prioribus libris, quos et esse bioticos voluit. nam singulis res singulas dedit, ut primo omina, secundo pathos, tertio errores, quarto ethos, quinto festivitatem, sexto scientiam. Heinze, *Virgils Epische Technik* (Leipsic and Berlin, 3d ed., 1915), pp. 448–53, names the books from the central events described.

Latins. The Twelfth is Tragedy and Fulfilment. The tragedy is that of Turnus; it was foreshadowed at the start, suggested by various touches all along, and now is brought to a climax. The Fulfilment is that of both the lesser and the larger plot. The lesser is fulfilled when Turnus receives his deathblow. The larger issue, the union of the two elements that make up the new nation, has already been assured. Aeneas has declared that he seeks no sovereignty, but that he will contribute religion, enlightenment, to this new civilization in which both races unvanquished shall be loyal to an eternal pact under equal laws. It is a noble peace without victory. The invaders will not dominate the conquered, but themselves will be absorbed. Virgil had recounted the limitations of his countrymen in the splendid lines at the end of the Sixth Book; he now makes amends — it is his larger and his truer meaning — by proclaiming the full majesty and the richness of the Roman ideal.

The Seventh Book and the Eighth Book, therefore, — Italy and Rome, — present unmistakably the chief actors in the larger drama of the *Aeneid* that becomes ever plainer as the poem sweeps to its close. The attainment of the goal is nothing easy. Various frustrations intervene. If in the first half of the poem an *Italia fugiens* is ever held beyond the hero's grasp, it is now *Roma fugiens* that eludes him. Thus is the solution of the larger plot postponed.

The Seventh Book sets before us no race of savages.

These aborigines are primitive; they are armed with un-couth implements and they are quick to quarrel. The late Richard Heinze, to whom every lover of our poet owes a lasting gratitude, admonished us not to associate the pious shepherds of the *Bucolics* and the *Georgics* with the hardened rustics — *duri agrestes, indomiti agricolae* — of the Seventh Book.[1] I venture to think, how-ever, that Virgil's chief interest is to show the inherent worth of this sturdy folk, from whom no less than from the Trojans the Roman lineage was to spring. They are a warlike race and have overcome valiant enemies. They are a religious race, with temples and decorous rites; yes, the ceremony of closing the temple of Janus in time of peace was established by these aborigines. To Virgil's contemporaries, hardly any religious or political event could have had a more spectacular importance than the closing of Janus's temple twice in the reign of Augustus, once after the victory of Actium and once in the year 25, not long after, perhaps very shortly after, the Seventh Book was written. Only once before in all Roman his-tory had this happy event occurred, namely, at the com-pletion of the First Punic War. The veritable founder of the custom, according to tradition, was King Numa. Virgil must have some deep-seated motive for refashion-ing tradition in a matter so momentous as this. What surer sign of his desire to shed the lustre of legend about these early times, which really were wrapped in dark-

[1] *Op. cit.*, p. 190, n. 1.

ness, and thence to ennoble the primitive people of Italy? They come of no mean lineage. The human and the divine mingle in their origin; Caeculus, one of their heroes, is sprung of Vulcan. Indeed, at the moment when the invaders arrive they are still enjoying the dispensation of the Saturnian, the Golden Age, constrained by no external laws, but bound to righteousness by their own character and their ancient faith.[1]

> Saturni gentem haud vinclo nec legibus aequam
> sponte sua veterisque dei se more tenentem.

This plain statement is reinforced by various echoes of the *Bucolics* and the *Georgics*, in particular a glancing back at the famous rhapsody on Italy in the Second Book of the latter poem. It is as though he meant to say, "Yes, it is the same Italy. Our own Saturnian land, land of nature's miracles and of men that I praised in a song of Ascra heard in Roman towns, was lovely and noble even then, in the days our ancestors,

> quibus Itala iam tum
> floruerit terra alma viris." [2]

Another magic touch that, with numerous others, helps to give the Seventh Book more of the pastoral charm of the *Bucolics* and the *Georgics* than is found in any other part of the poem is the creation of the hero Galaesus. He will not be found in any Roman history

---

[1] *Aen.*, VII, 203.
[2] *Aen.*, VII, 643. Cf. *Georg.*, II, 173:
> Salve magna parens frugum, Saturnia tellus
> magna virum.

of the day. He is the personification of the river Galaesus down by Tarentum, a locality which was dear for good reason, we have been tempted to infer,[1] both to Virgil and to his admiring Horace. The happy imagination with which Pontano and Sannazaro, exquisite masters of Latin verse in the Renaissance, transformed into nymphs the hills and streams and villas by the fair bay of Naples was partly taught them by Virgil.

Virgil, for all his sovereign contempt of tradition, is truer than the historians. They begin the history of Rome with Aeneas, since Latinus and his Aborigines are merely shadowy names. Virgil begins it with the Golden Age. He finds among this ancient folk a wealth of historical and religious tradition, to say nothing of forefathers who descended from the great Greek heroes and who founded Troy itself. His purpose is to show the strength and dignity and creativeness of Italy. He starts with long-established customs of the Romans, but instead of stringing them along in a more or less uncertain chronology he masses them in the period of his story, implying that their development had preceded. This readjustment gives a truer picture of the Roman genius and its expression in political and religious rites of great beauty and poetic charm than some careful *Religionsgeschichte* of today. We sometimes get the idea, because of uncertainties of chronology, because of the false at-

[1] See above, pp. 75 f.

tribution of many inventions to one man, — government to Romulus, religion to Numa, — that somehow the institutions so trusted are unsubstantial. We need a Virgil to give us a more critical account than that of the critical historians.

But Aeneas and his men are waiting to embark for their adventurous journey up the Tiber to seek allies in the spot where later stood the city Rome. The motive of their going is now, I hope, doubly plain. I have had to make it thus explicit that the full force of Virgil's magic may be appreciated. Aeneas sails up the waters of the kindly Tiber and finds Evander and his son Pallas making sacrifice to Hercules.[1] The heroes interchange greetings and identify their genealogies. In the larger plot of the poem, it is a meeting of Greek with Greek; they both are *optimi Graiugenarum*; and their union with the Etruscans, who were responsible for so many of the institutions of the young Roman state, is typical of the poet's plan.[2] The worship of Hercules is likewise a foreign affair, whether or not the story of Cacus, as the Augustan scholar Verrius Flaccus, reported by Servius, informs us,[3] was an old Italian legend in which the conqueror of Cacus was one Garanus, a shepherd of mighty strength. In any event the tale had become thoroughly Hellenized

[1] *Aen.*, VIII, 102.

[2] The importance of the Etruscan element in Virgil's idea of Roman culture is well brought out by Nardi in his article "Antiquam Exquirite Matrem," in *Virgiliana*, I (1930), 5–7. Not everything spiritual was introduced from outside. Aeneas's journey to Italy was a kind of home-coming.

[3] On *Aen.*, VIII, 203.

by Virgil's time, and Livy tells us [1] that the worship of Hercules was the only Greek rite adopted by Romulus. The rites celebrated by Evander are splendidly portrayed, and with them are associated, in Virgil's way, the Salii, the leaping priests of Mars. The poet would attribute to early Rome and its colony of Grecians no less than to Latium a wealthy liturgy of beauty.

The ceremony over, Evander escorts his guest through the city to his home. And here enters the magician. The sacrifice has been made on the Great Altar, Ara Maxima, which Hercules had erected and which had ever since been sanctified by his rites. Virgil and his contemporaries knew it well. The heroes are not far from what today is the square known as the Bocca della Verità, with the Palatine not far to the east, the Tiber not far to the west, and the Capitoline towards the north as their nearest objective. As they proceed, Aeneas looks about him in wonder. He asks many questions and receives many answers about the various monuments of the men of old —

virum monimenta priorum.

Rome is already ancient. But what a Rome do they see! I will not try to reconstruct the city that Virgil knew. It was a far simpler place than that which the traveller today can picture with the help of the Colosseum, the Arch of Titus, the Basilica of Constantine, and other well-known landmarks that seem eternally characteris-

[1] I, 7, 3-15.

tic of the eternal Rome. Nor had the chief improvements of Augustus been effected when Virgil was writing his *Aeneid*; for instance, the Temple of Mars Ultor had not been built. Architecture lagged behind literature in the Augustan Age; at the time of Virgil's death not all the brick had been turned by the Emperor to marble. For all that, Rome was a magnificent place; and if it did not contain some of the buildings that we can see, it had others that we cannot.

Evander and his guest move northward. The "monuments of the men of old" seem at first nothing substantial in brick or stone. Woods are all about, and they preserve the memory of fauns and nymphs. The Golden Age succeeded, and after Saturnus came Ausonians, Sicanians, Italians. A race of kings ensued, among them Thybris, who named the Tiber river. Evander speaks as an old man who is sounding the depths of history; even primitive Rome has its long perspective. He now points out the first bit of architecture that they have seen after the Ara Maxima. It is the altar in honor of his mother Carmentis, a nymph and prophetess; we are not far from the age of nymphs and fauns after all. Her prophecies were true, for she sang of the coming of Aeneas and his men and of the future destiny of the hill named for her son, Pallanteum, later Palatium, the imperial Palatine. Her gate is also there, the Porta Carmentalis; what though it be one of the gates of the later Servian Wall, our magician can pick it up and set it where he likes.

Now they look up at the wooded slopes of the Capitoline; the mighty grove there, though they know it not,
will be the site of the Place of Refuge established by
Romulus for refugees to swell the number of his citizens.
Across the way on the slopes of the Palatine is the Wolf's
Den, Lupercal. Evander can point it out. It was there in
his day, and named, from the rites of Arcadian Pan,
dweller on the Lycaean range, Wolf Mountain; later
the story of Romulus and Remus will give it a new
meaning — perhaps the poet is painting in, anachronistically again, just a bit of later Roman color. Off in the
distance, on the north of what Virgil knew as the Forum,
lies the Argiletum. This was, in his time, one of the
thoroughfares leading to that busy spot. The Romans
had a dozen explanations of the name, which the curious
will find in Servius. For Virgil's Evander it meant the
tomb where he laid the remains of his guest Argus, a
faithless guest who had plotted his murder but was detected and slain by the King's loyal friends. For all that,
the ruler gave him decent burial — not that he deserved
it, says Servius, but *hospitalitatis causa*; the sacred law
of guest-friendship must be kept intact. "And fittingly
does he dwell on that point," adds Servius,[1] "and explains the causes of the act, to allay any surmise of his
present guest."

And now they climb the Capitoline, famous later for
the rock of Tarpeia, the faithless Sabine maiden, and for

[1] On *Aen.*, VIII, 345.

Jupiter's gold-roofed temple that Virgil's readers knew. But the poet's magic showed these readers instead nothing but woods and bristling thickets. And yet there was some strange stirring of the divine; the rustics trembled as they gazed on the woods and the rock. Surely some god dwelt there. The Arcadians had tales of seeing Jove himself shaking his blackening aegis in his left hand and with his right summoning the rain-clouds; for so had they seen him in their native mountains near the sky. Off across the river is the hill of Janus, and another citadel is that of Saturn. Ah, here are veritably the monuments of men of old, the ruined walls on both these hills —

disiectis oppida muris
reliquias veterumque vides monimenta virorum.

They now direct their steps to the King's own dwelling, crossing what later was the bustling Forum, where they heard the lowing of the grazing kine. They pass the Carinae, the "Keels," name of what to Virgil's readers was a fashionable place of residence on the west slope of the Esquiline, but when Aeneas and Evander pass that way, there are the lowing kine.

They mount the Palatine on its eastern side and come to a modest house. Evander speaks:

"This threshold Hercules the victor crossed,
And this the palace that then sheltered him.
Dare thou, my guest, like him to scorn display.
Fit thyself, like him, for a life divine,
Nor come disdainful to a poor estate."

> He spake, and neath the rafters of his hut
> He brought the mighty hero to his bed —
> A bear-skin quilting on a pile of leaves.

This is the passage of which Dryden said, "For my part, I am lost in the admiration of it; I contemn the world when I think on it, and myself when I translate it."

> Aude, hospes, contemnere opes et te quoque dignum
> finge deo, rebusque veni non asper egenis —[1]

the words in their sheer simplicity startle the reader with the force of the Decalogue or the Sermon on the Mount. They come at the close of a climax, for the walk through Rome stops suddenly at the site of the palace of Augustus. It was a modest palace, Suetonius tells us;[2] the utterance of the poet is both admonition and acclaim. He speaks from the heart in a flood of repressed emotion. It is one of the rare lyrical moments in the poem, like the dirge on the young Marcellus at the end of Anchises' prophecy in the Elysian fields,[3] or the poet's vaunt that, if aught his songs should avail, the tragedy of Nisus and Euryalus, happy in their deaths, should live in the minds of men as long as the household of Aeneas held the firm rock of the Capitoline.[4]

While Aeneas sleeps in the King's hut, the scene shifts to the world of the gods. Venus spurs Vulcan, her spouse, to make new armor for her son. The Cyclops' forges are busy and the task is finished with the dawn.

---

[1] *Dedication of the Aeneis* (Cambridge Edition), p. 518.
[2] *Aug.*, 72. [3] *Aen.*, VI, 882 ff. [4] IX, 446 ff.

On the shield is engraven the whole history of Rome. The early legends of the early kings are there, the sack of the city by the Gauls, the punishment of Catiline in Hell, the exaltation of Cato in the abode of the just — and, yes, the full triumph of Augustus is there, and the defeat of Antony with his wanton queen at Actium, the defeat of the dog-faced Anubis and all the monstrous gods of Egypt, the defeat of all the hosts of wrong, the victory of Roman peace throughout the world. Small space for many scenes, small space for Virgil's epic on Augustus's deeds, the epic that he had once planned for a poem and now had confined within the border of a shield. Illusion masters the impossible, as with the scenes that Hephaestus engraved on the shield of Achilles. What would be impossible in description is set forth convincingly in narrative. Homer tells us of each marvel as the divine craftsman adds it; Virgil, with no less delicate an art, as Lessing ought to have seen, shows us the hero spelling out the mysterious stories one by one, delighting in the scenes that he does not comprehend and raising on his shoulders

> the fame and fates of his own lineage —
> attollens umero famamque et fata nepotum.

In this the last line of the book the diapason of the poet's song ends full in Rome.

The imagination displayed in this intrusion of actual history into the setting of myth in which the whole poem is placed is of a higher quality, if I mistake not, than that in the only other similar scene in the *Aeneid*, where Anchises in the Elysian fields unrolls the full history of Rome as he points to the line of heroes waiting for the draft of Lethe and the careers in store for them in the world of men — Platonic imagery appropriated for a dramatic intent, but no less expressive of the poet's inmost soul.

I have anticipated somewhat, neglecting for my purpose the moment when Aeneas wakes in his hut on the Palatine, roused by the kindly light and

> the morning songs of birds beneath the roof —
>
> et matutini volucrum sub culmine cantus.[1]

In this line of liquid music we have the supreme art of magic in the poem. At the waving of the master's wand, the splendors of the imperial city are dissolved, and the courtier's pride in the prosperity of Rome gives place to the prophet's summons to simple living and righteousness —

> aude, hospes, contemnere opes et te quoque dignum finge deo.

II

I have spoken of the imagination displayed in the Sixth Book of the poem as inferior to that in the Eighth. When we now turn to the earlier book, I am not so sure. It is hard to be sure of just what is best in Virgil. When Dryden says of the passage of splendid patriotism at

[1] L. 456.

the end of the First Book of the *Georgics* that "the poetry of this book is more sublime than any part of Virgil, if I have any taste," [1] I believe in his impeccable taste — until I read the praise of country life at the end of the Second Georgic, or see all Rome on the shield of Aeneas — or see it again in the vision of Anchises. There are many best passages in Virgil.

In the Sixth Book, at all events, another act of magic awaits us, of like nature to that which we have just observed. Before his descent to the world of the shades, Aeneas takes counsel of the Cumaean Sibyl. His fleet has come to anchor at Cumae. His first care is to visit the temple of Apollo, hard by the huge cave — *antrum immane* — of the Sibyl. On the temple doors he sees graven the whole story of Daedalus, who escaped from Crete and the Minotaur's labyrinth that he had constructed, flying on wings of his own workmanship. Aeneas is lost in the contemplation of this masterpiece of art, when the priestess of Apollo, the Sibyl herself, accompanied by the faithful Achates, reminds him of the sacrifice that he is neglecting. They approach the cave, cut out from the broad expanse of rock in which are perforated a hundred openings, a hundred doors, whence issue the responses of the Sibyl. As the virgin approaches the threshold, the power of the god comes upon her. Her face, her color, change; her locks are in a wild disarray; her breast heaves; a fierce frenzy pos-

[1] In his *Notes and Observations* on his translation of Virgil (Cambridge Edition), p. 710.

sesses her; her stature seems more than mortal; and no mortal voice speaks from her lips as she bids Aeneas pray. At the conclusion of his prayer, the raving priestess struggles against the flooding presence of the god, but in vain. The hundred doors of the cave open wide, and out is poured the response of the oracle. It is a grim prophecy of bloody wars, an ordeal harder than the perils of the sea through which the hero has passed. But he must steel himself to the task. "Go," she proclaims, in words as brave as ever uttered — words with which Aldus, greatest name in the history of the art of printing, was wont to cheer himself in the midst of his gigantic feats —

> To hardship yield not, but more boldly face it
> Than your fates let you.

> Tu ne cede malis sed contra audentior ito
> Quam tua te fortuna sinet.

All this sounds like a fairy-story, told in the epic key, a worthy prelude to the pursuit of the Golden Bough in the forest and to that easy descent through the opening by Lake Avernus into the realms of the dead. What is all this but the sublime imagination of the poet? So thinks the schoolboy, perhaps not feeling much sublime imagination in the lesson prescribed, but at least he knows that the poet is making these things up. And yet, the temple of Apollo, the Sibyl's cave, and even the entrance to Hell, can be seen at Cumae and Lake Avernus today. *Crede experto.*

To acquaint ourselves with the region, we cannot do better than consider what the ancient geographer Strabo has to say about various places that are near to the Sibyl's cave. Strabo was a contemporary of Virgil's, a Greek by birth but a Roman in spirit. He visited Rome several times, first in 44 B.C., not long after Virgil came down to the city from Milan. He thus describes Cumae.[1]

Next in order after these two cities comes Cumae, a city founded in most ancient times by people from Chalcis and the Euboean Κύμη; for it is the oldest of all the Sicilian and the Italiote cities. However, the men who led the expedition, Hippocles of Κύμη and Megasthenes of Chalcis, made an agreement with one another that the city should be a colony of Chalcis, and a namesake of Κύμη, and hence, although the city is now called Cumae, it is reputed to have been founded by the Chalcidians alone. In earlier times, then, the city was prosperous, and so was what is called the Phlegraean Plain, which mythology has made the setting of the story of the Giants — for no other reason, it would seem, than that the land, on account of its excellence, was a thing to fight for; but later on, when the Campani became established as masters of the city, they committed numerous outrages against the people. . . . Nevertheless, many traces of the Greek culture and usages are still preserved there. But according to some, "Cumae" is named after the κύματα, "Waves"; for the neighboring shore is surfy and exposed to the wind. And Cumae also has the best fisheries for the catching of large fish. Moreover, on this gulf there is a forest of scrub trees, extending for many stadia over a waterless and sandy tract,

[1] V, 4, 4. I use the excellent translation (very little modified) of H. L. Jones in the Loeb edition of Strabo, London, 1923. The reader should consult a map of Naples and vicinity for the places mentioned in Strabo's account. On Cumae and the Sibyl, see Professor Catharine Saunders's excellent book, *Vergil's Primitive Italy*, Oxford, 1930, pp. 13–29.

which they call *Silva Gallinaria* (Poultry Forest). Here it was that the admirals of Sextus Pompeius assembled bands of pirates at that critical time when he caused Sicily to revolt.[1]

Near Cumae is Cape Misenum, and between them is the Acherusian Lake, a kind of shoal-water estuary of the sea. After you double Cape Misenum you immediately come to a harbor, the base of which runs inland and forms a deeply indented gulf — the coast on which is situated Baiae, and those hot springs that are suited both to the taste of the fashionable and to the cure of disease. Contiguous to Baiae is Gulf Lucrinus, and also, behind this gulf, Gulf Avernus, which forms a peninsula of the land that is cut off as far as Misenum, beginning from the transverse line which runs between Cumae and Avernus, for there remains an isthmus only a few stadia broad, that is, reckoning straight through the tunnel to Cumae itself and to the sea next to Cumae. The people prior to my time were wont to make Avernus the setting of the fabulous story of the Homeric νέκυια (the invocation of the dead); and, what is more, writers tell us that there actually was an oracle of the dead here and that Odysseus visited it. Now Gulf Avernus is deep, up to the very shore, and has a clear outlet; and it has both the size and character of a harbor, although it is useless as a harbor because of the fact that Gulf Lucrinus lies before it and is somewhat shallow as well as considerable in extent. Again, Avernus is enclosed round about by steep hill-brows that rise above it on all sides except where you sail into it (at the present time they have been brought by the toil of man into cultivation, though in former times they were thickly covered with a wild and untrodden forest of large trees); and these hill-brows, because of the superstition of man, used to make the gulf a shadowy place. And the natives used to add the further fable that all birds that fly over it fall down into the water (Avernus, from ἄορνος), being killed by the vapors that rise from it, as in the case of all the Plutonia.[2] And people used to suppose that

[1] That is, at the time of the battle of Philippi, 42 B.C.
[2] That is, entrances to the realms of Pluto.

this too was a Plutonian place and that the Cimmerians had actually been there. At any rate, only those who had sacrificed beforehand and propitiated the nether deities could sail into Avernus, and priests who held the locality on lease were there to give directions in all such matters; and there is a fountain of potable water at this place, on the sea, but people used to abstain from it because they regarded it as the water of the Styx; and the oracle, too, is situated somewhere near it; and further, the hot springs near by and Lake Acherusia betokened the River Pyriphlegethon.[1] Again, Ephorus, in the passage where he claims the locality in question for the Cimmerians, says: They live in underground houses, which they call "argillae," and it is through tunnels that they visit one another, back and forth, and also admit strangers to the oracle, which is situated far beneath the earth; and they live on what they get from mining and from those who consult the oracle, and from the king of the country, who has appointed to them fixed allowances; and those who live about the oracle have an ancestral custom, that no one should see the sun, but should go outside the caverns only during the night; and it is for this reason that the poet speaks of them as follows: "And never does the shining sun look upon them";

οὐδέ ποτ' αὐτούς
Ἥλιος φαέθων ἐπιδέρκεται.[2]

But later on the Cimmerians were destroyed by a certain king, because the response of the oracle did not turn out in his favor; the seat of the oracle, however, still endures, although it has been removed to another place. . . . Such, then, are the stories the people before my time used to tell, but now that the forest round about Avernus has been cut down by Agrippa, and the tracts of land have been built up with houses, and the tunnel has been cut from Avernus to Cumae, all those stories have proven to be mere myths; and yet the Cocceius [3] who made, not only this tunnel, but also the one

----

[1] The fire-flaming river.   [2] *Od.*, XI, 15.
[3] Cocceius Auctus, an architect and engineer, employed by Agrippa.

from Dicaearchia [1] to Neapolis, was pretty well acquainted with the story just now related about the Cimmerians, and it may very well be that he also deemed it an ancestral custom, for this region, that its roads should run through tunnels.[2]

Gulf Lucrinus broadens out as far as Baiae; and it is shut off from the outer sea by a mound eight stadia in length and broad as a wagon-road. This mound is said to have been brought to completion by Heracles, when he was driving the cattle of Geryon. But since it admitted the waves over its surface in times of storm, so that it could not easily be traversed on foot, Agrippa built it up higher. The gulf affords entrance to light boats only; and, though useless as a place to moor boats, it affords most abundant catches of oysters. And some say that this gulf itself is Lake Acherusia, while Artemidorus says that Gulf Avernus itself is that lake. But Baiae is said to be named after one of the companions of Odysseus, Baius; and also Misenum. Next in order come the headlands that are in the neighborhood of Dicaearchia, and then the city itself. In earlier times it was only a port-town of the Cumaeans, situated on the brow of a hill, but at the time of Hannibal's expedition the Romans settled a colony there, and changed its name to Puteoli from the wells there — though some say that it was from the foul smell of the waters, since the whole district, as far as Baiae and Cumae, has a foul smell, because it is full of sulphur and fire and hot waters. And some believe that it is for this reason that the Cumaean country was called "Phlegra," and that it is the wounds of the fallen giants, inflicted by the thunderbolts, that pour forth those streams of fire and water. And the city has become a very great emporium, since it has havens that have been made by the hand of man — a thing made possible by the natural qualities of the sand, for it is in proper proportion to the lime, and takes a firm set and solidity. And therefore, by mixing the sand-ash with the lime, they can run jetties out into the sea and thus make the wide-open shores curve into the form

[1] Puteoli, the modern Pozznoli.

[2] In other words, Strabo suspects that these tunnels may have been antique.

of bays, so that the greatest merchant-ships can moor therein with safety. Immediately above the city lies the Forum of Hephaestus, a plain shut in all round by exceedingly hot ridges, which in numerous places have fumaroles that are like chimneys and that have a rather noisome smell; and the plain is full of drifted sulphur.

I have quoted thus at length from Strabo, who is always his own excuse for quotation, to let readers of Virgil see some of the actualities with which the poet was concerned. The most striking and, to us, unpleasant actuality that confronted him was a result of the improvements introduced by Agrippa. They are described by Servius, whose comment I will translate: [1]

Agrippa declares in the Second Book of his *Autobiography* that he had conceived the plan of turning the Lucrine Lake into a harbor, but the glory for this operation fell to Augustus. The poet speaks of the "chafing sea," because at the time that the sea was let into the Lucrine Lake and a channel was dug between the Lucrine Lake and Lake Avernus to effect the union of the two lakes such a storm arose that the event was regarded as a prodigy, and it was reported that the statue of Avernus had sweated; wherefore the pontifices proclaimed that expiatory rites should be performed in that place.

This feat had been accomplished while Virgil was at work on the *Georgics*. Our poet was no sentimentalist. He was ardently devoted to science. From the way in which he talks about the implements of the farm we have found reason to believe that he would have been highly interested in all the mechanical inventions which have made the farmer's life easier today, and in fact

[1] On *Georg.*, II, 162.

would have immortalized these useful novelties in his best epic verse, with some mention of the cruder devices of the days of Triptolemus and Ceres. At any rate, instead of bemoaning the barbarous desecration of Lake Avernus, in such strains as we pour forth when the beauties of Niagara or Hetch Hetchy Valley are made to contribute to man's necessities, Virgil exalts Agrippa's engineering feat as one of the glories of Italy. He has praised the wild lakes of the north in the ballad-burthen music of *Lari maxume*, that ran in Tennyson's heart all day when he set out in the grey dawn from Como, and now, in contrast, Virgil sings of the triumph of human ingenuity over nature shown in the union of two southern lakes into a land-locked harbor:

> anne lacus tantos, te Lari maxume, teque
> fluctibus et fremitu assurgens Benace marino?
> an memorem portus Lucrinoque addita claustra
> atque indignatum magnis stridoribus aequor,
> Iulia qua ponto longe sonat unda refuso
> Tyrrhenumque fretis immittitur aestus Avernis? [1]

> Why tell of harbors and Lake Lucrine's bars,
> That held the tumult of the chafing sea,
> Where the far-sounding Julian wave beats back
> And Tuscan billows flood the Avernan pools?

So speaks Virgil when his theme is the greatness of Italy and the triumph of recent improvement. But when Aeneas consults the Sibyl, the poet has quite a different attitude of mind. It would be easy to call Virgil a realist

[1] *Georg.*, II, 159.

from the lines in the *Georgics* — or even a mere modern, with an admiration of the mechanical and the new — were it not for the mood of primitive awe with which he bids us approach the Sibyl's cave and the corridors of Hades. If any poet needed to be judged not by isolated passages but by all that he wrote, it is Virgil, whose thoughts are actors in his drama of life.

This is not the place to speak of the excavations in progress at Cumae under the able guidance of Professor Maiuri. He will publish his complete results in due time.[1] I also will refrain from recounting a visit to the excavations made in April, 1927, when I also, on the back of a brawny guide, was conducted through the tunnel at Lake Avernus to the veritable entrance to Hades where I saw — *vidi egomet* — the three stone baths of the Sibyl, the Emperor Nero, and Cerberus.

From the narratives of ancient historians, and from the discoveries and the interpretations of archaeologists, we may draw a tolerably accurate picture of what the haunts of the Sibyl suggested to Virgil's contemporaries. There was a temple of Apollo at Cumae with which an oracle was connected. It was visited by pious folk—perhaps, however, only by *il basso popolo*, "the little people," as my guide to the infernal regions suggested to me. At least they heard megaphonic re-

[1] See his preliminary article in *Notizie degli Scavi* (1926), pp. 85–93, and his recent "Monumenti e Luoghi Virgiliani nella Campania," in V. Ussani and L. Suttina, *Virgilio*, Milan, 1930, pp. 22–28. The *London Illustrated News* (May 28, 1927), printed a popular account, pp. 964 f.

sponses,[1] and left an amount of coin with the attendants
at the temple, and with the keepers of inns and shops
round about. If the Sibyl could be seen in her calmer
moments, she probably was not averse to small gra-
tuities. A tunnel leading from Cumae to Lake Avernus
may have connected, I venture to suggest,[2] with that
which the visitor may penetrate for some distance today,
and thus have provided for her and the priests of the
temple a quick and unseen approach to that awesome
spot whose sanctity was an important asset for the cult.
This ancient underground avenue to the entrance of
Hell had been converted either by Agrippa into a military road or by somebody else into a romantic boule-
vard. Perhaps we may guess that an ancestor of my escort was on hand at the right spot to show the curious,
for a consideration, the bath of the ancient Sibyl, that of
Cerberus, and a third bath, not belonging, however, to
the Emperor Nero; possibly in those days it had been
recently assigned to Catiline. The awesome groves on
the slopes of Avernus had been shorn, and millionaires
were outbidding each other for sites for villas in the latest
est style. The new double harbor was pointed out by

[1] See an interesting note on an oracular, and megaphonic, cave in Malta
by E. Riess, *The Classical Weekly*, XIV (1920-21), 14.

[2] My friend Professor Walton B. McDaniel reminds me that a considerable stretch of bare country intervenes between the temple at Cumae and
the present entrance to the tunnel. I can only surmise that the character
of the land may have altered since the ancient Sibyl's day or that an underground passage awaits discovery. Maiuri (*Virgilio*, p. 27) believes that
after Agrippa's changes, Augustus restored the religious character of the
grottoes and the tunnels.

one-hundred-per-cent Romans as the finest harbor in creation. The place was thronged with soldiers, sailors, hawkers, and sight-seers. Not far away on the beach at Baiae strolled idle summer visitors, the *élite* of Rome. Avernus had become a bigger, and a busier, if not a better, place than it had ever been before.

The magician appears and waves his wand again. The new canal fills with sand. The new villas are metamorphosed into the forest primeval. Modern activities, modern amusements, modern vulgarities, fade into nothing. The voice of the god resounds in true omen from the hundred doors of the Sibyl's cave, and the prophetess directs the founder of the Roman race to the world of the shades, where the vision of his nation's destiny is revealed.

The foregoing pages have illustrated, not completely, but adequately, I hope, for my purpose, the epic quality of Virgil's temperament and the magic of his art, a magic that would leave his mediaeval counterpart gaping in amazement. The word is not idly used. All good poetry is magic in a way, since it involves the act of creation. But I have in mind that special gift of turning one substance into another, of blending the heterogeneous and incongruous into harmony. There is little of such magic in the minor poems attributed to Virgil. There are pretty poems among them, like the *Copa* and the little pieces in honor of the scarecrow-god. We note clever design, pleasantry, skilful verse, moral earnestness, and the foregleams of the poet's epic temperament. But attempts to associate the incongruous, to unify the multitudinous, resulted, as I showed from the *Culex*, in what Mr. Lowes calls "joiner's work." It is in the *Bucolics* that Virgil first reveals the magician's art, and in the poems that follow his power increases with the magnitude of the feats that he attempts. I have singled out some of the diverse strands of which these splendid tapestries are woven. The poet himself found enough short-comings in the *Aeneid* to determine him to burn it; among them were the inconsistencies occasioned by happy afterthoughts, the failure to make real certain moods or episodes bequeathed to the epic poet by tradition, the failure, — if failure he thought it, — to make Aeneas human and universally appealing like Dido. Then there were the fragmentary lines and the lines that served as scaffolding till the solid timbers should be hewn and set in place. In short, though he must have known that the dream of his boyhood had come true in the *Aeneid*, the conscience of the artist condemned his work for its flaws; it was not yet wrought out *ad unguem*, like the *Georgics*.

I have refrained, as I promised to refrain, from dwelling on the weaknesses of Virgil's epic, not being sure that I can point them out. Better is the naïveté of the Virgiliomaniac than the superiority of the Virgiliomastix, *qui dum poetae inscientiam vult insectari, suam confitetur*. It is both safer and wiser to study the nature of

Virgil's success, with the help of commentators new and old, Servius above all, but especially with the companionship of his peers in poetry.

> Still with itself compared his text peruse,
> And let your comment be the Mantuan Muse.

So Pope tells us to read Homer. The Maeonian Muse will be as useful a guide to Virgil. So will two above all others who looked to him as guide — Dante and Milton. To study the art and spirit of these four, Milton and Dante and Homer and Virgil, who takes the palm for the kind of magic that I have described, is to subject one's self to a pleasant incantation, which transmutes the shifting banalities of life into its lasting pleasures.

INDEX

INDEX